PROMISE TO MARY

PROMISE TO MARY

A Story of Faith in Action

Paul Jellinek

○

With a Foreword by
Della Reese

JOSSEY-BASS
A Wiley Imprint
www.josseybass.com

Published by Jossey-Bass
A Wiley Imprint
989 Market Street, San Francisco, CA 94103-1741—www.josseybass.com

Library of Congress Cataloging-in-Publication Data

Jellinek, Paul (Paul S.), 1951–
  Promise to Mary : a story of Faith in Action / Paul Jellinek ; with a foreword by Della Reese. — 1st ed.
      p. cm.
  ISBN 978-0-470-29268-6 (pbk.)
1. Faith in Action (Program)—History. 2. Faith-based human services—United States. 3. Church charities—United States. 4. Volunteers—United States. 5. Robert Wood Johnson Foundation. I. Title.

HV530.J45 2007
362.1'0425—dc22

2007049559

Printed in the United States of America
FIRST EDITION
PB Printing   10 9 8 7 6 5 4 3 2 1

CONTENTS

PART FOUR
Alaska

FOREWORD

I FIRST HEARD about Faith in Action when my television series *Touched by an Angel* came to an end. It's almost as if Faith in Action and I found each other. I was surprised to learn that the program had been going for quite some time and that many thousands of people were involved in communities all across the country. My immediate reaction was that more people needed to know—more volunteers were needed and more local Faith in Action programs needed to be created. And I was going to help in any way I could. I immediately signed on as the national spokesperson, helping to spread the word about how Faith in Action volunteers help their less fortunate neighbors.

I've had a blessed life. I have a wonderful family and a successful and fulfilling career. But it wasn't always like that. Growing up in the slums of Detroit, I saw firsthand the importance of people helping people. It was the only way we could survive. It was how I survived.

Many of you know me as a singer and an actress, but I'm also an ordained minister with an active congregation in Los Angeles, California. One of the most impressive aspects of Faith in Action is how it brings together people of diverse faiths and backgrounds, all dedicated to the same goal—helping others. It warms the heart and the soul. I've always believed that most people want to do good. . . most people want to help. . . they just don't know how to help. I call them "inactive angels." All of the wonderful Faith in Action volunteers out there are "active angels." You may not see their wings. But they are there.

When I first met with some of the Faith in Action volunteers in California, they kept referring to all the "little things" they do to help their neighbors in need like shopping, providing transportation, and visiting. I told them that to those they are helping, these are not little things. . . they are BIG things. It is really about love, respect and caring. . . doing God's work here on earth. I've been fortunate to meet hundreds of Faith in Action program directors and volunteers. Their dedication and humility move me every time. They truly put the Golden Rule into practice.

Paul Jellinek's odyssey to faraway places across America to gather just some of the thousands of Faith in Action stories is truly impressive.

Ironically, his journey starts in his own neighborhood. The heartwarming story of how Paul, his wife Susie, and their children befriend their elderly next-door neighbor, Mary, is something to which we all can relate. And then we learn how Mary inspired Paul to take action to put together a national Faith in Action movement. I was touched by her profound comment to Paul as she lay dying in a nursing home, "There are so many other people out there who are in the same boat as me, old and alone and forgotten," she said. "Only they've got nobody to look out for them. Nobody who cares."

We follow Paul from New Jersey to small towns in New England, then to the Deep South and, finally, to an amazing encounter in Alaska. Every story touched my heart. There's Harold, a 95-year-old volunteer in Woodlands, Maine, who calls Alan every morning at 10:00 to make sure he awakens. They've never met! Paul plays checkers with Harold (and gets beat), and learns this wonderful man's life story and his deep perspective on things.

In tiny Petal, Mississippi, Paul interviews Sylvia, who has a PhD from the University of Massachusetts and moved to Petal when her husband took a faculty position at nearby University of Southern Mississippi. Deeply concerned about those less fortunate, Sylvia had been struggling to provide social services to the many poor in the community. When she heard about Faith in Action, her response was, "This is it!"

Paul questions whether his encounter with George Mohr in Alaska is "coincidence or fate." You see, George is Paul's grandfather's cousin. Paul had met him only briefly thirty years before. Yet, Faith in Action brings them together again in, of all places, Anchorage, Alaska! George's story of escaping the Nazis in 1938 and eventually ending up in Anchorage is fascinating and heartbreaking, too, as Paul learns that George's parents and other relatives did not survive.

In his acknowledgment, Dr. Jellinek thanks many of the people who have been involved in Faith in Action over the years. I'd like to take this opportunity to thank him, as we all should, for his countless years of devotion to the cause, and for his dedication to sharing some of the inspirational stories of caring and compassion.

Della Reese
Los Angeles, California

ACKNOWLEDGMENTS

THE FIRST DRAFT of this manuscript was more than three times the length of the book that you now hold in your hands, but, sadly, it had to be shortened to its present length so that it could be read within the average life span. Consequently, while I am deeply grateful to all of the people who appear in this book for all of the time, the stories, the wisdom, the encouragement, and the inspiration that they so generously shared with me, I am equally indebted to the many wonderful people I met with in the preparation of this book whose stories, most regrettably, do not appear on these pages. In particular, I thank Lisa Carmalt, the foundress of our local Faith in Action program in Trenton, New Jersey; Leah Inverso, a long-time volunteer in the Trenton program who patiently endured my first caregiver interview; Nick Ridolfino, who has helped me to learn what interfaith volunteer caregiving is really all about; and Bill Grogan, a Faith in Action volunteer on the Jersey shore who was once my high school English teacher and who, early on, over a couple of cheeseburgers, gave me invaluable counsel on how to go about writing this book.

I also want to express my profound appreciation for the support and encouragement of my many friends and colleagues at the Robert Wood Johnson Foundation, past and present, without whom neither the Faith in Action program nor this book would have been possible, especially Terrance Keenan, who developed and pushed through the original demonstration program on which the Faith in Action program was based; Steven Schroeder, Richard Reynolds, and the foundation's trustees, especially John Heldrich and Linda Griego, who were willing take a very big gamble on Faith in Action; Vivian Fransen, Gail Benish, Lewis Sandy, Terri Gibbs-Appel, and Tito Coleman, who worked hard to help me get the Faith in Action program off the ground in the early 1990s; Elise Brown, Stuart Shear, Vicki Weisfeld, Frank Karel, Jan Opalski, Nancy Fishman, and James Knickman, who worked equally hard five years later to keep it going and to learn as much as we could from it; Judy Stavisky and Rosemary Gibson, who very graciously picked up where I left off when I left the foundation in 2002, and gave it their all; and Ruby Hearn, who boldly recruited me to the foundation in the first place and whose unflagging optimism, encouragement, and friendship saw me through some of those moments of bleak despair that are an inevitable part of any large and complex undertaking of this kind.

In addition, I want to express my sincere appreciation to Risa Lavizzo-Mourey, president of the Robert Wood Johnson Foundation, for her generous support for the writing of this book, which has been a dream come true for me in more ways than she will ever know; and to David Morse, Jane Lowe, Calvin Bland, and James Ingram for their steadfast support and assistance in making it a reality. And finally, my heartfelt thanks go to Liz O'Neill for her superb administrative and emotional support; Joy Neath for her exceptional dedication to the program and to the hundreds of local Faith in Action grantees for whom she truly *is* the Robert Wood Johnson Foundation; and especially Ann Pomphrey, without whose phenomenal commitment and hard work, the Faith in Action program would long since have run out of gas.

Outside the walls of the Robert Wood Johnson Foundation, Kenneth Johnson played a pivotal role, both in the original interfaith volunteer caregiver demonstration program and subsequently in the development and management of Faith in Action. For his vision, his leadership, and his tenacity, I will always be deeply in Ken's debt—as will the many thousands of families and individuals across the country who have benefited from the presence of a Faith in Action program in their community.

Stanley Jones and Judy Miller Jones also played a vital role, both in reminding the foundation about the potential of the interfaith volunteer caregiving model that it had already invested in and in helping to make the case for the continued expansion of Faith in Action in the late 1990s.

Arthur Fleming, Barbara Jordan, Bishop Kenneth Hicks, Rabbi Murray Salzman, and Della Reese each provided important leadership in advancing the vision and the goals of Faith in Action, as has Cardinal William Keeler, who graciously hosted a high-level interfaith summit of national religious leaders at his residence in Baltimore in support of Faith in Action.

I am also deeply grateful to Burton Reifler, who, together with Sarah Cheney, Larry Weisberg, and others in the Faith in Action National Program Office at Wake Forest University Baptist Medical Center, stepped in at a critical juncture in the program's history, and especially to Tom Brown, who has done a terrific job of continuing to move the program forward during these final years of the foundation's funding. I should add that I am delighted to see that as the National Program Office has begun winding down its operations, a number of veteran local Faith in Action directors from around the country have come together of their own volition, with generous support from the National Program Office, to form a Faith in Action National Network that, together with existing state and regional networks, will strive to provide continuing assistance to the field in the years to come.

As for my work on the book, I benefited tremendously from the astute editorial advice and unflagging encouragement of Stephen Isaacs, a seasoned writer and editor (as well as my partner in the foundation consulting firm of Isaacs-Jellinek), and from the editorial services of Pat Crow, a *New Yorker* veteran who tackled my early drafts with remarkable patience, forbearance, and good humor. At Jossey-Bass, Andy Pasternack and Seth Schwartz provided first-class editorial support, and Kelsey McGee, Stan Shoptaugh, Beverly Miller, and Susan Bennett brilliantly transformed a series of very raw computer files into the finished product now before you. Michael Cook did a super job on the cover. Rich Barber worked hard to promote the manuscript, and in the process convinced me to edit it down to a readable length. Digby Dichl, Buzz Bissinger, Mike Tidwell, Irene Wielawski, Roger Cobb, John Milward, Efrem Marder, Derek Bok, Stephen Payne, Paul Rimassa, Joan Hollendonner, Michael Beachler, Amy Jellinek, Lisa Jellinek, Michael Jellinek, and Robert Jellinek also made valuable tactical and editorial suggestions at various stages of the process (some of which I actually heeded), and David Rosenbloom and Alice Richmond got me off to a wonderful start with their warm hospitality at the outset of my travels on a particularly cold and rainy Boston night. Martin Jellinek and Bill Branch fed me barbecue and made me feel right at home in Memphis after my swing through the South. Elizabeth Dawson very graciously took care of all the administrative headaches that come with a project like this and magically made them disappear. Also, for sharing their recollections and for the important roles that they played during the early years of interfaith volunteer caregiving, I thank Robert Blendon, Leighton Cluff, James Firman, Teresa Langston, Margaret Mahoney, and Rebecca Rimel. Tom Armenti and Annie Pecan at Fred and Pete's Deli here in Mercerville, New Jersey, kept me fed each morning before I started writing, and Jake Wig, who knew all the old cowboy songs, kept me company.

A special word of thanks to my mother, Elvira Myers, who has always encouraged and supported me in every way; and to my father, Joseph Stephan Jellinek, who, with great patience and affection, plowed through draft after draft of what, after all, started out as an exceedingly long manuscript. His gentle but keenly insightful questions, comments, and counsel have beyond question made this a better book than it would otherwise have been. That said, neither my father nor any of the other people whose contributions I have acknowledged here bear any responsibility whatsoever for what I have written.

Finally, for everything that matters most in my life, my very deepest gratitude goes to my wife, Susan Jellinek, who has been a tireless and devoted Faith in Action volunteer since 1995. This book is for you, Susie.

For Susie

THE AUTHOR

Paul S. Jellinek is a native of Madison, Wisconsin, and a founding partner of Isaacs-Jellinek, a consulting practice that works with private foundations and nonprofit organizations. He has a background in public health, health economics, and journalism and served on the staff of the Robert Wood Johnson Foundation for almost twenty years. He and his wife, Susan, are long-time Faith in Action volunteers, and he currently serves on the board of the Faith in Action National Network. A father of four, he and his wife live in Mercerville, New Jersey.

PROMISE TO MARY

PART ONE

A PROMISE

A DREAM COME TRUE

ONE PERVERSELY SUNNY afternoon in the fall of 2002, more than nine-teen years after I had first arrived as a wet-behind-the-ears program officer, I left my job as vice president of the Robert Wood Johnson Foundation, a casualty of one of those periodic internal shakeups that have become an unhappy hallmark of modern organizational life.

That was the bad news.

The good news was that several months later, I received a call from the same foundation telling me that I was about to be awarded a generous grant to write a book about one of its signature programs: Faith in Action.

I was thrilled. For one thing, the grant would give me some additional breathing space to think about what, at the not-so-tender age of fifty-one, I wanted to do next with my life.

But more than that, Faith in Action was a program that I was passion-ate about. Not only had I been involved in its development at the foun-dation, but—in a somewhat unusual twist—through our church, my wife, Susie, and I had also become active volunteers in a Faith in Action pro-gram in our own community of Mercerville on the outskirts of Trenton, New Jersey. For me, the chance to write this book was a dream come true.

So what exactly *is* Faith in Action?

First, let me say a word about what it *isn't*, because that's often the first question that people ask me when I start to tell them about Faith in Action: *it is not a government program.*

Rather, Faith in Action is a privately funded program developed and supported by a private foundation—not by the government. Moreover, the work that led to Faith in Action began more than twenty years ago, long before the government had any interest in faith-based initiatives. And Faith in Action itself was launched in 1993, seven years before George W. Bush took office as president and began talking about such initiatives.

Faith in Action is a nationwide grant program, funded by the Robert Wood Johnson Foundation, that brings together local congregations of different faiths to provide volunteer help to people who, because of a long-standing health problem or disability are largely confined to their homes. They are mostly frail elderly people, but also people with developmental disabilities, people with AIDS, people who are terminally ill, people with mental illnesses; even children.

Burton Reifler, a doctor and a former national director of Faith in Action, put it even more succinctly: "It's about neighbors helping neighbors."

What do the Faith in Action volunteers do?

"It all depends on what people's needs are," Burton said. "They'll give them a ride to the doctor, take them shopping, help them with their laundry, cut their grass, fix a broken porch step, change a light bulb—or just come by for a visit."

Simple things, on the face of it. But as Burton was quick to point out, sometimes these seemingly simple things could make a big difference—especially to people who lived alone.

MARY

I FIRST NOTICED MARY not long after Susie and I moved here to Mercerville in the fall of 1983, shortly after starting my new job at the Robert Wood Johnson Foundation. She was our next-door neighbor.

An elderly widow, Mary lived alone. She didn't come outside much those first few months, and when she did, she would never look my way or acknowledge me in any way. She kept strictly to herself. When I asked Paul, our other neighbor, about her, he grunted. He said she had lost her husband twenty years ago and that she had been that way ever since.

Mary didn't look particularly friendly. Her face was hard, even bitter, as if she was angry at the world. (It wasn't until later, after we got to know her, that I found out that she was in almost constant pain from a bad back.)

Once spring arrived and the weather warmed up, she did come out more often. But even then, I would catch only an occasional glimpse of her, lurking behind the dense row of forsythia bushes that stood like a bright yellow wall between her back yard and ours. I couldn't help feeling that she was always watching us from behind those forsythias, keeping a suspicious eye on us.

Fortunately Susie's impression was completely different. Although she didn't specifically remember the first time that she talked with Mary, she said it was probably on one of those spring mornings when they were both out back hanging the laundry to dry. Before long, they got to know each other. "We'd talk like neighbors do. You know, out at the mailbox, in the yard—that sort of thing."

Mary was constantly on the go. To the store, to the hairdresser, to the senior center. She'd take the bus wherever she wanted to go and prided herself on being independent. After all, she was still in her seventies at that time, still a real go-getter.

From time to time, though, Mary would ask for help. For instance, because of her bad back, it was hard for her to pick up all the bits and pieces of bark that came down from the big sycamore tree in her front yard. So she would ask Susie if our boys, Mike and Rob, would mind picking up the bark when they came home from school.

"We didn't mind most of the time," Mike told me. "But then she'd insist on paying us. We tried telling her no, but she'd always give us an envelope with maybe thirty cents in it, sometimes all in pennies."

In the summer, Susie would bring Mary strawberries or blueberries that she'd picked at one of at the local farms. And whenever she fixed a special meal, she would send one of the kids over with an extra plate for Mary. In return, Mary would keep an eye on the house for us when we weren't home.

When Mary reached her eighties, she began to slow down. Her chronic back pain was getting worse, and then her heart started acting up. At one point, she was diagnosed with cancer and had to go in for surgery.

After that, everything was more difficult for her. Just walking the two blocks down to the bus stop had become an ordeal. So now Susie would drive her to the doctor's office or to the hairdresser or to the Acme, where she did her shopping. And from time to time Mary would call and ask me to change a light bulb or turn on the furnace or turn over her mattress—little things that she couldn't do for herself anymore.

We also spent more time visiting with Mary. She had two middle-aged daughters who came by every now and then to take her out for the day, but most of the time she was alone—sometimes for weeks on end. Her television was on pretty much all the time, with the volume turned up so loud that you could hear it all over the house. Most of the time she didn't really watch it, but she said it made her feel less alone.

She loved to talk. When we would go over to visit with her, we'd sit on her old living room sofa, and she would tell us stories about growing up in Trenton—about some of the hard times she had lived through as a young girl and about how she hadn't finished high school because she and her sister had gone to work to help support the family. But she also talked about the good times, especially the dances down by the Delaware River.

Often Mary talked about her husband—how much she missed him and how he had been a "real handyman" who had always kept everything "just so." That was why she wanted to stay in her house, she said, and why she always tried to keep it nice: "Because that's how he would have wanted it."

As time went on, there were more and more pills to keep track of, and I remember once there were some pretty serious interaction effects. Mary had trouble standing up and complained of feeling "all woozy." It took a lot of calls to her various doctors to get that straightened out.

Slowly but surely, Mary was becoming depressed. "I feel like the world has just passed me by," she told Susie over and over. She said it was a very different world from the one that she had grown up in.

Eventually Mary wound up back in the hospital, and from there she was taken to a nursing home across the river in Pennsylvania. That was the beginning of the end. Before long she was in another nursing home, and then a third, each more depressing than the one before. Susie and I would go to the nursing homes to visit her, and often we would find her in tears.

"I wish the Lord would just take me," she'd sob.

Then one gray Sunday afternoon when I went to see her by myself, Mary and I had what for me turned out to be a pivotal conversation.

Despite the bleak skies outside her window, she seemed less depressed than usual. In fact, it struck me that for the first time in a long time, she seemed at peace, as if she knew that her long ordeal was finally coming to an end.

I talked for a while, telling her about the kids and whatever else I could think of that might interest her, and then, having run out of things to say, I just sat quietly. She had hardly said a word, and I thought maybe she wanted to rest. For several minutes, we were both completely still.

Suddenly, she broke the silence. "Paul, I know I don't have much time left," she said, her voice perfectly clear and steady. "And don't try to tell me different. I know that the Lord is finally coming for me."

I didn't say a word.

"I want you to know," she went on, "and I want you to be *sure* to tell Susie, how much I appreciate everything your family has done for me." She paused and glowered at me with some of her old fire, daring me to contradict her. Then she added, "I do have one regret though."

"What's that, Mary?"

"Well, you know, there are so many other people out there who are in the same boat as me, old and alone and forgotten," she said. "Only they've got nobody to look out for them. Nobody who cares."

"I know," I said.

Of course I knew. How could I not know? All I had to do was walk down the halls of that dreary nursing home—or pretty much any other nursing home that I had ever been in. Moreover, I knew from some of the presentations that I'd heard at the foundation that it was a problem of staggering proportions. In all, almost a hundred million people in the United States had one or more chronic health conditions, and more than

40 million of them—one in seven Americans—had some kind of functional limitation as a result of their condition, including 12 million children.

These huge numbers came as a surprise to a lot of people. They certainly surprised me when I first saw them, probably because I was used to thinking of these kinds of chronic conditions in terms of specific diseases rather than as a group: arthritis, asthma, heart disease, diabetes, paralysis, multiple sclerosis, Alzheimer's, Parkinson's, Huntington's, AIDS, blindness, deafness—the list went on.

Yet while these conditions might be distinct biologically and clinically, their impact on people's everyday lives was often depressingly consistent. People with serious chronic health problems, no matter what their particular condition might be, often needed some level of assistance with ordinary activities of daily living, such as eating, bathing, dressing, housekeeping, transportation, and, perhaps most important for the many who, like Mary, lived alone, companionship.

Suddenly my mind was racing. I thought about conversations that I'd been having over the past several months with some of the people I worked with at the foundation—conversations about interfaith coalitions of volunteers who helped homebound elderly people, about doing things on a large scale, about finding new ways for the foundation to have a national impact, and about what it is that makes a foundation great—a jumble of seemingly disconnected thoughts all swirling together.

"Mary," I said, "you know that I work at a big foundation."

She nodded.

"The foundation has a lot of money," I went on, "and its purpose is to help people." I paused, choosing my next words carefully. "I'm going to see what the foundation can do to help all those people you're talking about. I can't promise that it will actually happen—that isn't up to me—but I can promise you that I'll try."

That was it. That was the promise. I'm not sure that she understood what I was talking about, but it didn't matter. It was a promise to myself as much as to Mary.

After that, Susie and I visited Mary a few more times, but she was fading rapidly, and it was increasingly hard for her to talk. So we would just sit with her.

Then one day, one of her daughters called to tell us that Mary had died. She said that her mother had given her our telephone number some time ago, and she thought that we would like to know.

FAITH IN ACTION

SO NOW WHAT? How in the world was I going to find a way for the Robert Wood Johnson Foundation to help all of those forgotten souls Mary had been so worried about—a largely hidden population that I knew numbered in the millions? I didn't even work with the elderly. My main area of responsibility at that time was children. Fortunately, though, it turned out that the foundation had *already* funded a program that had done precisely the kinds of things that my family had done to help Mary. It was called the Interfaith Volunteer Caregivers Program.

In the late 1970s and the early 1980s, the foundation had become increasingly aware of the growing challenge of caring for people with serious chronic health problems. Until then, we as a society had relied largely on family and friends to do the caring. In fact, for seven out of ten people with chronic conditions, family and friends were the *only* source of support.

But gradually that traditional approach was starting to break down. Already, one out of four Americans was providing some form of assistance to a person with a chronic condition, and with the baby boomers aging and life expectancy rates for the elderly continuing to rise, the need would only continue to grow.

At the same time, the capacity of family and friends to shoulder the burden on their own was declining. The proportion of Americans who fell into the average age range for caregiving—between fifty and sixty-four—was shrinking, and women, who had always done most of the caregiving, were entering the workforce in record numbers, sharply reducing the amount of time that they could make available to care for ailing family members or friends.

Nor was this a problem that, as a nation, we could easily buy our way out of. Political leaders were desperately looking for ways to *reduce* future spending for health and social programs, not expand it.

9

So new ideas were needed, and one potential resource that the foundation had decided to explore was the nation's 330,000 religious congregations. The basic notion of helping a neighbor in need was deeply rooted in the world's major faiths as a path to spiritual fulfillment, and in fact the foundation discovered that many congregations already offered at least some opportunities for members to volunteer their time in the service of others—often including caregiving.

But usually this caregiving was on a small scale, no more than a handful of people doing what they could on an informal basis. Partly this was because there was often a range of volunteer opportunities for people to choose from, so that those who were interested in volunteering dispersed themselves accordingly. But the more fundamental problem was that most congregations by themselves simply didn't have the resources to pay someone to oversee their volunteer programs adequately. And without a paid staff person to organize and manage their caregiving efforts, they almost invariably fell short of their true potential.

It was here that the concept of interfaith volunteer caregiving came into the picture. Rather than each congregation trying to develop and sustain its own volunteer effort to help its chronically ill and disabled members, the idea was that a group of congregations representing the community's various faiths would come together, collectively hire a paid director, and establish a single caregiving program that would draw its volunteers largely from the participating congregations to serve the entire community. By banding together in this way, the congregations would be able to create a program large enough to justify hiring a paid director, and together with other organizations in the community, they would be able to share the cost of that position.

Having a paid director would in turn make it possible to have a better organized, more structured program that could actively recruit, train, and supervise a lot more volunteers than would otherwise have become involved. Moreover, because these programs were interfaith in nature, religious proselytizing would be prohibited, which would tend to make their services more acceptable to those in need of care.

And so, in 1983, the foundation had awarded three-year Interfaith Volunteer Caregiver grants in twenty-five places around the country to see whether this idea could work in real life: to find out, that is, whether it was possible to mobilize volunteers from congregations of different faiths to help people who—like Mary—were homebound with chronic health problems.

It was. Not only did twenty-four of the twenty-five communities succeed in setting up effective programs, but at least twenty of them had found other sources of support to keep them going after the foundation's grants had been spent and were still up and running five years later.

Unfortunately, back in 1983 when the program had first started, I had been only dimly aware of it. The money involved wasn't a lot by the foundation's usual standards—only about $4 million over a three-year period. And Terry Keenan, the person on the staff most directly responsible for the program, was one of the most modest, self-effacing people I had ever known—hardly someone to trumpet his new program from the rooftops.

And so it wasn't until the early 1990s—not long before I had my pivotal conversation with Mary in the nursing home—that several things happened that finally got me to start paying attention.

One was a letter that Steve Schroeder, the foundation's new president, had received from Judy Miller Jones shortly after he had arrived at the foundation. Judy was a consummate Washington insider who ran a high-powered forum for Capitol Hill staffers and federal officials involved in health issues—usually big, important issues, like how to fix Medicare or Medicaid.

Only this letter wasn't about Medicare or Medicaid. It was about a small nonprofit organization—grandly titled the National Federation of Interfaith Volunteer Caregivers—that had started five years earlier with a little bit of money from the foundation at the end of the Interfaith Volunteer Caregivers Program.

In her letter, Judy told Steve that while he had probably never heard of the National Federation of Interfaith Volunteer Caregivers, she was convinced that it was one of the most important organizations the foundation had ever funded. But the federation was just about flat broke, she said, and unless the foundation took immediate action, it would soon cease to exist. This, she added, would be a tragic loss—not just to the organization but to the nation.

Steve was intrigued. The foundation routinely received cries for help from small nonprofits on the brink of financial ruin, but generally the letter would come from the organization itself. And in most cases, the foundation's response was that, regrettably, it simply could not bail out every distressed nonprofit that came knocking at its door. But this was different. Why on earth was Judy Miller Jones—a hard-nosed Washington realist—so concerned about this small nonprofit in upstate New York?

The reason—as it so often is—was personal. One of the places that the federation had picked to start up a new interfaith coalition was Shepherdstown, West Virginia, a small rural community where Judy and her husband, Stan, lived when they were not in Washington. Like Judy, Stan was well respected in Washington's health policy circles—in his case, for his expertise in health insurance.

But Stan wasn't just a health insurance expert. He was also an Episcopal priest. And it was in his capacity as a priest that he had become actively involved in Shepherdstown's new interfaith volunteer caregiver coalition.

Before long, he and Judy were enthralled, not only because of what this particular coalition was doing for the homebound elderly in Shepherdstown, but because as health policy experts, they understood that the kinds of simple support services provided by the interfaith volunteers could never be provided by the nation's formal health care system, nor were they likely ever to be financed by any of the big federal health insurance programs like Medicare and Medicaid.

Shortly after Judy wrote her letter to Steve, Stan came to the foundation and gave a talk in which he made just that point. Stan told us a story about Miss Lillian, an elderly woman who lived alone in Shepherdstown, and who sounded to me very much like Mary. He talked passionately and persuasively about what a difference the interfaith volunteers had made in Miss Lillian's life.

It wasn't long after Stan's presentation that the foundation approved an emergency grant to keep the federation's doors open for another five years.

The other person who played a major role in bringing interfaith caregiving to my attention was a doctor by the name of Ken Johnson.

I'd always enjoyed hanging out with Ken. Gruff, opinionated, charming, smart, proud, impatient, funny, and, above all, fiercely committed to making the world a better place, Ken had started out on the streets of Brooklyn and had eventually wound up on the faculty of the medical schools and hospitals of Yale and Dartmouth, where he had been the chairman of community medicine. He had worked with the foundation since the early 1970s, helping to develop, manage, and oversee a number of its programs.

One of those programs, which I worked on with Ken during the early 1990s, was an initiative in the foundation's home state of New Jersey to improve the kind of care that high-risk pregnant women and their newborns were getting. Because most of the hospitals being funded through the program were within easy driving range, I joined Ken on many of his periodic visits to the hospitals to see how things were going. This gave Ken a golden opportunity to bend my ear about one of his all-time favorite programs: the Interfaith Volunteer Caregiver Program—which, as it happened, he had managed for the foundation. Moreover, Ken had been instrumental in setting up the National Federation for Interfaith Volunteer Caregivers, with which he was still deeply involved. In fact, he was relentless on the subject. Over breakfast, over lunch, over dinner, and in between, it was interfaith, interfaith, interfaith.

One thing that Ken was especially excited about was the funding that the federation had received from the Public Welfare Foundation, in Washington, D.C., which, despite its government-sounding name, was a private foundation just like Robert Wood Johnson, only smaller. In fact, because its resources were more limited, the Public Welfare Foundation had decided to try to replicate the original interfaith model with one-year $20,000 seed grants, a fraction of the three-year $150,000 grants that had been awarded under the original Interfaith Volunteer Caregiver Program.

Miraculously, it seemed to be working. Not only were these new coalitions getting off the ground, but, like the original Robert Wood Johnson–funded prototypes, most of them were being sustained by local funders after their one-year seed grants expired. "Just think what that means!" Ken exclaimed.

Finally, he talked me into an early-morning breakfast meeting in a Washington hotel where, for over an hour, he and his good friend Arthur Flemming double-teamed me on the subject. Arthur Flemming was an extraordinary man who was in his eighties at that time but still had the vitality of a man a third his age. Over the course of his long and distinguished career, he had been, among other things, President Eisenhower's secretary of health, education and welfare, the chairman of the national Civil Rights Commission, and president of several universities.

More recently, Arthur had served as chairman of the national advisory committee for the Interfaith Volunteer Caregivers Program, and now he was chairing the board of the National Federation of Interfaith Volunteer Caregivers, with Ken Johnson as his vice chair. As Arthur talked, it soon became clear that he was every bit as passionate on the subject of interfaith volunteer caregiving as Ken was. At one point, he actually banged the table with his fist, rattling the silverware and freezing half a dozen somnolent waiters in their tracks.

"This could become a national movement!" he thundered.

And for a moment it was as if his audience was a crowd of thousands, and not just Ken and me and half a dozen startled waiters.

Finally, in addition to Judy's letter, Stan's talk about Miss Lillian, Ken's incessant lobbying, and Arthur's oratory, there was one final element in the mix: the rather strange question, posed by Dick Reynolds, the foundation's executive vice president, of what it is that makes a foundation great.

"We're a *good* foundation," Dick would say again and again. "But we're not a *great* foundation."

It was maddening. What on earth did he mean?

Because of Dick's position, you couldn't just blow him off. But when I pressed him for an explanation, he just grinned and said, "That's your job, Paul. You figure it out."

Then one day, thankfully, Terry Keenan wrote an essay on the subject that helped to clarify things. Terry had worked with foundations for more than thirty-five years: the big national and international foundations, community foundations, conversion foundations, corporate foundations, family foundations—you name it. If anyone knew what made a foundation great, it was Terry.

And Terry, in looking back over the history of American philanthropy, singled out the Carnegie libraries as his choice for the outstanding example of great philanthropy. Early in the twentieth century, when it was just getting off the ground, Andrew Carnegie's foundation had funded the construction of public libraries in communities all over the country that had made a difference in the lives of tens of millions of people. It was a legacy, Terry said, that persisted to the present day. And so it all fell into place. All I would have to do would be to convince the Robert Wood Johnson Foundation to replicate its interfaith program in hundreds of communities all over America—just like Andrew Carnegie's libraries. Only instead of buildings full of books, these would be networks of volunteers, recruited from congregations of all faiths to reach out to their frail elderly and disabled neighbors who needed a helping hand in order to cope with their day-to-day needs.

Of course, the notion of making hundreds of grants under a single program—even if the grants themselves were relatively small—would be a giant stretch for us. Typically the foundation made only about ten to twenty grants under its national programs. But wasn't that what being a great foundation was all about: taking risks?

In my excitement, I burst into my friend Vicki Weisfeld's office down the hall. As quickly as I could, I told her what I'd been thinking about, and then I gave her the punch line: "We could fund a thousand of them!"

Vicki looked up from her mountain of papers and shrugged. "Aren't you worried that people will get it confused with the Bush administration's Thousand Points of Light program?" she asked (this was back during the first administration of George H. W. Bush). "You know, the one that recognizes all those exemplary volunteer programs?"

"Okay, so we'll make it nine hundred," I said. "Or eleven hundred. The exact number doesn't matter. The point is to do a lot of them, so that we can really have an impact. Think about it, Vicki. Hundreds and hundreds of grants. Thousands of people being helped."

She peered at me over the top of her glasses. "Well, I guess it sounds okay," she conceded. "But you know, Paul," she added with a deep sigh, "it isn't going to be easy."

Vicki was right: it wasn't easy. But in the end, after a good deal of effort by a lot of dedicated people both inside and outside the foundation, the idea *did* become a program, which, at Ken's suggestion, we called Faith in Action. And over the course of the next decade, starting in 1993, the foundation awarded almost seventeen hundred Faith in Action grants to local interfaith volunteer caregiver coalitions that have served many thousands of homebound elderly and disabled people all over America.

And now, more than ten years after my promise to Mary, I would finally have the chance to get out on the road and meet face to face with some of the volunteers and the people they were helping.

PART TWO

NEW ENGLAND

TRAVELS WITH PEARLCORDER

IN THINKING ABOUT how to write this book, one of my inspirations was *Travels with Charley,* John Steinbeck's account of his 1960 journey around the country with his poodle, Charley. Only instead of one long cross-country trip, I would pick several regions of the country and visit Faith in Action programs within each of those regions. Like Steinbeck, I decided to start in New England.

Of course, there were plenty of differences between my trip and Steinbeck's. Instead of a customized truck fully outfitted with sleeping and living accommodations to my personal specifications and christened *Rocinante* in honor of Don Quixote's horse, I rented a Chevy Malibu from Avis. Instead of spending my nights beside bubbling brooks and under star-spangled skies, I stayed in a string of anonymous motels that were at least of sufficient quality to make it into the pages of my Triple-A Tour Books—meaning that they did not as a rule rent rooms by the hour. And instead of having "an old French gentleman poodle known as Charley" as my traveling companion, I had an Olympus Pearlcorder J500 micro-cassette recorder so that I could record my interviews.

I decided to begin my New England trip in Boston partly because it had one of the original twenty-five Interfaith Volunteer Caregiver programs and partly because I was going to be there anyway for parents' weekend at our son Rob's college.

From there, I would head to Presque Isle in northern Maine. Presque Isle's Faith in Action program served Aroostook County, a huge rural county bigger than the entire state of Connecticut—quite a contrast to the Boston program or our program in the Trenton area. And once I'd decided on Presque Isle, choosing the rest of the places to visit was just a matter of geography and convenience. Presque Isle was on Route One, and there were several other towns along or near Route One in Maine that had also received Faith in Action grants, including Calais and Bar Harbor, so those were the ones I picked.

BOSTON, MASSACHUSETTS

IT WAS ONLY a ten-block walk from where I was staying to Janet Seckel-Cerrotti's office in downtown Boston, but the rain that had blown in the previous afternoon was still coming down hard, so I was pretty well soaked through by the time I reached the old brownstone YWCA building where Janet's interfaith caregivers program, called Match-Up, was housed. The friendly young woman at the front desk said that Janet was on the phone and would be right with me, then showed me the coat rack full of wire hangers at the back of the office where I could hang my dripping jacket. The hangers jingled like bells as I reached for one of them.

As I waited for Janet to get off the phone, I looked around the office. Metal filing cabinets, metal desks, pipes with flaking paint hanging from the walls and the ceiling, buzzing neon lights, and an ancient desktop computer with a tangle of wires spilling out of its back onto the floor: it was not the Ritz. The windows were insulated with strips of silver duct tape and were so smudged with grime that you could barely see daylight.

Janet's personal office space consisted of her desk, a big metal filing cabinet, and a chair with its stuffing falling out the bottom. Pictures of her children brightened the wall beside her, and hanging in a row were framed certificates of appreciation from, among others, the Multicultural Coalition on Aging, Central Boston Elder Services, and, of course, the National Federation of Interfaith Volunteer Caregivers.

I took a seat.

I could tell from the resolutely patient tone of her voice that Janet was talking to a potential funder. She was trying to make the case for flexible operating support—always a real need and always a very tough sell for community agencies like Match-Up. After almost twenty years as a funder myself, it was strange—and a little embarrassing—to hear the conversation from this end of the phone. She sounded as if she were talking to a child.

Her call finally finished, she hung up and heaved a deep sigh. Then she turned to me with a big smile. "You made it!"

I didn't really know Janet apart from our phone conversations in preparation for my visit, but from the outset, it felt as if we were longtime friends. Her black hair cut short, she wore a black and white top with black pants—more New York than Boston, I thought. We moved from her desk to the "conference table"—two beat-up metal tables pushed together that looked as if they had done a lot of years of hard duty in a high school cafeteria. The tables were surrounded by seven stained blue chairs, with a small desiccated cactus plant for a centerpiece.

Janet started by apologizing for the mess. The office would be relocating to Chinatown soon, she explained, because this entire building was about to be renovated—after which Match-Up would no longer be able to afford the rent. "At least it's better than the boiler room in the basement of the Church of the Covenant where we started out when we first spun off on our own," she laughed. "We were only one and a half staff then. Now we're up to seven."

For the next several minutes we talked logistics. One of her volunteers was scheduled to come into the office later in the morning to meet with me; then I'd have lunch with some of her staff, meet some more volunteers in the afternoon, and have dinner with somebody by the name of Linda.

After that, provided that I still had the strength to keep going, she was trying to set up a meeting for me in the evening with an elderly blind man by the name of Doug Barker who lived in an assisted living facility in Concord, twenty miles outside Boston, and had been served by the same volunteers—a family by the name of Donoghue—for the past seventeen years.

"So how does that sound?" she asked.

"Great," I said. "But before I talk to the volunteers, I want to interview you."

"Me?"

"That's why I'm starting here in Boston," I told her. "I wanted you to be the first interview of the book." Although twenty of the original twenty-five Interfaith caregiver programs were still active, along with hundreds of Faith in Action programs, Janet was the only director who had been with the program since its inception in 1983.

It turned out that I was right in thinking that Janet seemed more New York than Boston: she was born in Queens. She went to college at Temple University in Philadelphia, with a major in cultural anthropology, but when she returned to New York for graduate school, she switched from cultural anthropology to social work.

"I would have loved to stay in cultural anthropology," she said. "But I realized that in order to be Margaret Mead and study different cultures, you had to live on grants for the rest of your life."

"And you don't?"

Janet laughed. "I guess I was interested in being a change agent."

"And where did that come from?"

"My passion? I think it comes from my family background—being a first-generation American and having parents who had to leave their homes because of World War II. And having a mother who'd lost her family at fourteen because of the Holocaust—realizing what prejudice can do, and people's misunderstandings of other cultures and other people."

She paused.

"And I guess part of my being in Match-Up is that being in an interfaith group is really something I wanted to do. To try to bring people of different faiths together to understand one another. That's probably it as much as the aging piece. I love elders, and my own grandparents were killed at a very young age. So the combination here in Match-Up is a good fit for me in terms of my own passions."

After graduate school, Janet came to Boston, where she slept on the floors of various friends' apartments until she landed a part-time job at an organization called Boston Aging Concerns. "At first, I was their drop-in center coordinator," she said. "The drop-in center was where homeless people would come in for coffee. Then I became their volunteer coordinator part time. I also taught Sunday school part time, and did yoga, did calligraphy—you know, a little bit of everything pulled together."

In 1983, when she'd been at Boston Aging Concerns for about two years, the organization received a grant through the Robert Wood Johnson Foundation's new Interfaith Volunteer Caregivers Program, and she became the volunteer coordinator under the grant.

Although delighted about the grant, Janet faced a number of challenges right off the bat. For one thing, a lot of the people attending the city's churches didn't actually live in the city anymore. They lived in the suburbs, sometimes more than an hour away, making it much more difficult for their members to serve homebound people in Boston through a program like Match-Up. Also, it turned out that there was a long-standing division between Boston's Protestants and Catholics—something that, having grown up Jewish, she hadn't really been aware of before becoming involved in the program.

But despite the obstacles, she'd persevered, even through the traumatic transition period in the early 1990s when Match-Up was dropped by Boston Aging Concerns and had to learn to stand on its own two feet as a fledgling free-standing agency.

And now, Janet said, twenty years after receiving that first Interfaith Volunteer Caregivers grant, Match-Up was still going strong, with almost two hundred regular volunteers and about a dozen congregations that she counted as actively involved.

Still, along with the triumphs, Janet continued to have her share of frustrations. One that especially weighed on her was the fact that over time, the coalition had become less, rather than more, diverse.

"I think that as we've grown, we've become more white," she told me. "We *were* much more diverse. If you'd go to our events, people would notice and say, 'Wow, in the city this is probably one of the most diverse, comfortable, warm kind of places there is.' And I would feel really good, because that's kind of what my own personal mission is—my own personal passion. But I think that as we've grown and our budget has gotten bigger, we've needed to have people who were of more means and who were more sophisticated about how we did our fundraising and things like that—and we've lost some of the community base."

Another frustration for Janet, also related to Match-Up's growth, was that increasingly she had had to put much more of her time into administration and fundraising, leaving her less time to be out in the community connecting with the congregations, the community groups, and the volunteers themselves.

And fundraising, of course, remained a never-ending challenge—even after twenty years. She got some money from the congregations, from Match-Up's annual fundraisers, and a small amount from local corporations. But the bulk of the money still came from local foundations, and that could be hard to sustain, especially given the recent downturn in the economy.

"So what's kept you going all these years?" I asked.

"Well, first of all, I like my job," she said. "As much as I say that we're not succeeding in the way that I'd like us to, I really like what we do, working with different religions. At most places where people work, they talk about sex and money over lunch. But here we can talk about things that matter. And I like the people I work with—our board of directors, for instance. I feel like when they come in, they leave their egos at the door and they're there for Match-Up. It's very special to work with people who are committed to bettering the lives of other people. And I like older people.

"But mostly, I feel like we're making a difference in people's lives every day. And I think it's a privilege to do work that you think is making a difference in people's lives. Because I think that's what we're here for. Maybe it's not on a big scale—you know, when I was younger, I had that I-want-to-change-the-world kind of thing. But it's the hope that through what we do, we are changing the world in small ways, one by one."

Doug and the Donoghues

Doug Barker was waiting for me when I walked into the lobby of his assisted living facility in Concord that evening. Only I didn't recognize him—he recognized *me*, which impressed me all the more because, after all, he was blind.

"Are you the writer?" he said, getting up from his chair and walking up to me with his cane. He was a big man with shaggy eyebrows that reminded me of Andy Rooney on *Sixty Minutes*.

I introduced myself. "You must be Mr. Barker," I said.

"I can't hear too well," he said. "What did you say your name was?"

"Paul," I said, raising my voice a notch.

"Well, come with me, Bob," Doug said, shaking my hand. "We can talk in my room."

I followed him as he turned and slowly walked toward the elevator.

"That's quite a rain," I said loudly, as we went up the elevator.

He didn't respond, and I realized that he probably hadn't heard me—or the rain. This could turn out to be a long interview, I thought to myself. Or a very short one.

We got off at the second floor, and Doug led me straight across the hall to his room. For a moment, I had the impression that he was doing all of this navigating the geography of the building purely by memory rather than by the use of his senses.

Doug's room was neat but spare. There was a bed, a desk, a table, and two plain wooden chairs. The walls were bare except for a wooden crucifix hanging over his bed and a wall hanging that said, "Love Shows Best By Giving It." And—rather incongruously, I thought—there was a television. Everybody, it seemed, had a television.

Doug sat down at his desk and told me to pull up a chair. He had a small electronic device on his desk with an amplifier and an ear plug that he said helped him to hear, but it didn't seem to help all that much.

"Let me first just introduce myself to you," I began, trying to speak slowly and clearly, "so that you'll know who I am and what I'm doing."

"I don't know," Doug said.

"I will explain to you," I said. "My name is Paul."

"Paul?"

"Paul, right. And I am writing a book."

"You're what?"

"I'm writing a book . . ."

"Oh, yes, yes," he said.

". . . about interfaith caregiving," I said, sounding the words out slowly.

"Interfaith . . .?"

"Caregiving," I said.

"Spell it."

I did, but it didn't help.

"I don't know if I know that word," he said.

I tried another tack. "You know, you're connected with the Donoghues," I said.

"Yes, right."

"The Donoghues have been helping you, and they are volunteers in a program called Match-Up."

"Called what?"

"Match-Up," I said, and I started spelling it.

"Oh, Match-Up. I'm sorry."

"No, no, that's okay."

It was a struggle, but gradually I was able to explain to Doug what I was doing and what my purpose was in coming to see him. "What I'd really like to do," I told him, "is to learn a little bit about you. So let me start by asking you, Where were you born and where did you grow up?"

"Where what?"

"Where were you born?"

"Where was I what?"

I glanced at my watch. It was only a few minutes after 6:30, and the Donoghues weren't scheduled to join us until around 8:00. How in heaven's name was I going to do this? How could I possibly keep going like this for another hour and a half?

Yet already I liked Doug. There was something about him—a blend of gentleness and sadness—that drew me to him despite our frustrations in communicating. So I tried again.

"Where did you grow up?" I said, trying to speak very clearly.

"Where did I grow up?"

"Yes."

"Well, as a very small child, I was in Middleton for a while with my parents. And then we moved to Lynn. They wanted to help some family that was in difficulty. And then at the end of the year, my mother died. That was in 1926."

"And how old were you?"

"Nine years old," Doug said. "And then my father and I moved back to Middleton. And in the meantime, arrangements were made that I go to Perkins School for the Blind in Watertown."

I was glad he was talking, but I was having some difficulty understanding him. Not only did he have a strong Boston accent, but his speech was thick, probably because of his hearing impairment, and some of the words were slurred.

"Of course, when I got to Perkins, I didn't have any formal schooling, because I wasn't able to see the blackboard and so forth. So I had to start with about the first grade, I guess. At that time, it was very common that the students at Perkins graduated several years after their companions would have at the public school because they didn't know where they could be educated. When they got to Perkins, they were three or four years behind."

"So when did you finish at Perkins?"

"At Perkins?" he said. "1940." That meant Doug would have been twenty-three years old when he graduated from high school.

"And then what did you do?" I asked.

"The first thing I did was I worked at a box factory for about a week," he said. "Then I worked at a state hospital—a cancer hospital—just outside of Norwood. I was there for about seven or eight months. Well, I didn't care for it there, so I went up to Cambridge and roomed at the YMCA. And then I decided to look for a job outside, so I worked in the union offices, and they sent me to the Hathaway Bakery. And they hired me, in spite of my vision problems and all. I think what happened was the superintendent—his wife was having trouble. So I guess he figured he'd be helpful to somebody else. I worked for them for about twelve years."

"What did you do there?"

"I was a general baker of all the bread departments. I used to be in charge of making sure all the bread went through the ovens and was baked properly. And I'd make sure the men got their reliefs and their breaks."

But by the early 1950s, the bakery started having financial problems, so Doug left to take an office job in Boston. "I was the office manager for about a year," he said. "I wasn't really trained for it, and I didn't exactly like it anyway. So I left there, and I took over the Newton branch—the building and grounds, the maintenance, checking the fire alarm systems, and so forth. I worked eight or ten years for them. And from there I went to Perkins. I worked for Perkins for nineteen years."

Back to his alma mater—Perkins School for the Blind.

"And what did you do there?"

"Primarily grounds and buildings," he said.

Doug retired from Perkins in 1981, which brought us close to the time that he was first matched with Daniel and Ann Donoghue, the family he had been paired with through Match-Up. I asked him to tell me about that.

"Well, about that time, my wife was having asthma quite a bit, and it was starting to develop," he said. "She was coughing a lot, and she found it hard to go out too far because of her breathing. So we had a foster son who got in touch with Match-Up. He knew them because I guess they'd helped him with readers once in a while. And then they contacted Dan and Ann and asked if they'd be volunteers for us."

When the Donoghues first came over, their first son, Nathaniel, had just been born. "So when they came over, we became acquainted with him. They left him with us when they wanted to go shopping at the mall one time. That was the beginning of it. So it worked out that way, and it continued on."

Every so often, the Donoghues would invite Doug and his wife, Steph, to plays at Harvard, where Dan was on the faculty of the English Department. They would pick up Doug and Steph on Sundays to come with them to church. When Doug had gone into the hospital for heart surgery, Dan came to visit him. And when Steph died a few years ago, the Donoghues again were a big help to Doug.

"Dan did a lot of running around and a lot of time was spent to help me move here from the old house," Doug said. "An average person wouldn't have put the time in." In fact, according to Janet, a big part of the reason that Doug had sold the house in Watertown and moved to this assisted living facility was to be closer to the Donoghues, who had moved to Concord years earlier.

"They must be like family to you," I said.

"Yes," Doug replied. "They're very good."

I asked Doug whether the Donoghues were religious.

"I do know their *religion*," he responded after thinking it over, "but I won't assume the privilege of offering an opinion on that."

He talked about how considerate Dan was—how if there was something in the apartment that needed attention, he might mention it. "I guess all I can say is he's been extremely thoughtful and helpful. And," he added, "he never makes you feel small by anything he might say."

I asked Doug how often the Donoghues came to visit.

"Not too often. No, they really don't come that often. If I want something, I can call them up, and they'll bring it down, but they really don't come that much." He paused. "And I can understand why. Because we had a foster son, and he became quadriplegic. And when that happened, the hospital and the doctors, they told us, 'Don't go and visit too much. Because then he'll become dependent.' And I think it's the same thing here. You've got to just *live* with what's happened. You've got to live the rest of your life, you know. But it is very difficult here to make friends."

"You've been here a year now?" I asked.

"Over a year," Doug said.

"So tell me a little bit about what your day is like here."

"My day?"

"Yes."

Tomorrow morning, he said, he would get up at seven o'clock and go down and have breakfast in what they called the country kitchen. There was a long table where people could sit together, and you could get a pastry and something to drink. At nine o'clock, he would get a haircut on the premises. At 10:30, there might be exercises downstairs in the activity room. Then in the afternoon there would be a program of some sort.

"You said that it's hard to make friends here," I said.

"I think so," he said. "They don't seem to have the interest."

"And so it's hard to have a conversation?"

"It's impossible," Doug replied gruffly. "Overall, I find a lot of them are very difficult to converse with around here. And then, of course, the hearing problem is not helping any. You have to take that into consideration."

"So do you have any friends here?"

"I haven't got any friends at all," he said.

"So how *do* you spend your time?"

Well, he was doing more reading in braille, he said, but even that was becoming increasingly difficult. "My fingers are getting numb. Like when you see and your page gets blurry. It's the same thing with your hands. When it registers on your brain, it's all fuzzy. You can't make out the letters."

As I looked at Doug there sitting motionless at his desk, I realized that despite his openness with me, I couldn't begin to imagine what he was thinking or feeling—an eighty-six-year-old widower living alone in this little room with nobody in his life other than a family he had been matched with through a volunteer program many years ago. Yet he didn't seem to feel sorry for himself.

"Tell me about your wife," I said, after a while.

"About Steph?" he said. "She went to the same Catholic church that I did. So I'd be down at the church and I'd be talking all the time. Confessions or whatever. I'd be there talking and having a good time—and she didn't like it at all."

He chuckled.

"I didn't see any more of her for quite a few years. And then I was supposed to double with another fellow on a blind date. I was supposed to go with Steph, and he was going to go with some other girl. Well, he never showed up. So Steph and I went out together."

They got married a year later, in 1947, and a few years later bought a big house on Summer Street in Watertown.

Then a priest whom Steph worked with and who had something to do with the Veterans Administration asked Doug and Steph if they would be willing to take in one of the blinded veterans who had come back from the Korean War and now needed to learn to cope with his blindness. They did, and as time went on, they took in others. Then they began taking in blind foster children who were referred to them by the Perkins School.

"Vernon was the first boy," Doug said. "Perkins asked if we would take him for a short time, just for the summer. We said yes, and they said, 'Well, he's the worst kid we have here. If you can't take care of him, call us up and we'll pick him right up.' And I said, 'If we take him, we're not sending him back.'"

There were several more foster children after Vernon, including Barbara and Joe, the quadriplegic young man Doug had mentioned earlier.

"He was in Kenmore Square," Doug said. "He had a part-time job over there. He already had a full-time job at Perkins working at the library, but I guess he wanted the extra money. So anyhow, they attacked him over at Kenmore Square and threw him up against a post and broke the vertebrae in his neck."

"Oh, my God . . ."

"So he collapsed, and a woman came by and called the police. Well, they took him to the hospital, and then they called the house. So we went right over to the hospital, and we stayed all that night. Then around five o'clock in the morning, they decided to do surgery. We went in every day to see how he was doing. And of course they had to teach him how to breathe all over again, because he couldn't breathe normally. Then he went into a rehabilitation place in Roxbury, and after he was there, they told me he wanted to have an apartment. So they trained him to manage people, and he got an apartment on Temple Place in Boston. We used to see him quite often."

"Is he still in touch with you?" I asked.

"He died," Doug said. "A year or two ago. He had two heart surgeries within twenty-four hours, and I guess it was too much."

Doug's window was partially open behind me, and the rain, which hadn't let up all day, seemed to have intensified since we'd started talking. I pulled the window down to keep it from splashing in.

"Doug," I said, "does anybody visit you here besides the Donoghues?"

"Oh yes, other fellows and other couples have come in. But the way I feel now, I am very distraught with everything. You know, they say you can make friends. But you don't make friends like that—you know, like drawing them out of a hat. So really, it's a case of *existing*. I tell Dan that, but he doesn't approve. But it's true nonetheless. Because I'm not doing any services for myself or for anybody else. I'm really not.

"And my balance is getting worse—I notice that. I've noticed the last couple of days, when I go to stand up to walk around, my balance isn't good at all. So you see this gradual deterioration . . . they call it peripheral neuropathy. I think that's what I have. And what can you do? It's going to gradually creep up and creep up. You know, I went to a psychiatrist and he said, 'Take this medicine.' And I said, 'But that's not going to cure me.' And he said, 'Well, it'll make you more relaxed and you'll probably be able to accept it better.'" He laughed, but it was a pinched laugh—not like before. Doug fell silent for a minute, and then said, "The thing is, you get sluggish if you don't keep active in the community. Even if you're home, you've got to be out in your community doing something." He went on to tell me that he had spent eleven years in scouting.

"Oh, really?"

"I was chairman of the committee," he said proudly. "You had to work with the church because the church was the sponsor, and you had to get a group of men who could work together. And it worked out that we had a very good group of men—eighteen men and sixty-five boys."

"It sounds like you've done a lot of good in your life," I said.

"Well, I've enjoyed it," Doug said. "And the thing is, it was no effort. You see, my wife had a bad start too. Because her parents didn't want *her* either. So she'd had a hard time of it to begin with. That's why Perkins is a great school. Because they went beyond just what a school is asked to do. For instance, after my mother died, I lost my father. What happened is that I was home from Perkins for Easter when my father died of pneumonia. They notified the school, and I stayed with one of the neighbors until the next day. And then the school called to see if I was being taken care of.

"So then I went back to the school, and the director said, 'You can go on to the state and become a state ward, or we can see if we can get you independent by having a guardian and an administrator appointed.' Well, the school had Marjorie Hurd as a guardian, and some man as an administrator—so the school did all that."

"So that you could be independent?"

"Yes, well, they left a lot of it up to me. The guardian—she was a lawyer in Boston—she said to me, 'You know, you can't depend on me too much. You'll have to be independent.' And so I was pretty much independent."

"How old were you then?" I asked.

"When my father died? About fourteen or fifteen. And of course I had to work during the summer because I had no place to go. So Father Conway in Boston, he got me a job on a chicken farm."

"A chicken farm?"

Just then, the doorbell rang.

I opened the door, and before me stood a petite woman dressed in pale blue and a tall, lanky teenager with slightly curly hair and glasses. "Hi," the woman said. "I'm Ann Donoghue and this is our oldest son, Nathaniel."

She shook my hand and stepped into the room.

"Hi, Doug!" she said, going up and giving him a hug.

Doug was thrilled.

"Oh!" he said. "I didn't know you were coming. I would have baked a cake!"

We all laughed.

"It's been a while since you've baked a cake, hasn't it?" Ann said.

Nathaniel came up and gave Doug a hug too, although he seemed a little embarrassed—probably because I was there.

"Dan will be right in," Ann said, speaking slowly and clearly. "He's parking the car."

Just then Dan walked in. He was more compact than his son, but he had the same curly hair and wore a blue blazer. "How are you, Doug?" he said, his voice loud and clear.

Doug gave him a big smile. He was obviously delighted that Dan was there. "Well," he said, "I've been doing a lot of talking."

"You're looking good, Doug."

"I guess I feel pretty good," Doug said.

Ann and Dan pulled a couple of chairs over to where Doug and I were sitting, while Nathaniel remained standing near the window.

"Ann, why don't we start with you?" I said. "Tell me about yourself."

"I grew up in Scranton, I have three children, and I work as a part-time reading tutor in a local community school," she began.

"And did you get into volunteering as a child?"

No, she said, not really. She had participated in the occasional food drive at the church, but her family never did much volunteering.

"So how did you get involved in Match-Up?"

"We were living in Watertown, but we were attending the Paulist Center, which is a church in downtown Boston. And one day when we were down there, we noticed a poster asking for help: an elderly couple in Watertown needed help with groceries. So we contacted the person on that poster—the Match-Up person at the Paulist Center—and asked her if we could help out."

"Why?" I said, interrupting. "I mean, what possessed you?"

"Well, we lived in Watertown, and we figured . . ."

Dan jumped in, interrupting Ann. "What I remember is a little more cynical. My feeling at the time was, 'We don't want to be yuppies. We don't just want to be out for ourselves and improving our style of life and our quality of life.' I remember that I felt there should be something more that we do."

"Let's back up a little," I said. "Dan, please give me the same information that Ann . . ."

"All right," he said, with a straight face. "I was born in Scranton . . ."

All of us laughed, including Doug.

"Actually," Dan said, "I grew up in Oregon, just outside Portland. A large Roman Catholic family. I was one of eight kids."

"Was there any tradition of volunteering in your family?"

"I guess there was. For instance, we all played musical instruments of one kind or another, and at Christmas our parents would gather all of us together to play Christmas carols at one of the old folks' homes."

"That's great," I said.

"Actually, we were of two minds about it at the time," he said. "It wasn't exactly a cool thing to do."

I brought the conversation back to Doug and Steph. "Do you remember your first visit?" I asked.

"Oh, yes," Ann said, adding that she thought it had helped that they had brought their three-month-old son—Nathaniel—with them. "That might have helped ease their anxieties."

"So what happened?"

"Well, we knew they needed help with their groceries," Dan said. He turned to Doug. "By the way, how *did* you and Steph do your grocery shopping?"

"We did it ourselves," Doug said. "We would just take a shopping cart around and take all the things that we needed off the shelves."

"But how did you get home?" Ann asked.

"We would come back along the river," Doug said.

"So you would *walk*?" Ann said. "That's quite a ways."

"On the other side of the river, yes," Doug said.

"That's quite a ways," Ann repeated.

"It was a walk," Doug said.

"That would have been over a mile," Dan said. "But I guess I didn't actually realize that until now."

"We used to put it in one of those old supermarket baskets—you must have seen it," Doug said. "We would fill it up and take it home. We'd usually buy enough for two weeks, you know."

It had turned out that grocery shopping wasn't the only thing Doug and Steph needed help with. They also needed help with reading and with paperwork. So as things developed, Ann would stay with Steph and read her the newspaper and the mail while Doug went to the store with Dan and Nathaniel.

"And when they came back," Ann said, "we always stayed and had . . ."

"Ice cream!" Dan exclaimed.

"And what about you, Nathaniel?" I asked. "How did you get involved?"

"Nathaniel was a great shopper," Dan said. "He used to ride in Doug's shopping cart. Do you remember that, Nathaniel?"

Nathaniel didn't, but Doug did. "He used to ride all through the supermarket in the cart, but then he started eating so much, we had to take him out."

We all laughed.

As I listened to the conversation and watched the Donoghues interact with Doug, I realized that this relationship ran considerably deeper than what people usually think of when they think about volunteers. "Now, this is something that started out as a kind of anti-yuppie rebellion," I said. "But it sounds like it turned into something much more than just doing somebody's shopping every so often."

"Oh, yes," Dan said.

"When did you realize that?" I asked.

Dan guessed that it was probably after about two years. After two years, he said, if you were doing something just to be doing it, you might say, "Well, that's enough. I'll do something else now." But they hadn't felt that way about Doug and Steph.

"Doug and Steph became almost family," Ann said. "Exactly when that happened I don't know. But our kids . . ." She turned to Nathaniel. "You probably know them better than your own grandparents." Dan's mother was still in Oregon, she said, and her mother was still in Scranton.

"There was one point where there was a possibility that we might be moving away to Virginia," Ann went on. "And I think at that point, it struck us that if that happened, it would impact Doug and Steph in a big way. It turned out that that didn't happen, but I guess that's when it really dawned on me."

"And would it have had an impact on *you*?" I asked.

Dan thought about that for moment before answering. "I think *that* part of it sort of crept up on us. I mean, from the beginning, it was a very friendly relationship, although, you know, to be honest, occasionally it felt like a chore—like if we wanted to do something else that day. But for the most part, no," Dan said. "So I think it just developed slowly over time. And the year that Ann was talking about—when there was a chance that we might have moved to Virginia—that was 1990. So that would have been, what? Less than three years into our time with Doug and Steph?"

"So I guess by then, we already sensed that the relationship was about more than just the volunteering," Ann mused.

"Sometimes we'd get things in the mail from Match-Up," Dan said. "You know, they'd want to keep track of things, like how many hours we were spending. And we'd say, 'Well, why do we need this? *We're* not volunteers.'"

"And actually we still feel that way," Ann said. "I mean, I guess we're on the books, but it's gone way beyond that."

After we finished talking, Doug came with us down the elevator to the lobby. Before we left, he gave us a guided tour of the entire first floor, including the "country kitchen" where he had his breakfast every morning. Then he walked out the front door with us, where we stood together for a few minutes under the awning before braving the rain.

But finally we had to say good-bye. As I shook Doug's hand, I wondered how much of my handshake he could actually feel. And when I pulled out of the parking lot, soaked through from my dash back to the car, I could see Doug still standing there, alone under the awning, facing out into the night.

PRESQUE ISLE, MAINE

THE NEXT MORNING, I left for Presque Isle, Maine. Janet had estimated that it would take from eight to ten hours, depending on my willingness to risk a speeding ticket. By the time I pulled onto Route One north, the sky had cleared, the humidity had blown out to sea with the clouds, and I had the front windows down to let in the cool fall air.

Half an hour later, after crossing the Picataqua River into Maine, I stopped at the Welcome Center on I-95 and asked the man behind the desk whether he could give me the latest weather report for Presque Isle.

"Sure thing," he said, bringing up weather.com on an old desktop computer that was even slower than mine at home. "Looks like today there's a high of fifty-four and a low of thirty-four. And there's a 90 percent chance of rain tomorrow. But hey, last week they had a foot of snow."

It was about 5:30 when I reached the end of I-95 near the Canadian border and got back onto Route One, turning north toward Presque Isle. Route One along the Canadian border was a far cry from the chronically jammed six-lane highway back in New Jersey. Up here, it was down to two lanes, divided by a dotted line. There wasn't much of a shoulder on either side and not much lighting apart from the occasional neon sign. And while there were plenty of trucks on Route One in New Jersey, up here it was *all* trucks, many of them piled high with freshly cut timber.

I stopped at a roadside place called the Blue Moose for dinner, so it was almost 7:30 by the time I finally got to Presque Isle. From several hundred yards down the road, I spotted the yellow electric sign for the Northern Lights Motel where I had booked my room. Not quite the Plaza, but at seventy-nine dollars for two nights, I was relieved to find that it was clean, neat, and comfortable. A framed cross-stitch of brightly colored flowers adorned the wall, and a big sign over the desk warned: FOR YOUR OWN PROTECTION NO SMOKING IN BED.

Elaine

The next morning, the sky was gray and bleak, and—sure enough—it was raining again, although not as fiercely as it had in Boston. Just a cold, steady, depressing rain that makes you want to stay inside and drink coffee all day. According to the electric sign in front of the People's Bank, it was forty-one degrees.

But as if to spite the weather, Elaine Briggs, Presque Isle's Faith in Action director, wore a brightly flowered skirt and a bright red enamel apple brooch on her jacket lapel. Even her smile was bright—an act of open defiance on such a miserable morning.

Based in a converted mobile home that housed the Aroostook Agency on Aging, Elaine's office was tiny, made even smaller by the rows of cardboard file boxes stacked against the wall. She motioned for me to sit in the chair beside her desk while she finished a phone call.

"Well, we'll do what we can," she said patiently to whoever was on the other end. "We'll try to have somebody there to take her. . . . Sure thing. . . . You're very welcome."

Elaine spoke with a twang that didn't sound like New England; it turned out that she was originally from Wyoming. Her husband, she said, had been in occupational medicine in the military, and when he'd retired nine years ago, he had wanted to settle down in a small, rural community where he could practice occupational medicine in peace. Elaine had fond memories of a weekend that they had spent on the Maine coast years ago when they were first married, so when a position came open in Caribou, they decided to take it.

"I told him I wanted to be in Maine," she laughed, "but I forgot to be specific about *where* in Maine." Caribou, which I would be passing through later that day, was even farther north than Presque Isle and had to be a good four-hour drive from the nearest town on the Maine coast.

After a brief stint at a local newspaper, Elaine had taken a job here at the Agency on Aging, running the federally funded Retired Senior Volunteer Program, known as RSVP. Through that experience, she said, she had begun to understand the needs of Aroostook County's sixteen thousand older residents, many of them isolated and scattered across this sprawling sixty-five-hundred-square-mile county.

It was also through RSVP that she had started to realize that volunteers from the area's many churches could play a role in helping to meet those

needs. Church volunteers often helped out with things like medical transportation, minor home repairs, and putting up people's storm windows—
services that the county's elderly very much needed. "But," she said, "it
was very spotty. It would work in some places, but it was hard to get it
going in others." And so about three years ago, Elaine had given up her
job as RSVP director and applied for a Faith in Action grant.

"There's one story that really sticks in my mind about why this is so
important," she said. "We had this lady up around Caribou who'd called
us for medical transportation. Meanwhile, her son, who lived down in
Boston, had called me because he was very concerned about the condition of her home. Some of the windows were broken out, and we needed
to get someone out there to take care of that.

"So what happened—and it was kind of on two parallel tracks—is that
we had a volunteer who went out to provide medical transportation to a
doctor's appointment for this lady. He went to pick her up, and she came
out with nothing but a little scarf around her shoulder—and this was in
the dead of an Aroostook winter. He said to her, 'Don't you have a coat
that you need to put on?' And she said, 'Well, I think I have a coat, but I
can't find it anywhere.' And that obviously alarmed him.

"Then, when the other volunteer who was going to take care of the
windows went in, he discovered pretty much of a deplorable situation.
There was a large number of animals living in the house, the lady was
obviously not eating well, and there were serious problems with the house
itself. So we communicated these things to the son, and he was very concerned. Ironically," Elaine said, shaking her head, "across the road was
the daughter—living in a house right across the road from the mother.
And she actually worked for the Department of Human Services."

"You're kidding!"

"And when we made a referral to Human Services, the daughter was
aware that we were working through it. Ultimately, the lady was removed
from the home and put into a nursing home—because she just could not
stay there in that house. And it was directly because of these volunteers
going in and becoming aware of the distress. Now, the lady wasn't *happy*
about having to leave her home. But it was truly in her best interest to
have her needs cared for, because there was just no way to see to her needs
in the home."

"But what about the daughter?" I asked, incredulous.

"Well, I don't understand that either," Elaine said, suddenly sounding
very tired. "Because that was a really serious situation. But we run into
that a lot—where there's actually family, but for some reason they absent
themselves. And so it made me realize that there are an awful lot of peo-

ple out there that appearances would say don't need any help. But until you get in and know the *real* story, you don't know what their situation is. And just because they have family across the road doesn't mean that they get the care they need."

I nodded.

"And if we hadn't had volunteers . . ." Elaine paused. "Because you see, this lady would *not* let an agency in. She was refusing Meals on Wheels because she was saying, 'I don't want the government involved.'"

"But with this program, they think 'church'?"

"Right. Because these were people who were coming via a church mechanism—somebody whom maybe they could link to somebody else who they knew in the community. Then it was less threatening."

I glanced at my watch and was amazed to see that we'd talked for over an hour. "I need to get going," I said.

"Oh, my gosh," she said. "You sure do."

Elaine had scheduled me to meet with the pastor of the United Baptist Church in Littleton, and she was anxious for me to get there on time since he had only half an hour free to talk with me. Then at one o'clock, I was to meet with an elderly woman who was being helped by a Faith in Action volunteer from the church.

Elaine had tried to set up an interview for me with the volunteer too, but the volunteer had flatly refused to be interviewed, telling Elaine that she didn't want any publicity for what she was doing. Elaine told me that the volunteer worked at Wal-Mart and that I could try to call her over there if I wanted to try to change her mind. (I didn't.)

Finally, Elaine said, she'd scheduled an interview for me for the next morning with Harold Rasmussen, a ninety-five-year-old volunteer—not a care receiver, she emphasized, but a volunteer—who lived by himself in an area called the Woodlands, just west of Caribou.

Harold

The next morning, after checking out of the Northern Lights, I drove north up Route One through Caribou, following the directions that Elaine had given me to Harold Rasmussen's place. The rain had finally let up, but the air was still raw, with heavy gray clouds flying in endless waves up toward Canada.

Harold's address turned out to be a small house on a corner lot. There were other houses scattered up and down the road, but it was basically rural out here. Trees seemed to be creeping up from all sides, as if, many years ago, someone had started to build a new development and given up before the job was halfway done, relinquishing sovereignty to the Great North Woods.

There was something forlorn about the place: weeds sprouting up from the paving stones and along the sides of the house, birches and pines and some kind of deciduous scrub crowding in from behind, the house's blue and white paint smudged with grime as if some giant child with dirty hands had picked it up and played with it. Naked wires hung from one of the windows and from the roof, and there was what appeared to be an old iron sink near the back door with tall weeds growing out of it like a bad haircut.

I knocked on the front door.

No answer.

There was a small window in the door, so caked with grime that it was barely translucent, but there was a corner on the bottom that I could still see through, and there, sure enough, across the hall in what appeared to be the living room, sat a rather large bald-headed man wearing khaki pants that were a little too wide and too short, a striped dress shirt open at the collar, a red-checkered wool hunting jacket, and big square black-framed glasses that made him look a little like a high school science teacher.

Harold.

I remember feeling, even at that first glance, that there was something so sad about him as he sat there, utterly alone in that empty house.

I knocked again, but again there was no response. He was just sitting there, motionless, staring blankly across the room, not even looking toward the door.

Was he dead?

This time I pounded the door hard with my fist, but when I peered back inside, he still hadn't moved. I was really starting to worry.

I could see an old black telephone on the table next to him, so I decided to try calling him on my cell phone to see whether maybe that would get his attention. But my cell phone said NO SERVICE.

Then, suddenly, he turned toward me. He seemed to be reaching for something on the table beside him, next to the phone. Hugely relieved to see him move, I waved my hands frantically in front of the little window, hoping that maybe the motion would catch his eye.

It did!

Slowly Harold got up from his chair, grasped a wooden cane that was leaning against his chair, and lumbered toward the door. He put his face up to the grimy window, squinted out at me, and motioned for me to go around to the back. Apparently this particular door no longer worked.

"Come on in," he growled as I came around to the back of the house. With a hard shove, he pushed the rain-warped wooden back door open for me.

"Thank you," I said, following him through a musty kitchen and into the living room. "And thank you for inviting me into your home."

Harold grunted. "I'm very happy to have some company," he said, carefully lowering himself back into his chair, an old recliner with a stained blue blanket thrown over it.

I could see now that his chair faced the television. It was tuned to one of the morning talk shows, but with the sound turned off. The item that I'd seen him reach for on the table beside him turned out to be a coffee mug, which appeared to be empty. I sat down across from him and started to try to explain who I was and what I was doing there.

"I assume you talked to Elaine Briggs," I began.

"Did I talk to whom?"

That's when I noticed his hearing aid.

"Did Elaine Briggs call you?" I asked, louder this time. "A lady from the aging agency?"

"Oh, yes," he said. "Sure."

But I wasn't convinced that he really understood what I was talking about.

Still, I told Harold about the Robert Wood Johnson Foundation and the Faith in Action program and said that I was interested in talking to some of the Faith in Action volunteers. "And I understand that you're a volunteer," I said.

"Oh," he said, choosing his words carefully and speaking at about half my speed. "I don't know about that. I have a man here that I call at ten o'clock every morning so that he can get up. Five days a week I call him at ten o'clock. That's all the volunteering I do."

"How long do you talk to him?"

"Very little. I say, 'Good morning, Alan.' He says 'Good morning.' And then I say, 'Good-bye.'"

"That's it?"

"We don't go far beyond that," Harold said. "But I am planning on getting in contact with him and going to visit him—if he wants me to."

"You haven't met him yet?"

"I haven't met him yet, but the lady said he was sixty years old. I think he's a veteran, and he's in a wheelchair."

Elaine had told me that in fact the man was something of a recluse, and that minimal telephone contact was as much as he would tolerate at this point. But she was hopeful that he would gradually warm up to Harold and that eventually he would become sufficiently comfortable with the relationship for them to meet face to face. As for Harold, Elaine said, he was always on the prowl for somebody to play checkers with. He *loved* to play checkers. In fact, she had warned me to be prepared for a game or two myself.

Taking my cue from what Elaine had told me, I suggested to Harold that maybe he and Alan could get together to play checkers.

"He doesn't play checkers," Harold said sadly. "I asked him if he played checkers. But," he added, brightening a little, "I might *get* him playing checkers."

"You'll have to teach him," I said.

"If he is interested, I will."

"That sounds terrific," I said. "And if you'd like, maybe you and I could play checkers later on this morning."

"We can?"

"Sure. Before I go, we can play."

"I like to play with people," he said. "I'm a poor player, but I like to play checkers."

"I'm a poor player too," I told him, which was true. "But I like to play too," I added—which wasn't quite as true.

Harold told me that he was born on the thirteenth day of July in 1908—so he really *was* ninety-five years old, just as Elaine had said. He was born nearby on a farm in Caswell Township, just north of Limestone. He had lived on the farm until he was eleven years old, and then his father had moved the family to Tangle Ridge. He had four brothers and two sisters, one of whom—an eighty-six-year-old widow—was still living in an apartment in Caribou.

"How often do you see her?" I asked.

"Oh, I see her often. Once or twice a week."

"That's nice," I said. "Nice for you *and* for her."

"She's very happy where she is," Harold said. "I love the town, so I suggest that we go out to lunch. But she's not interested to go out for lunch." He paused and chuckled. "But I do have a lady I take out for lunch occasionally."

"Oh, and who's that?"

"An old friend. We go out and spend the day."

"That's very nice. Is this someone you've known for a long time?"

"I've known her in a small way for a long while," Harold said. "But then after I got to be a widower, I became reacquainted with her, and then we started going out. She's a woman eighty years old. Never was married. A retired school teacher. She likes to talk. She studies astronomy, so she's kind of an interesting woman to talk to." He chuckled again. "She's not much of an astronomer, but when I want to talk about astronomy, why then she has no trouble talking at all."

I asked Harold whether he got out much aside from visiting with his lady friend.

"I get out about every day," he said. "Practically every day."

"Where do you go?"

"I go to town shopping, and I just drive around in the area. I don't have many people to visit. Because . . ." He smiled sadly. "My friends are all dead. And who wants to bother with an old man?" There wasn't any self-pity in the way he said it. He was just explaining the situation.

"Years ago, before I become a widower, I had a couple of old guys who just loved to play checkers," he went on. "And we'd get together—two or three of us, we'd get together once a week, and we'd play checkers all afternoon. But they're dead."

"So you're the last checkers player," I said.

He smiled, nodding his head.

"I guess I am."

It turned out, though, that Harold did still have one friend up in a place called New Denmark whom he said he played checkers with from time to time. They would play a couple of games, drink coffee, and talk about religion. "I'm very interested in religion," he said. "It's a great mystery to me. My faith in Jesus Christ changed my life when I was twenty-one. That was the first time that I learned that I was a sinner. The first time I knew that I was bound for hell."

I asked Harold whether his parents had been religious.

"They were Lutherans," he said. "My father was an ugly man and a rough man to live with, but he was an honest man. He couldn't hear. Lost his hearing when he was forty. Probably that's why he didn't go to church. But he believed in the Bible. Both my parents believed in the Bible."

Harold didn't go to church much either when he was growing up. The roads were closed in winter, and the winters were long up here. But he did go to Sunday school, which was held in the nearby schoolhouse.

I asked him what had happened when he was twenty-one that had changed his life.

"Well, you see," he said, "I was a railroad man by then, and I had a brother who'd become converted, and he said to me, 'Why don't you come down to the service with me?' So I did. And I'd never heard a man preach the way that man preached. He was what you call a lay preacher. A farmer. And when he preached, I could see what kind of shape *I* was in. There was nothing good *in* me. And I thought, Well, I don't want to live that way. I don't want to help tear the world down. I want to be an *asset* to the world. And I *surely* don't want to go to hell."

He looked at me to see how I was taking it, and then went on, "As I think about it now, what bothered me most was not the life I'd lived *before* that. I'd lived a pretty good life for a non-Christian. I didn't use tobacco, I didn't use liquor, I didn't gamble, and I didn't run around with bad company. But when I think about the poor *example* I'd been . . ." He stopped midsentence and laughed. "But I don't want to preach a sermon to you!"

"You mentioned that you were a railroad man," I said. "Which railroad?"

"The B&A," Harold said. "The Bangor and Aroostook Railroad. Ran all the way from St. Francis, about seventeen miles up the river from Fort Kent, down to Bangor. I was a fireman. Fired the old steam locomotives. There's an old saying: all you need to be a fireman is a strong back and a weak mind." He chuckled.

"I was with them for eighteen years," he went on. "After ten years, I became a diesel locomotive engineer. And then I lost my hearing. It was hereditary, just like my father. So I quit before they had to let me go. I was thirty-five years old." He shook his head. "One thing about the railroads. You have to know *everything* about the railroad when you're working for them. But you can't use that knowledge anywhere else. So I had to start my life over again. And that hurt me. I had a lot of seniority."

I did some quick math in my head—1908 plus thirty-five—and calculated that at least by that time—1943—the Great Depression had pretty much come to an end. I asked Harold about the Depression.

"Well, I generally worked," he said. "I worked at the railroad, and I went home and helped my father on the farm. We had cattle and potatoes and timber. But farming was rough. I helped my father keep his farm, but a lot of people lost their farms. I didn't spend any of my money from the railroad on women because my father needed the money for the farm. And then when I got through railroading, I bought the farm from my father."

It was a hundred-acre farm, and soon afterward. Harold had bought an adjoining hundred-acre farm. About half of the two hundred acres was tillable, the other half forested. His father kept a small five-acre tract and built himself a house on it, where he retired.

What about school?

"I did not graduate from the fifth grade," he said, chagrined. "When I got that big, I spent my winters on the end of a crosscut saw with my father." He had started working on the farm when he was eight years old, doing chores while he was still at school. But as soon as he left school, at age twelve, he said, "Then I took a man's place."

After he left the railroad and bought his father's farm, Harold farmed for the next seventeen years. It was hard going.

"I was working my head off just to hold my own," he said. "I wasn't getting ahead. I just kept thinking, 'If I could get out of here . . .' Well, then the Soil Bank come along. Boy, I thought, here's where I get out. They paid me eighteen hundred dollars a year, and that was real money in the late 1950s."

He quit farming in 1960 and finally sold the farm ten years later.

"A fellow bought it in 1970 with a government loan and farmed it for about two years before he went under. So they put it up for sale again. I thought about putting in a bid for it, but then I thought, What'll I do with it?"

Besides the farm and the railroad, Harold had also worked in the woods—on both ends: cutting down the trees with a crosscut saw and then milling them at a small sawmill that he had up on the Van Buren River. Summers he worked at the mill; winters, he was back at the railroad.

It was at about this time that another big change occurred in Harold's life.

"I went to Crouseville one day, and my father came with me. While we were there having dinner, he says to me, 'Why don't you get married?' I was in my thirties then. 'Well,' I said, 'I can't afford a wife.' And he says to me, 'Well, you don't want to go through life single. You want to get married and establish a home. You have no life living alone.' So I thought it over, and I said, 'I guess you're right, Dad.'" Harold looked up at me with a grin. "So I said yes to the first woman who asked me."

"You're kidding!"

"Her name was Marian. She was brought up in Fort Fairfield, and she was a dental technician. I lived with her for forty years and then she died. And . . . I didn't like that when she died. I cried a little bit every night when I went to bed, and I cried a little bit every morning when I got up."

They had no children of their own, but they did adopt a son.

"I didn't want any children," Harold said. "But my wife wanted a son. I said, 'All they are is just a bother and a worry to their parents.'"

"So did he worry you?"

"No," Harold admitted. "He was a good boy."

After leaving home, his son had served as a paratrooper for twenty-one years, moved to North Carolina, and driven a long-distance truck until he'd had a major heart attack that had required six bypasses within the past year. "He's a sick man now," Harold said sadly.

But, he said, in spite of his health problems, his son had come up from North Carolina for a visit this past summer—just like he used to when the trucking company would send him up to Aroostook County on some of his runs. And there was a bright green birthday card from him on the table near the telephone that must have been there since July. Harold picked it up and read it to me, word for word.

"So, Harold," I said, "how have things changed around here since you were a boy?"

Well, he said, he didn't see his first airplane until he was twelve, and you hardly ever saw a car in those days. There weren't any roads, really. Everybody used horses. When he bought his father's farm, he used a trac-tor, but his father had always farmed with horses—said that was the only way to farm.

"What about television? How much do you watch it?"

"Oh," he said, "I watch it a lot. Mostly the world news and Bill Reilly on Fox. I like to watch Reilly. And *Forensic Files*—that interests me."

He brought up Iraq.

"It's just another Vietnam," he said, with some bitterness. "Meanwhile, we're spending ourselves to death. Do you know that over in China, they make only two dollars an hour, but they've got money invested in our country. We're the richest country in the world and *they're* lending *us* money. Our national debt—and the interest on it—is getting so high I don't know how we're going to get out of it. You know, this democratic system we have over here has worked very well, but I don't know if it can survive."

"Why do you say that?"

"Because at the rate it's going, all this debt is taking something away from us. A lot of us who are on pension, we had a dollar or two put aside. And we depended on that interest. I was getting 5 or 6 or 7 percent interest on my CDs—and now it's nothing. That hurts me, you see. I am surviving without it, but I planned on that. So it's hurting me. And I'm just one—that's just one example. There are many, many people in the same situation."

I nodded.

"Things are different now than when we migrated to America," he continued. "We had so many resources here. Minerals and woods. But we have dissipated it, don't you see? Now we don't have that to fall back on. You look at the candidates for office. It seems all they have to do is make a lot of promises. But there *are* no free gifts. Like the new sidewalks in Van Buren. That's just buying votes," he said, his voice filled with scorn. "What I say is, if the people in Van Buren want new sidewalks, let them build their *own* sidewalks."

I asked Harold whether there were any presidents or other political leaders, past or present, that he thought were any good.

"Well," he said, "I have less respect for them all the time. When I talk to our local representatives or senators, they always say, 'One man can't do anything.' And I tell them, one man *can* do something: he can speak out!

"So I have a very poor opinion of elected officials. Bush gets all the blame for invading Iraq, but he didn't do it alone. A president cannot start a war alone. If Congress can't do anything else, they can cut off the money supply. So he's not alone. He's got the majority behind him."

I was ready for a break, so I took a chance and asked Harold if he was up for a game of checkers.

He broke into a big grin. "Are you sure?"

"You bet," I said.

He grasped the armrests of his recliner and pushed himself up onto his feet. "We can play in the kitchen," he said, reaching for his cane. He said that he had fallen and hurt his hip three years ago. "My walking hasn't been so good since the surgery."

He paused on his way to the kitchen and pointed at a big framed black-and-white photograph on the wall. "That's one of the steam locomotives at Van Buren. And that's me right there in front of it."

I went over and looked at it more closely. The locomotive was positively majestic, standing on the tracks with its black iron flanks gleaming, clouds of steam pouring from its top and from its sides. And standing beside it, barely taller than the huge steel wheels, was a young man dressed in what appeared to be some kind of uniform.

"I loved those steam engines," Harold said. "Those trains, when they got going, they were hungry. Used a ton of coal in twenty minutes."

"You're kidding."

"It broke my heart when I had to leave them," he said, shaking his head sadly.

There were other pictures, but they were of people, not locomotives.

I asked which one was his wife, Marian.

He said there wasn't one. "I've been married three times," he explained. "Each time I had to get rid of my old pictures."

His second marriage, after Marian died, had lasted fourteen years. He'd met his third wife when he was eighty-seven. "She was a lot younger. I said to her, 'Is it worth it? You can't expect me to be around more than five years.' And she said, 'It's worth it.' Evidently, I don't like to live alone. But now my niece—she's really good to me—she says, 'I don't care how many girlfriends you have, but you can't get married again!'"

We went into the kitchen and sat down at a rickety table covered with what appeared to be an old flowered oilcloth. Harold put a folded cardboard checkers board and a box of big wooden red and black checkers pieces in front of us. "I am not a good player," Harold assured me again.

We set up the board, and he told me to go first, so I did. I moved one of my two center pieces.

"Well, well, well," he said ponderously, as if I had just made a particularly interesting first move—when, in fact, in checkers you only have four choices for your first move.

"Well, well, well," he said again.

In fact, that was pretty much the extent of our conversation for the next ten minutes. By the end of the ten minutes, I had a sinking feeling that this could turn out to be a very long morning.

I decided to break the silence and asked him about his parents.

"My father was from New Denmark, but my mother was from the Old Country," he said. "She came over when she was a little girl."

"From Denmark?"

"That's right," he said, as I made another move. "Well, well, well."

"What about the farming up here? Has it changed since you were a boy?"

"Oh," he said, "it's way down. They used to farm two hundred thousand acres up here. Last year it was down to about sixty thousand."

I asked him why.

"Price of potatoes," he said, frowning thoughtfully at the board. "Now, there . . . I did something I shouldn't have done."

I looked at the board, but didn't see anything wrong.

"I did something I shouldn't have done," he muttered again.

He started whistling softly to himself. It was as if I wasn't even in the room. I realized that he took his checkers a lot more seriously than I did.

"Well," he said after a while, "I made mistakes. Big mistakes."

For a moment, I thought he was talking about his life, but then he said it again: "Well, well, well . . ." And I realized he was talking about the game.

"I've gotten myself in a jam here," he said. "A terrible jam."

Mercifully, the game ended in a draw soon after that. It was 10:15.

"Oh," he said, as he looked up at the kitchen clock. "I've got to call Alan. I'm fifteen minutes late."

Slowly, Harold got up and dialed the old black wall phone. "Good morning, Alan," he said cheerfully. "I'm a little late in calling you . . . Yup . . . Good-bye."

He hung up.

"You're right," I laughed. "That *is* a quick call. You've never had a longer conversation with him?"

"Yes," Harold said, "I have had a *little* longer."

He sat back down heavily at the kitchen table, and we played a second game of checkers—but I'll spare you the details. Suffice it to say that this time he beat me—clobbered me, in fact, with a triple jump that came out of nowhere.

"Well," I said, "that was a great game. You absolutely got me that time. But I enjoyed it. Thank you very much."

He chuckled kindly.

"Well," he said, "at my age, you know, it's an odd time of life. But," he added, "we only have to go through it once."

Not sure what he meant or exactly what had prompted his comment, I asked Harold whether he'd enjoyed his life so far.

"Well," he said, "I am living comfortably, yes."

"Is there anything you would have done differently if you had it to do over?"

"Oh," he said, "I've made some very poor choices."

"Such as?"

"Oh, business deals that I've made," he chuckled. "And then the other thing is," he said, suddenly turning serious, "I've been mean to people at times. Railroading is . . . Well, you have to fight for your rights. You have to fight for your rights or certain people will walk right over you."

"Did people walk over you?"

"They will if you don't fight for your rights," he said fiercely, though not quite answering my question. Calming down, he added, "But of course railroad men are like other men: there are good men, and there are men who will walk over you."

I asked Harold if he would like to go out to lunch. He said sure, he would enjoy that, so I asked him to recommend a place.

"You've never heard of Stan's, have you?' he said.

"Stan's? No."

"It's about twenty miles from here, by Madawaska Lake."

We took my car. We could have taken Harold's—a '91 Plymouth the color of poorly brushed teeth that was parked in the gravel by the road. But when I offered to drive, he eagerly accepted. In fact, it was hard to believe that he could still drive at all at his age. A lot of people ten years younger than Harold had long since given up their cars. But at least Harold was not a prisoner in his own home, like so many of the others.

As we started down the road, he began talking about the fall of man. I couldn't quite follow what he was saying until he said, "I carry no grudges now."

"How do you let go of a grudge?" I asked him.

"It's come over the years," he said. "Just reading my Bible."

We turned left onto New Sweden Road.

"I imagine you've heard all about the poisoning we had up here," Harold said as he looked out the window.

"You had a poisoning up here?"

"At the Lutheran church up there, they were having a feed," he said. "And somebody put poison in the coffee."

"You're kidding."

"A lot of them were taken to Bangor," he said. "They had a hard time surviving."

"Did they ever find out who did it?"

"Yes, sir. One man—he died. He either committed suicide or somebody killed him."

"The one who did it?"

"Yup."

"Why did he do it? Do they know?"

"As far as they could find out, it was because of the church," Harold said. "He was dissatisfied. There was more than one involved, and people say they know who the other ones are. But they're not ready to release that yet."

"When did this happen?"

"Oh, it happened this summer sometime."

We kept driving north up New Sweden Road.

"They had a killing up here once," Harold said after a few minutes, pointing to a side road on our right. "Right here. They found a man in that field, and he had three bullets in him. He had a jacket on," he added, "but there were no holes in the jacket."

"Did they ever solve that one?" I asked.

"Never did," Harold said. He seemed pleased by the fact that the mystery remained unsolved.

A few minutes later, Harold told me to turn off onto a narrow dirt road that led up to a big windswept lake edged by pines and birches. The waves slapped at the rocks along the lakeside.

"This is Madawaska Lake," he said. "And right there, that's Stan's."

The place was straight out of Walker Evans: a rundown, ramshackle old building of crumbling brick, cracked wooden shingles, and peeling paint. It looked as if it was slowly beginning to sink into the dirt, as if all it wanted to do was die and rest in peace. The gutters had long since fallen by the wayside, leaving the bare wooden underside of the roof exposed to rot in the rain. An old rusted fuse box to the left of the front door sprouted wires and cables in every direction, and beside the fuse box was a large wooden bulletin board plastered with signs, notices, certificates, brochures, advertisements, bulletins, and warning notices of all kinds, some of which looked as if they had been there since the Great Depression. The front windows were boarded up, and on one of them was a sign: TAYLOR'S WORMS AND CRAWLERS. Mounted on the roof overhead was a larger sign with big block letters stenciled onto a bare wooden board that read: STAN'S GROCERY.

Inside it was like no other grocery store I had ever seen before. It was as if a hardware store, an Army-Navy store, a bait store, a grocery store, and a truck stop had thrown everything they had into one big heap and then randomly stacked it on every shelf, counter, and table in the place: a row of red ketchup bottles standing beside packets of bright plastic fishing lures, camouflage rain ponchos over by the Cheerios, and a big display of hunting knives on the counter where you ordered your lunch.

Behind the counter, grim and unsmiling, stood Stan.

"Stan," Harold said, "this is my new friend Paul. He's writing a book."

Stan, who wore a faded gray T-shirt stretched taut across his formidable girth, grunted at me in what I took to be a form of greeting.

"Nice to meet you," I said.

"We'd like to have some lunch," Harold said. "Any specials today, Stan?"

"Meat loaf."

"Well," Harold said, "I don't care much for meat loaf myself. I guess I'll have my usual."

"Bacon, lettuce, and tomato?"

"That's right. And not too much mayonnaise."

"You?" Stan asked me.

"I'll try the meat loaf," I said.

Harold led me past the counter to a booth beside a big grease-streaked window that looked out over the silver-gray expanse of Madawaska Lake. There were three local ladies at a table across the room who all seemed to be talking at once, and two couples in another booth who, judging from their L.L. Bean caps and sweatshirts, appeared to be tourists.

I asked Harold whether he came here often.

"Every now and then," he said. "Stan's a good man, you see."

I asked him about the railroad. He said that he had wanted to be a railroad man ever since he saw his first real live steam locomotive when he was eight years old. He told me about some of the winters back in the 1930s when the snow was five stories deep and the railroad workers had to shovel it out by hand for the trains to get through. "And it was cold," he said. "It would get down to fifty over by the river." Meaning fifty below zero.

I asked Harold whether he had ever lived anywhere outside Aroostook County.

"No," he said.

"Have you ever wanted to?"

"No, not really. I've traveled some. I've been to Florida, and I've been to the West Coast. But you see, this is where I had my livelihood."

Stan brought over our food. Harold's BLT looked pretty good, with plenty of bacon and a big slab of ripe tomato, but my meat loaf looked like it had seen better days—probably last week sometime.

I asked Harold whether he cooked for himself when he was home.

"I get five frozen meals at the start of each week that I just warm up," he said. "Costs me $2.75 because it's subsidized. I don't eat it all, so I give some of it to my sister."

I asked him how spent his days.

"Well, I get up at nine o'clock. I have my doughnut and my coffee, and then I call Alan. By the time I get dressed, get my paper, and read that, it's about lunchtime. Oh, and I always watch *Gunsmoke*. Then in the afternoon, I'll go out in my car. Just to go somewhere, you know. Or I might be down in my basement working. And then I'll eat my dinner at about three o'clock. That's the way I fill my afternoon. But I'm always ready for the news at six o'clock. I watch TV a lot at night. And then somewhere in the evening, I'll have an orange."

"Every night?"

"Yes."

I wondered whether that was the secret to reaching age ninety-five.

And then suddenly we were back to religion again.

"I'm very perplexed about the whole thing," he said.

"What's that?"

"Well, we have people that go to church and they follow the rules and they're just as happy as can be. I think with a lot of them, there's never a doubt in their minds. But now the woman I go out with, she's interested in astronomy."

"I remember you mentioned that."

"Well, this business of how we are born sinners because of Adam's sin . . . You know, when Jesus died, it *didn't* take care of Adam's sin. We never get rid of that. I think it's a constant fight. Because the flesh—the flesh wants its way."

Even at age ninety-five?

"I think the world is becoming . . ." Harold paused, trying to come up with the words. "It's a *doubting* world," he said emphatically. "When I was a boy in the neighborhood, on Sundays we would gather somewhere. It might be somebody's stable in the wintertime because it was warm in there. A lot of them didn't have any Christianity. But they were *believers*. They still *believed* in heaven and hell. They *believed* in right and wrong."

He paused again, catching his breath.

"But now that is changing," he said. "And I think the reason it's changing is because we see what a complex universe we have. You see, if you want to go back far enough, they thought the earth was the nucleus of the universe—and so you see how far we've gone beyond that."

I was finally beginning to understand why Harold kept alluding to his lady friend's interest in astronomy.

"And I think that has a tendency to make people change their minds," he went on. "You see, the Bible is very simple about the beginning. There's not a lot of detail. But there are always those who are glad to fill in the details. And you know, people don't interpret it the way they did once.

"But there's one thing," he said firmly. "If I have to live another life, I want to live it with Christian people. I don't want to live it with the Hitlers and the Saddams. In spite of the shortcomings of churchgoing people, I'll pick them just the same."

I got up and went back to the counter to pay Stan for lunch. It came to $7.44. As I walked back to our booth to get Harold, I saw that he had pulled up a chair and joined the three ladies across the room, laying on the charm. He was trying to persuade one of them to move in with him.

"I'm a lot of fun," he was telling her.

The woman was laughing, but her face was red with embarrassment. Her two friends were laughing, and so was Harold—but I wasn't entirely convinced that he was just kidding.

"Did you ask her if she played checkers?" I asked him as we got back in the car.

"I didn't get that far," he chuckled.

As we were driving back, it started to rain—not hard, but enough that I had to turn on the windshield wipers.

"Well," Harold said after we'd driven in silence for a while, "it's been good to talk to you."

"I've really enjoyed it too," I said.

"I'm not built to live alone, you know."

"Does it get lonely for you?"

"It does," he said.

We turned onto another dirt road.

"This is the Bunderson Road," he said. "This is where the man got shot."

"And they never figured out who did it?" I asked, not sure exactly which shooting he was talking about.

"Well, the man who committed suicide, he left a note saying that he was one of the perpetrators. But they don't even know if he wrote the note or if it was a homicide."

It was beginning to sound like a recent episode of *Forensic Files* that Harold might have seen on TV.

"Make a right turn here," he said. "The man who lives here used to teach school. He had cattle too. I don't really know what breed they are. They're shaggy. Built for cold weather and rough feed." He pointed up the hill. "There's some of them there." About a dozen shaggy longhorns were scattered up and down the steep hillside, mournfully chewing the weeds. "It's hard raising cattle up here. They'll get along all right until the snow comes. But when the snow comes, then you've got to feed them."

He pointed to another house at the end of a long dirt driveway. It looked abandoned. "Now the man that lived here was in a wheelchair. He went fishing one day, slipped on the bank, and never walked again. He was right in the prime of life when that happened."

"I thought fishing was pretty safe," I said. "You never know, do you?"

"No, you never do."

We drove on.

"Now this here is the Tangle Ridge Road where I used to live," he said as we made another turn. "It's seventeen miles long, and it was once a very busy road because of all the farming. Now there's not *any* farming up the whole road."

"All because of the price of potatoes?"

"Because of the price of potatoes and what it costs to grow 'em. This is not choice land, you see. We have some choice limestone land down by the river—potatoes like limestone land. But this area's not that type of land. We *were* making a living here, and we were raising crops. But it's not choice. The only farms now are on choice land.

"Our farm started right about here," Harold said, pointing to an overgrown stretch of forest to our right. "We planted potatoes right there, see? All gone to forest now."

"All that's left is that potato barn?"

He chuckled. "Yup. That's all that's left."

We drove past a small pond where he'd learned to swim, and past the abandoned railroad siding where he used to bring his potatoes and lumber to be shipped off to Presque Isle and points south. "There were times during the Depression and right after the war when we got only forty cents for a barrel of potatoes. And it cost us several dollars to raise 'em. The wood business kept us alive during the Depression."

The railroad track itself was gone now, its bed converted to a recreational trail marked with yellow snowmobile signs.

"A lot of the people up here, well, at times all they had to live on was potatoes," Harold commented. "Reminds me of a story about a fellow who wasn't feeling too good. So he went to see the doctor. And the doctor says, 'What did you have for breakfast?'

"'Taters,' the man says.

"'What did you have for dinner?'

"'Taters.'

"'Well, what are you going to have for supper?'

"'I don't know,' the man says. 'The taters is all gone.'"

Harold burst out laughing at the old joke.

I drove on in silence.

"So I guess you've seen a lot of changes up here," I said after a while.

"It's not the same life at all," he said. "We used to have a big neighborhood up here. We had thirty people in that little school room. Most of the people who live here now, they come from out of state. Nurses and other professional people, you know."

We turned back onto Woodland Road, and as we drove, Harold talked about how things were always changing. He said he believed in evolution and the idea that everything changed. Even in the heavens, he said, new stars are born and old stars die out. People change, too, he added.

"How do you mean?"

"When I was young, everybody had to work hard, he said. "Now a lot of the young people can't find work. That's partly why you see so many of them obese—that and the tube. We used to be outside running around all the time when I was a kid, but now they just sit in front of the television."

I asked Harold whether he knew his neighbors where he lived now.

"No, not really," he said. "I know who they are, but we don't neighbor."

"Don't neighbor?"

"We don't get together," he explained.

I asked him how long he'd lived in his present neighborhood.

"Thirty years," he said. "My wife and I used to neighbor with people, but after she died, they weren't interested."

Harold talked about his hip surgery three years ago. There had been some complications, he said, and three days after his operation he'd had to have gall bladder surgery. "I was pretty sick then, and I said, 'Lord, I wish you'd take me out of this body.' You see, my wife was in a nursing home with cancer, and I knew *she'd* never come home. So what did I have to go back to? I said, 'Lord, take me out of this shell. Just take me out of this old shell.'"

"But He didn't," I said.

"No," Harold chuckled. "He didn't."

"And how do you feel about that?" I asked. "Do you wish He had, or are you happy to be home again?"

"Oh," he said, "it would have been better if He had. You see, I'm not used to it. I don't enjoy living alone. And I'm not contributing. I know I'll just get more feeble all the time. I'll never get better." He chuckled again, as if it were all some great cosmic joke.

As we pulled back up to his house, he invited me in. As he pushed hard on the warped back door and we walked back into the kitchen, he talked about how the price of heating oil was going up again this year. "Guess I'll just have to put on an extra set of long johns this winter."

He wanted me to stay longer, but it was time to go. Calais was at least four hours away, and I wanted to get there before it got too dark. I told Harold that I wished I lived nearby so that we could visit more often.

"Then we could play checkers," he said.

"You'd have to teach me," I said.

"Well," he said, shaking his head, "you shouldn't feel bad. I know what it's like to get beat, believe me. One winter when I was doing spare work, there was this fellow who used to play checkers with me four or five days a week. And he would beat me *every* time. I never *once* beat him." Harold paused—and then broke into a big grin. "But I kept on playing," he said, chuckling to himself. "Just kept right on playing."

CALAIS, MAINE

FOUR HOURS LATER, I was in Calais, Maine, which, despite the presence of large numbers of French-speaking Canadians in the area, rhymes with *Dallas,* not *ballet.* I had booked a room at the Calais Motor Inn on Route One, about a mile south of the border crossing into Canada. You couldn't miss it: a big modern-looking structure with its own Olympic indoor pool and a health spa. Its brochure proudly proclaimed: IF IT'S HAPPENING IN CALAIS, IT'S HAPPENING AT THE CALAIS MOTOR INN.

For dinner, I picked a Mexican restaurant on North Street, where the air was thick with diesel fumes from the semis that rumbled back and forth across the border in a never-ending stream, day and night. I went in and sat at the bar, had a drink, and ordered the burrito dinner. After he took my order, the bartender, who had a shaved head and an earring, asked me where I was from.

"New Jersey," I said.

"Well," he said, "you've got to get out of this place."

"What?"

"Listen," he said fiercely. "These people here are crazy. Look, I'm from Orlando. I'm not from around here. But, man, you'd better watch your step. You'd better just go back to New Jersey. You can't trust these people."

He proceeded to tell me how "they" had videotaped him with a local girl and how "they" were now making threats. I was seriously beginning to wonder whether maybe I shouldn't have just paid the few extra dollars and gone to the steakhouse up the road. Meanwhile, two very large police officers strode into the bar and started questioning some of the people at the other end of the bar. It began to dawn on me that not necessarily everything that happened in Calais happened at the Calais Motor Inn.

The next morning there wasn't a cloud in the sky. I could hear the cries of the gulls from the waterfront nearby. Calais, I discovered when I looked at my map, sits at the mouth of the St. Croix River where it empties into Passamaquoddy Bay. Passamaquoddy Bay in turn flows into the Bay of Fundy and the Atlantic Ocean.

Barbara Barnett, the Faith in Action director in Calais, was waiting for me in the lobby of Calais Regional Hospital with a plastic photo-ID badge clipped onto her navy blue turtleneck. I followed her down a flight of stairs to her office.

The first order of business was reviewing my itinerary for the next two days. The one thing that she wasn't sure about yet was whether I would be able to meet with Arlene Smith, a woman in East Machias with amyotrophic lateral sclerosis (ALS), also known as Lou Gehrig's disease. Arlene had her good days and her bad days, Barbara said, but she hoped I would be able to visit her tomorrow.

In addition to running the local Faith in Action program, Barbara was the director of Down East Hospice, a small nonprofit organization that had been around for more than twenty years to support terminally ill patients and their families in Washington County. The organization had gotten its Faith in Action grant eight years ago, when Barbara was a part-time volunteer with the organization. She said that the grant had given the organization the chance to work more closely with the churches and that this had generated a lot more volunteers, as well as more referrals. "We were very small back then, but now we have more than a hundred volunteers. The other counties around here are just stunned when I tell them that, especially because we have just myself and a part-time office person."

Linda and Lou

I interviewed several of Barbara's volunteers that morning, including a retired army major and his wife, and Linda Gralenski, who was both a volunteer and president of the board of Down East Hospice. After her interview, Linda invited me to join her for lunch at the Calais Motor Inn with a man she told me was her favorite client. His name, she said, was Lou Viscovitch.

Lou was already at a table in the dining room when we arrived. "He's always early," she whispered as we made our way to his table.

Linda had told me a little about Lou before we got there. Technically, she said, he probably shouldn't have been a hospice client at all. For one thing, the hospice had been helping him for about three years now, way beyond the six-month norm for hospice patients. For another, it was his wife, not Lou, who had received the "poor prognosis" designation from her doctor that normally triggers a hospice referral and who was now in a nursing home. But the doctor, who was Lou's doctor too, had become increasingly concerned that Lou, who had health problems of his own, was gradually killing himself under the strain of taking care of his wife. And so he had ordered hospice for Lou too.

Maybe that's why I was so surprised when I first laid eyes on him: I had expected a little old man, gray and feeble, bowed down under the weight of all these years of caring for his dying wife. Instead, I got Rodney Danger-field—or at least his cousin. Lou was a big, bluff, hearty-looking guy in a boldly striped short-sleeved shirt with a quick smile, a firm grip, and slightly bulging eyes that seemed to be in a perpetual state of astonishment at the wonders of life.

It wasn't until I sat down beside him that I spotted the small green oxygen tank on the floor behind his chair. And there was the clear plastic oxygen tube that snaked up around from the tank to his nostrils, without which he couldn't have functioned.

"So tell me about yourself, Lou," I said, after I introduced myself and explained what I was up to. "Are you from around here?"

Of course I'd known the answer to that question the moment he opened his mouth. He not only *looked* like Rodney Dangerfield: he sounded as if the New York comedian was dubbing all of his lines.

"No," he said, "although I'm *affiliated* with the area because my wife was born in Eastport, Maine, and we've shared thirty-five years of marriage together. Unfortunately, now she's in a nursing home."

A waitress came over to our table.

"Hi, Lou," she said. "You're not going back in the hospital, are you?"

"Just for the day," he said. "Got to get my tank filled again."

"Well, take care of yourself, will you?"

"So anyhow," I said after the waitress had gone back to the kitchen with our order, "where *are* you from, Lou?"

"Originally, New York State."

"Where? What part?"

"Upstate and downstate," he said.

It was like playing Twenty Questions.

"Where upstate and where downstate?" I persisted.

"From Hell's Kitchen to Catskill," he said. "I was born and raised in Hell's Kitchen, and I was schooled in Hell's Kitchen—if you know where that is. Believe me, I know where it is. Had to fight my way just to get across the street half the time."

"What street was that?"

"Forty-Seventh," he said. "Number 316 West Forty-Seventh. That's one of those things you don't forget."

"And how old were you when you moved?"

"In my thirties."

"Oh really? And that's when you went up to Catskill?"

"Yeah. I had a wife and two kids all of a sudden."

"Just like that?"

"Well," he said dryly, "it took a couple of years. I'm quick, but I'm not *that* quick."

But his wife and kids weren't the only reason he left. "I decided to get out of the city for prejudicial reasons," Lou said cryptically, adding: "I was being overrun by somebody I didn't like." He fell silent.

A radio in the kitchen was playing "A Must to Avoid," by Herman's Hermits. Apparently somebody back there liked it because they turned the volume up a notch.

"So," Lou said, "I packed up my bags, hopped on a train at Grand Central, and took off. Got off in Hudson, New York, and was met by somebody that was a friend of ours—my first wife's. I've been married two times. Anyway, I didn't have the proverbial bottle or a window to throw it out of, so I just got up there on nerve alone—or whatever you want to call it. I had letters of recommendation, etcetera, etcetera, but the company where I'd worked was being sold. That was another thing that pushed me out of the office." He stopped. "You want to hear the whole story? It's boring."

"It's not boring."

"Okay. Well, I got there and, as I said, I didn't have the proverbial bottle or a window to throw it out of. But I was an *ambitious* young man. Jack of all trades, master of none. When I left, I was the production manager of a pharmaceutical company—and I'd started there as a box boy back in shipping. When I left, they did not want me to leave, but I said, 'Sorry, Jack. I'm on my way.'

"So, anyhow, I took off and got up to the town of Catskill and went to the unemployment office. The unemployment office was on Main Street, and about three doors down there was a Ford dealership. So I went over there and talked to the man whose father owned the dealership. We went round and round, and finally he says, 'Well, I was supposed to give this job to my son who's just coming out of college.' And I say, 'But I got a wife and two children.' I didn't burst into tears, but I did pour it on a little. I said, 'My children have to eat. I'll do anything—sweep the floors, anything you want me to. But I *have* to have a job. Because I'm *not* going back to unemployment every week and getting a check for doing nothing.' So he says, 'All right, you're hired.' That was back in 1960."

"And you were how old?"

"I was born in '20," Lou said. "So I was forty years old. Older than I thought I was."

I was astonished. "Are you telling me you're eighty-three years old?"

"Eighty-two," Lou said blandly. "So anyway, I talked myself into this job—sweeping the floor, whatever. I was a gofer. And the gofer job lasted about two weeks. Then I became the assistant grease monkey. And then, once I found out a few more things—bang, bang, bang, bang—I was *running* it. When I left the company, I was general manger."

"So how long did you wind up staying?"

"Twenty-five years. When I turned sixty-five, I said, 'I'm out. I'm done.'" That was in 1985.

Soon afterward, Lou and his present wife, whom he'd married in the late 1960s after losing his first wife, moved to Maine, which was where his health problems began.

"What kind of health problems?" I asked.

"Heart. I was out in the yard with a pickax digging a hole, and all of a sudden: aaaahhh. . . 'Holy Mackerel! What was *that*?' I went and sat down on the steps, but when I got up, it started doing it again. Nevertheless, I finished the hole. Then I got hold of my doctor."

"Was it a heart attack?"

"Angina. It was angina," Lou said. He chuckled ruefully. "Still is."

"So then what happened?"

"Nothing really *happened*. I had to watch myself, that's all. I slowed down. Did what my doctor told me to. I did stay active in the church, though. I'd been active in the church a long time. I also used to do a lot of volunteer work when I was in New York. I organized and ran a group called JIFFY. I was the chairman of JIFFY. It stood for Joint Intergenerational Friends for Youth."

"Tell me about that," I said.

"It was just a bunch of senior citizens that I conned. That's what I did—I conned them. I got a gift for that. Twisting people's arms and getting them to volunteer. 'You, you, and you—okay?' Well, why not?" Lou smiled broadly. "Anyhow, we got together, we organized, we put it together. I had to go over to the schools and talk to the principals and the superintendent, and I conned them into letting us into the schools. So they did. They opened their doors, and we wound up tutoring—no, excuse me: *mentoring* the kids. You know, they wanted us to work with the little kids, but I said, 'No, that's not who I want.'"

"You wanted the teenagers?"

"Right. I said, 'Give us the teenagers in school that are giving you a little bit of trouble. The ones that need to be talked to or need somebody to listen to them.'"

"Were you a volunteer yourself?"

"I *had* to be," he said. "You know, if you're going to be the heavy, you got to *do* it. You got to teach by example."

I asked him if he had enjoyed it.

"I *loved* it. Loved every minute of it. And the legislature of New York State, in its wisdom or whatever, gave me a great big framed citation. It's hanging in my office. Senior Citizen of the Year for New York State."

"No kidding!"

"Mario Cuomo gave me this thing to sign, and then he signed it. Let me tell you, they did everything. Threw a party for me. It was great!"

Lou's face fell. "When I left, I really didn't want to leave that," he said. "I had big hopes of doing it when I got here. I really did. I brought all my paraphernalia with me, and I wanted to go to all the schools up here. But then *this* happened to me," he said despondently, pointing at the small green oxygen tank as if it were a ball and chain.

The waitress came back with her tray. "Sorry it took so long," she said. "It's been busy."

I looked around. It *had* gotten busy—and noisy too. It was getting harder to hear over all the other conversations and the clatter of dishes and silverware.

"You here by yourself all morning?" Lou asked her. "That's kind of hard." As she started back to the kitchen, he muttered, "I do need my decaf, though."

"It's coming," Linda assured him. I realized that she had hardly gotten a word in since we'd sat down.

"You mind if we say the blessing?" Lou asked me.

"Please," I said.

The three of us bowed our heads.

"Heavenly Father," Lou began, his voice pure New York, "I thank you for this wonderful and beautiful day you've given us. And I'm so glad we could meet this afternoon and talk about the things that have been done in the past, and we hope and pray for things in the future. We know that whatever it is, it's in your hands. You know everything that was there. You knew me in my womb and you know me now. And you know that I'm here to serve you, Lord. So is Linda. Linda has been serving and serving and serving. But she's still my guardian angel. I thank you for her. For her care, her compassion, and her really keeping after me. And as for this gentleman here today"—meaning me—"I hope he puts his book together the way he wants to, and that you will guide everything that he does and says. We give you thanks in Jesus's loving and precious name. Amen."

It turned out that Lou was, among other things, a lay preacher. "I can get up in front of a congregation and just do it: zing, zing, zing! Right?"

"Right," Linda said. "Old Fire and Brimstone himself."

"Is that right?" I said. "What denomination?"

"Methodist," Lou said. "But I've been affiliated with the Congregationalists too. In fact, I've probably preached in every church down in this end of the county at one time or another in the years that I've been up here. I did a lot of preaching in New York too. I've been doing it for over forty years."

"He'd visit the prison," Linda said.

"I was in the prison chaplaincy at a maximum security prison back in New York before I left," Lou explained, chewing his turkey club. "I hated to leave that."

"Now where does *that* come from?" I asked. "Were your parents religious?"

"No, no," Lou said. "I was an orphan. Raised in foster homes. It was a very terrible childhood. Very terrible. Bounced around from one foster home to the other."

He was silent for a few moments.

"But at least I got a fairly good education," he said, brightening. "Mostly parochial. Lady of Sorrows. Holy Cross. St. Michael's."

"Those sound like Catholic schools," I said.

"They were."

"But you're a Methodist."

"I am *now*, but I was Catholic then. I even had some of the nuns that I had at Our Lady of Sorrows in the Bronx later on again when I went back to New York. I think they were following me."

"Keeping an eye on you," I said.

"They looked at me like: 'What? *You* again?' But the yardstick did get my attention. It wakes you up. You pay attention."

I asked Lou whether he had ever been in the military.

"Six years in the United States Navy," he said. "From 1943 to 1949. Based on an aircraft carrier most of the time."

"In the Pacific?"

"The Atlantic. The Mediterranean, the North Sea, et cetera. I did get out to the Pacific briefly, but it was a mistake, and they shipped me back right away. Anyway, I spent seven months in a naval hospital in St. Albans, New York, but I went back on active duty—because I wanted to."

The waitress finally brought Lou's decaf. "Sorry about that," she said. "No problem," Lou said.

"So when did you become a Methodist?" I asked.

"Oh, that happened because of my wife that I presently have," he said. "When I married her, she was a faithful Methodist. And I got involved in her church. People took a liking to me, I guess. Found out I was a little gifted—that I had a big mouth."

"Speaking of your present wife," I said, "what's the situation?"

Lou heaved a deep sigh and took a sip of his decaf. "My wife got very sick and she wound up in the hospital—a triple bypass and all that good stuff. Then she needed to stay at home. She couldn't do anything. So naturally I became her twenty-four-hour caregiver."

"And this was when?"

"Three, four years ago?" he said. "No. Longer. Time goes so fast. Probably more like five years ago."

His wife had had her bypass operation in Bangor, after which she had spent three months receiving skilled nursing care back here at the Calais Regional Hospital. It was when she came home after those three months that Lou had become her full-time caregiver.

I asked him what it was like.

"Terrible," he said. "It was a job and a half. I had aides who came in and washed and cleaned her, and I took advantage of *that* time to do a little shopping. But I had to be home before they got done—and they were quick. Sometimes I had to move her by myself. I shouldn't have been doing those things, of course, on account of my heart. But I had to. And it went on and on. I was weak. I was tired. Tired all the time. My doctor told me, 'Lou, you gotta watch out.' And then, the next thing you know, he told me about hospice."

"What was your reaction?"

"Yippee!"

"Really?" I said.

"Because I knew what hospice was," Lou said. "So I said, 'Do you really think she needs *hospice*?' You know, you think of hospice, you think of people who are dying."

"Right."

"But the doctor said it isn't necessarily always the case. My wife was very, very ill. She couldn't do anything. I mean *nothing*. And then the dementia came in. And that only made it worse. And I *do* mean worse."

He took a sip of his decaf and didn't say anything.

"Tootie had very vivid hallucinations," Linda broke in. "Hallucinations where she saw and heard people in her house."

"Singing," Lou added.

"And she would get up and bring them dinner," Linda went on. "Which was not good. All hours of the day and night. So Lou couldn't get *any* rest."

"It's true," Lou said.

"So, Linda," I said. "Tell me about your first visit."

"My first visit with Tootie . . . Hmm," she said, thinking back. "Well, you know, Tootie wasn't always lost in space, and we would actually have fascinating conversations. She'd had a really fascinating life."

"She did," Lou agreed.

"She was gutsy, and she would try anything," Linda said. "And she had run a funeral home in New York."

"An undertaker," Lou said.

"So we had wonderful times," Linda continued. "She had a *great* sense of humor—and even when she was down in the dumps, you could usually get her to perk up."

Lou reached into his wallet and pulled out a photograph of a vibrant woman in the prime of life. "That's my baby right there," he said proudly. "She's precious. She is to me. And she hasn't changed any. She still looks the same."

"That's wonderful," I said, handing the picture back to Lou.

"And *she* is ninety-four years old," he added.

I was stunned. "Did you say *ninety-four*?"

"Yup," Lou said.

"Wow!"

Ninety-four? That would make her twelve years older than Lou.

"One of those May and December marriages," Lou said.

"You'll have to tell him how you met," Linda said.

"Oh, sure," Lou said. "Well, we lived right across the street from each other. Her husband had died. I knew her husband. I went fishing with the guy. We were friends. But his wife and I—we weren't friends, even though we lived across the street from each other.

"But then, after he died, she decided that she wanted to drive. And she needed somebody to help her learn how. So she comes over to me—I'm always the volunteer, you know—and so I say, 'Okay, I'll give it a try.' And after a while, she took her driver's test and she made it, which I was grateful for. But in the meantime," Lou added, arching his brow, "Cupid had stepped in."

None of us said anything for a while. The place was beginning to empty out, and it was a little quieter now.

"I was down to see her on Sunday," Lou said. "And, believe me, she was all excited when she saw me. All lit up like a Christmas tree. So I sat down with her and told her what was happening—that I hadn't been doing too well and all that. Because the people in the nursing home hadn't told her, and she kept wondering why I hadn't been in to see her. So I told her the reason: that I'd been sick and that I didn't feel up to driving the seventeen miles out to Eastport. Not that it's such a big deal, but for me, I was too weak. This is what happens when you run out of gas."

For a moment, he looked defeated.

"But anyhow," he said, pulling himself together again, "I *did* get out to see her, and I told her what was going on. And then I wrote out a whole list for her of where I was going to be every day."

"She worries about him," Linda said.

"Yeah," Lou agreed.

"So how often do you get out to the nursing home, Lou?" I asked.

"About two or three times a week. At least I try. I try to make it every Sunday, Tuesday, and Thursday."

"You're able to drive okay?"

"Oh, yeah," he said. "I can *drive* to California. I just can't *walk* to my mailbox. I can't. My legs are very bad."

"So what is your life like now on a day-to-day basis?"

"Lonely," he said.

"You're lonely?"

"Very," he said. "I miss my wife terribly. I don't have anybody to take care of. As a result, I don't take care of myself very well."

"Do you have any friends or neighbors around here?"

"Oh, yeah. I've got a *lot* of friends and neighbors. I'll give you a little incident that just happened. About a week ago, we had a terrific storm. The lights went out. And I went to the telephone, sat down on a chair to call somebody, and I fell off the chair. Hit my back. You've heard that advertisement: 'I fell down and I can't get up.' That was me. It's happened a couple of times before. I have a history of falling down and being picked up by the ambulance and taken to the hospital. And they know where I live, believe me. They don't need a card with my name and address or nothing. 'Oh, him?' they say. 'Yeah, sure, we'll go get him.'

"Anyway, I fell down, and I'd brought the telephone down with me as I fell. So I called my mechanic, who lives right down the street. I said, 'Scott? Bring Tony up with you. I fell down, and I can't get up.' I hung up the phone and—bang, bang, bang—they were there. They picked me up, shook the dust off me, and I was all right."

Linda added that Lou was on the phone a lot just keeping in touch with people.

"Yeah," Lou said. "I'm in the loop."

And although his son and his daughter both lived far away, Lou had a thirty-three-year-old grandson who lived nearby in Machias and came to see him on a regular basis.

"But still," Linda said to me, "he has many hours alone."

"What do you do during those hours?" I asked Lou.

"Watch TV. Read."

"What are you reading now?"

"Junk," he said.

"He reads his Bible every day," Linda said.

"I do read my Bible," Lou acknowledged. "I read Scripture. I start my day doing that. I *am* quite religious. I have a great deal of faith that I could move mountains if I wanted to. And I've *moved* a couple of mountains in my time, believe me. I've been very successful in doing the things that God wanted me to do."

I asked him whether he was able to get to church.

"Oh, yes," Linda said. "A couple of weeks ago he was the *preacher.*"

"Two weeks in a row," Lou said.

"Now *that's* moving mountains," Linda said.

I asked him what he watched on TV.

"Junk," he said again.

"What about the news?"

"Oh, yeah. I watch the news. I'm a big Fox fan. Fox News. That's my favorite."

"So what do you think about what's going on in the world these days?"

"It stinks," he said.

"Do you want to elaborate on that a little bit?"

"No, not really," he said. "It's just in a mess—an awful mess. This war in Iraq. It probably shouldn't have happened, but it did. I'm not *against* it, but I wish they'd get it straightened out a lot faster. Stop the killing. And those fires in California—my God! I pray for those people morning, noon, and night that it doesn't go any farther. God didn't do it, so don't blame it on Him. People are always blaming God for this and blaming God for that. If *I* did that, I'd be a very mean old man—not that I'm *not.*" He grinned at Linda. "What are you making that face for over there?"

"*I* didn't say anything," she laughed. "Anyhow, 'mean' doesn't come to mind."

"What does?" I asked.

"Stubborn," she said, still laughing.

"No," Lou said, "I have a better word than that."

"What?"

"Determined."

Arlene

The next morning after breakfast, I checked out of the Calais Motor Inn and headed south down Route One, toward Eastport and East Machias, which was where Arlene Smith lived. Barbara Barnett, in Calais, had suggested that I give Arlene's nurse a call in midmorning to see how Arlene was doing and to find out what the best time would be for me to come over. So I figured that I had plenty of time for a detour through Eastport, the easternmost town in the country.

Just south of Calais, I passed the St. Croix Country Club and a red, white, and blue roadside sign that urged me to ELECT EARL JENSEN TO CITY COUNCIL. A couple of hundred yards past Robbinston Elementary School, I spotted a group of hunters wearing iridescent orange vests and carrying their deer rifles at their sides. Well, at least it was Saturday, so the school was closed.

I opened the windows and began to sense a change in the quality of the air as I got closer to the Atlantic—not the smell so much as the feel of the air. It felt softer as I got nearer the ocean.

I turned onto Route 190 and followed it through Point Pleasant to its end in Eastport, where I parked by the old pier on Water Street. The fishing boats moored along the pier rocked peacefully in the swell, and there were a couple of cars besides my own parked along the street.

I walked out to the end of the pier, which must have been the easternmost place in the nation's easternmost city, and stood for several minutes watching a lone cormorant flying in a long straight path just a few feet above the surface of the water, on and on, until I finally lost sight of it in the distant haze.

As I stood there gazing across the water, I realized that I was thinking about my upcoming interview with Arlene Smith. I was uneasy about it. I'd never met anyone with ALS, but by all accounts it was a terrible disease. Your muscles got progressively weaker and weaker until eventually you couldn't even breathe without a mechanical respirator. It was as if you were slowly being strangled by your own body. Most people with ALS died within ten years of diagnosis; about half died within three.

And then there was the fact that, according to what Barbara had told me, Arlene couldn't speak any more. The only way she could communicate was through some kind of computer keyboard. So how was *that* going to work?

But most of all, I felt uneasy about imposing myself on someone so sick and intruding on her privacy. The truth is that I was hoping that her nurse would tell me that Arlene just wasn't feeling up to it today and that I'd be off the hook.

When I got to Arlene's house—a pale yellow one-story ranch across from a big empty field, with black shutters and a black metal eagle mounted over the garage door—I was greeted by a pert, no-nonsense woman with short brown hair, glasses, and a black sweatshirt with a picture of a housecat embossed on its front. Her name, she said, was Nancy. She was Arlene's nurse.

Before letting me into the house, Nancy handed me a couple of disinfectant wipes to clean my hands. She watched me carefully to make sure I was doing a thorough job. "Can't let you in without that," she said.

I followed Nancy through the clean but lifeless living room around the corner into Arlene's bedroom. There were a couple of chairs and a couple of dressers, but the room was dominated by Arlene's big hospital bed. The rest of the room was jam-packed with medical equipment and medical paraphernalia, most of which was a complete mystery to me. One item that I did recognize was the mechanical ventilator, a small green machine on the dresser beside the bed that was pumping quietly but steadily as we entered.

On the other side of the bed from the ventilator stood a computer, its screen mounted on the side of the bed and a black keypad placed on a tray that extended over the bed within easy reach. A thin black cord with a white medallion at its end hung from the arm of an overhead reading light. The medallion had a black button at its center and taped on the cord was a handwritten label: "Life Line." Also taped to the cord, just above the label, was a photograph of a little girl. Seated in the hospital bed in the midst of all of this technological clutter was Arlene.

The very first thing that struck me about Arlene—because, under the circumstances, it was the *last* thing that I had expected—was her smile. It was radiant. Instantly, all my fears and misgivings vanished.

Arlene was petite and had reddish-brown hair—the same color, I noticed, as the little girl in the photograph taped onto the Life Line cord. She wore wire-rimmed glasses and a pale purple dress with old-fashioned white ruffles on the sleeves. There was a white bandage wrapped around her throat with a blue and white plastic tracheostomy tube protruding from it that was plugged into a mechanical breathing machine at her bedside.

"What I'd really like to know, Arlene, is a little bit about you," I began after introducing myself. "Where are you from? Are you from Machias?"

She couldn't respond, of course—at least not orally—and so I waited in silence as she typed her reply on the black computer keypad perched on the tray in front of her. The only sound in the room was the soft clicking of the keys and the steady pulse of the ventilator. Gradually, a letter at a time, the words appeared on a small screen: N-E-W—P-O-R-T-T-LAND . . .

"New Portland," Nancy read out loud.

"And how long have you lived up here in Machias?" I asked her.

Nancy answered for her. "Thirty-some years, right?"

Arlene nodded.

I was beginning to see that Nancy had worked out some kind of non-verbal means of communication with Arlene, and that she would be answering some of my questions on Arlene's behalf—presumably to lessen the strain on Arlene

"Okay," I said. "Now tell me a little bit about when you got sick."

"Can't help you with that one," Nancy said. "I've only been here a few months."

We both waited as Arlene typed her answer.

DIAGNOSED JANUARY 2002 . . . BUT HAD PROBLEMS BEFORE THAT.

"Oh, I see," I said. "And when did you get your first volunteer from Down East Hospice?"

NOT SURE.

"Was it after you became bedridden—or before?" Nancy asked her.

Arlene nodded her head vigorously at the second choice.

"Before," Nancy said. "Okay."

"And what do the volunteers do for you?" I asked.

TALK & OFFER TO RUN ERRANDS.

Nancy added, "They've also made a few suggestions. Like they came in one day with a sheet—I'll show you the sheet." She went out into the living room and came back with a sheet of paper covered with small pictures. "This is so that when she can no longer type, she'll be able to point. See? It's got a picture of a bottle of pills for when she wants her medicine, and a bathtub for when she wants her bath."

"That's great," I said. But it was terrible to realize that at some point, Arlene's muscular control would be reduced to the point where she would be forced to resort to these pictures in order to communicate. I asked Arlene whether she had any family nearby.

"She has a daughter who lives in Biddeford," Nancy said. "About five hours away. In fact, she'd supposed to be coming up this afternoon."

Arlene nodded and smiled.

"So your daughter comes up to visit you?" I asked. "How often does she come up? Every week? Every month?"

EVERY WEEKEND RIGHT NOW.

Nancy said that there were other family members—aunts and uncles—who also came to visit from time to time, and that about once a month Arlene's daughter would bring her children, Arlene's grandchildren, up for a visit too. I was surprised that someone so young had grandchildren, but Nancy said that Arlene was sixty-three years old—about ten years older than I had guessed.

"Is that your granddaughter?" I asked Arlene, pointing to the photograph of the little red-headed girl in the photograph taped onto the Life Line cord.

She smiled proudly and nodded.

I asked Arlene whether, even with all the visits, she ever got lonely.

She shook her head and typed on the keypad: I'M USED TO IT.

"She has a caregiver with her all the time," Nancy explained. "Like today, I'm on for twelve hours, and then a girl will come in tonight and she'll do twelve hours."

"So you're never really alone," I said to Arlene.

"No," Nancy said. "Never."

"What's the hardest thing for you about being sick?" I asked Arlene.

"Not being able to do the things she used to do," Nancy said.

WORKING OUTSIDE AND COOKING, Arlene wrote.

"And sewing," Nancy added. "She loved to sew." But she could still play video games on the computer, Nancy said, and she watched TV and listened to music.

"What kind of music?"

"Daniel O'Donnell," Nancy said. "Isn't that right, Arlene?"

"He's your favorite?" I'd never heard of him.

Arlene grinned and nodded vigorously.

She also liked to read, Nancy said: magazines, newspapers, books— lots of books. "She used to work in the college bookstore over at the Machias campus of the University of Maine until she retired."

"How long ago was that?" I asked Arlene.

4 YEARS AGO.

I asked Arlene whether she kept up with what was going on in the world.

She nodded.

"What do you think about Iraq?" I asked her.

Again the room was silent, except for the tapping of her fingers on the keyboard and the steady beat of the ventilator.

A BIG . . . BLUFF . . . WASTING TOO MANY . . . LIVES.

"A big bluff wasting too many lives," I repeated.

She nodded again, her face grim.

"Now tell me a little bit about your volunteers," I said, changing the subject. "You have two volunteers. What are their names?"

SUZANNE AND SANDRA.

Nancy said that Suzanne and Sandra used to come on the same days, but that they had changed it so that now they came on different days. "The reason being that it takes a lot out of her in the mornings to do her bath, to go through her meds, to change the bed. And it just makes it easier if she has one person come one day and one another. That way she doesn't get too tired out."

I asked how long Suzanne and Sandra stayed when they came over.

HALF HOUR TO AN HOUR.

"It's according to how she's feeling," Nancy said. "If she's having a crappy day, they come in, ask if there's anything they can do, and they leave early. If she's having a good day, they sit here and visit and talk."

"Now is today a good day or a crappy day?" I asked Arlene.

She smiled broadly.

"So I lucked out," I laughed.

I asked Arlene whether she was active in her church, or whether her volunteers were.

NOT ME BUT SANDRA IS.

"O.K. . . . "

Arlene was still typing.

THAT'S NOT TO SAY . . . I DON'T DEPEND ON GOD . . . TO HELP ME.

"I understand," I said. "You just don't find it useful to attend . . . "

All of a sudden, something—probably the ventilator—started beeping furiously. What had I done? Had I said the wrong thing?

"No, it's all right," Nancy assured me. "That's just because she was moving."

Sure enough, the beeping stopped.

Arlene, meanwhile, pointed at the screen. She'd written: IT'S IN MY HEART.

Then she asked *me* a question: What was my book about? My answer, which I could have given in one or two sentences, went on for at least five minutes. While I was talking, Nancy left the room to turn up the fan in the living room because apparently it was getting too warm in the house. While she was out of the room, Arlene typed out: THAT'S QUITE AN UNDER-TAKING. Only this time the words didn't just appear on the screen; a woman's voice actually *said* the words out loud.

For a split second, I actually thought it was Arlene speaking—as if she'd been waiting for Nancy to leave the room so that she could reveal to me the secret that she could in fact speak. But then I realized that it was the computer talking, not Arlene.

Shortly after Nancy returned to the room, she signaled me that it was time to wrap up.

I nodded. "Okay, Arlene," I said, standing up, "I'm afraid it's time for me to hit the road. Thank you so much for having me over. It's been such a pleasure to meet you. The one regret that I have is that I don't live around here. I live all the way down in New Jersey, and so I won't be able to see you again—at least not in the near future," I quickly added.

She understood.

And then she did something that moved me profoundly: with visible effort, she reached out to shake my hand goodbye. As I felt her soft, almost lifeless fingers weakly gripping my hand, it was all I could do to contain myself.

As I was writing a few words for Arlene in a little guest book by the front door, Nancy, keeping her voice low, said, "I've only been working for her since August, but I can tell you this: they gave her eighteen months to live, and she's already gone over two years."

"That's terrific," I said. "And she looks good. Is she usually in such good spirits?"

"Yesterday you wouldn't have thought so."

"She seems very upbeat," I said. "She's smiling all the time and . . . "

"That's her personality. But yesterday the doctor was here to change the tracheostomy, so it was a rough day. It drains her, just drains her," Nancy said, shaking her head. "And of course, after he does it there's a lot of bleeding, so you have to constantly suction her—and it wears her out."

I asked Nancy whether she had worked with any other ALS patients before Arlene.

"No," she said. "She's my first. But she's a peach."

"So you enjoy working with her?"

"Very much. She's a wonderful lady." Nancy lowered her voice still further and leaned toward me. "Last week was like a reality check for her," she murmured. "They came in and told her what to be expecting as far as her body failure is concerned. Her *mind's* fine. It's her *body* that's going."

That, I had learned, was where the true horror of ALS lay: that you were fully alert and aware as, day by day, your body slowly but surely shut down.

"She had a few days after that where she was really down in the dumps, you know, and so I asked her, 'Is there anything I can do?' And she says to me, 'No. I'm just not ready to go yet.'" Nancy gazed past me out the front door at the barren brown field across the road. "It's like reality had just set in," she said.

BAR HARBOR, MAINE

AS I CONTINUED down Route One toward Bar Harbor, my next stop, I was struck by how many roadside Pentecostal churches there were up here—matched only by the surprising number of places offering "therapeutic massage." I hadn't realized that there were so many bad backs in this part of the country.

A little farther down the coast, I started seeing the tourist places, most of them long since closed for the season: The Puffin Gift Shop. The Ol' Salt Cafe. The Wild Blueberry Motel. Best of all was the big sign at the outskirts of the town of Cherryfield: WELCOME TO CHERRYFIELD—BLUE-BERRY CAPITAL OF THE WORLD.

By the time I turned off Route One and headed south down Route 3 toward Bar Harbor, it was already dark. Fortunately, the sign for the Atlantic Oakes By-the-Sea Resort and Conference Center, where I had my reservation, was well lit—unlike a lot of the other places I'd passed, which had shut down for the season and had their signs turned off. As it was, there were only three other cars in the parking lot of the Atlantic Oakes when I pulled in, and by the time I left a few days later, it was down to two. You had to wonder how they could afford to stay open.

Holy Redeemer

The next day—Sunday—was a day of rest: no interviews. For one thing, I knew when I'd planned my itinerary that I would need a break by this point in the trip. For another, I didn't like the idea of imposing on people on a Sunday. Besides, Bar Harbor bordered on Acadia National Park, a fabulous place that I had last visited fifteen years ago with Susie and our kids. It would be fun to see it again.

I woke up a few minutes after seven and stepped out onto the small balcony outside my window. My room was on the second floor and looked out over the water—Frenchman's Bay, according to the map on the wall. The sky was clear except for a few high cirrus clouds lit from below by the rising sun, and there was a brisk morning breeze coming off the water stirring the leaves of the maples and birches that were scattered across the property. The insistent cawing of a crow perched in a nearby maple mingled with the cry of the seagulls coasting above the bay in search of their breakfasts.

After my own breakfast, I still had a couple of hours before mass at Holy Redeemer, Bar Harbor's only Roman Catholic church, so I decided to take a quick ride into Acadia. There was nobody in the gatehouse to take my money, so I just drove on through and followed the winding road into the park. Before long, there was a turnoff to the left with a sign for Cadillac Mountain.

Actually, as mountains go, Cadillac Mountain is strictly minor league. At 1,532 feet, I'm not sure that it would even qualify as a foothill west of the Mississippi. But it does have the distinction of being the highest point along the North Atlantic coast. And depending on the time of year, the summit of Cadillac Mountain is said to be the first place in the entire United States from which you can see the sun rise.

It took me about twenty minutes to drive the three and a half miles to the top, winding my way through a forest of spruce and pitch pine that gradually gave way to large expanses of bare granite and twisted dwarf trees beaten down and stripped of their bark by the wind. I parked the Malibu in the empty lot at the summit, pulled on my jacket against the wind, and started carefully walking up a narrow footpath across the rocks.

Climbing to the top of a massive naked boulder just off the path, I felt for a moment as if I were standing on the edge of the world. The wind was fierce, whipping in from the ocean and so cold that it brought tears to my eyes. And the Atlantic itself was overwhelming: an immense, seemingly limitless expanse of blazing silver that almost blinded me as it reflected the fiery morning sun from a million different angles all at once. It was like looking God in the face.

The Church of the Holy Redeemer was in sad shape. Built in 1907 according to the cornerstone, some of the stones had literally fallen out of the walls, leaving what looked like gaping wounds, and the wooden doors and archways were badly in need of a fresh coat of paint. There was scaffolding all along the front face of the church, belted in by a long strip of yellow caution tape that made it look more like a crime scene than a house of worship. But I saw a couple of people going in, so I followed them.

It was about twenty minutes before mass. A small group of elderly women was practicing the hymn, "All Creatures of Our God and King," near the altar. Their quavering, slightly off-key harmonies echoed from the church's dingy plaster walls. As I knelt in prayer, I noticed that the only cushioning on the hardwood kneeler was a narrow strip of carpeting nailed onto it. It was almost like kneeling on the bare wooden floor. This was definitely old school.

Yet to my surprise, the priest wasn't. A big man, he seemed a little awkward, the way big men sometimes do—not only in his physical movements but also in his speech, almost as if he were nervous speaking in front of the congregation.

But as I listened, I liked what he had to say. Some of it was hard to understand because of the echo in the cavernous, near-empty church, but I was moved by his plain way of speaking and his obvious conviction.

After the mass, as I was walking back to my car, I realized that I wanted to talk to him. I wondered whether he was involved in Bar Harbor's Faith in Action coalition and, if so, what he thought about it. But also I was curious to know more about him as a person, so I turned around and walked back into the church. He was standing in the vestibule, sipping coffee and talking to a parishioner. I waited while he finished his conversation.

When I asked him if we could talk, he seemed to think that I wanted him to hear my confession. He took me by the arm and led me into a small room with a worn red carpet and two heavy oak chairs.

"What can I do for you?" he asked.

After introducing myself, I explained that I was writing a book about a program called Faith in Action and that I wondered whether he had been involved with it here in Bar Harbor.

"You're a writer?"

"In a way," I said cautiously.

He nodded thoughtfully, as if he were trying to decide something.

No, he said, he had never heard of Faith in Action. But then he had been here in Bar Harbor for only about a year, and he had three other churches to take care of in addition to Holy Redeemer.

"You're kidding."

"I'm afraid not," he said.

With four churches assigned to him, he hadn't had time to get involved in community programs—or much of anything else, he added ruefully. "But tell me about this Faith in Action. I kind of like the name."

So I told him about the program and about my travels of the past week, winding up with my visit to "a woman with Lou Gehrig's disease up in East Machias."

"Oh, you mean Smith," he said.

"You know her?"

"Oh, sure," he said.

Apparently Maine was smaller than it looked on the map.

I asked him whether—based on what I had told him about Faith in Action—he thought there might be any interest in it here at Holy Redeemer.

"Well," he said, "it's an uphill battle."

"In what way?"

"Just look around. There's just this one mass—the eleven o'clock—and what did we have? About a hundred people altogether?" He shook his head. "And quite a few of them elderly," he added.

He told me that St. Peter's, another one of his churches, had about the same number of parishioners, although at least they were younger. And at St. Ignatius in Northeast Harbor, where he said mass on Saturday evenings, not more than ten people showed up. "Ten people. Can you imagine?" His face was a mix of pain and anger. "We should be able to fill these pews!" he burst out. "Not just the Catholic churches. All of them! Every church on this island!"

I nodded.

"But it's become a very secular society," he said sadly. "People just aren't going to church anymore."

And then, almost as if he were trying to explain the decline to himself, he started talking about his own frustrations with the church. "I try to tell them what's happening out here in the real world, but they don't listen. You get a form letter that says, 'Thank you for your input.' But nothing else. No real response."

As he went on, I was beginning to feel as if I were hearing *his* confession. He talked about how the world had changed since he was a boy in Boston.

"You know," he said, "last night I was flipping through the channels on TV and they had *lap* dancing going on. On *television*! I mean, it was like a *bachelor* party—only right there on television, where any kid could see it. It was just *appalling*! I just couldn't believe I was seeing this stuff."

And yet, he said, the world wasn't all bad. You had to remember that. He told me about his mother, who still lived in Boston, and how she used to love to play bingo at the church with her friends. A while ago, the church had stopped the bingo games, but the woman who had run the games had some of the old-timers come over to her house, where she would fix meals for them and give out prizes. "She didn't have to do any of that. But it made such a difference to these people, including my mother. It really was a wonderful thing."

And, he said, you had to have faith.

Once when he was saying Easter mass in one of the large parishes where he had served in the past, he'd looked out and suddenly realized that there were a thousand faces out there looking up at him. "But they all looked so glum!" he cried. "And I just wanted to say to them: 'Don't you realize that Christ *died* for you? And that Christ is *risen*? That he died for your sins and then he rose from the dead? This is a time for joy! Why are you all looking so glum?' But then a voice said to me: 'No, that's not it. Have *faith* . . . and they will come to you.'"

Michael

The next morning, I drove across town to meet with Michael Reisman, director of Bar Harbor's Faith in Action program, which was called Island Connections. When I got there, Michael's phone was relentless. He would hang up, and in less than a minute it would ring again.

"Ten o'clock tomorrow? Sure, we'll have somebody there at about quarter to ten to pick you up."

"Yeah, she doesn't eat fish . . . No, really. So see if you can get her something else . . . I don't know, maybe the vegetarian plate."

"Right . . . The meeting is at 7:30, over at the Y . . . You're going to bring the coffee? Great. No, we don't need any cookies . . . I'm sure . . . Yeah, thanks."

Michael hung up and grinned at me. Short, trim, and dressed in khakis and a tan corduroy shirt, he was all energy. "Maybe we should go to the community room," he said. "It'll be quieter in there."

He was right. The room was deserted. There was a big unused brick fireplace, a pool table that had seen better days, an old unplugged electric fan on a stand, a black upright piano with a vase of artificial flowers perched on top, and a card table covered with a partly completed jigsaw puzzle. We sat on two plaid sofas in the middle of the room that faced each other at right angles. He began by telling me that he was from Philadelphia.

"So how did you wind up here?" I asked him.

"I came up here in 1973 and worked for a month at a summer job," he said. "I thought it was the most beautiful place I'd ever seen. Then I went back to the University of Michigan that fall—it was supposed to be my last year—and wound up with a bunch of incompletes. Which meant that I had a choice of either going back home and telling my parents what I'd done *or* coming back up here to Bar Harbor, getting a job in a restaurant, and living in a nice place."

Michael worked in Bar Harbor's restaurants for about six years, but in 1975, he also became the commissioner of the local softball league. "That was my first experience working with the community. Then I did some volunteer work with the Y, and I became the program director at the Y in 1979," he said. "I did that from 1979 to 1986. And then in 1986, they made me the executive director of the Y, which I did until 1994."

"So you'd become a pillar of the community."

"Yeah," Michael said ruefully. "But then I left the Y and ran a small bagel shop for several years."

"How did that go?"

"Well, I always say that I've worked for three nonprofits in my life: the YMCA, Island Connections, and Reisman's Bagel Bistro." He laughed. "And so then, in 1997, *this* opportunity came up to run Island Connections. I saw an ad in the paper, and I really did need a job, so I applied. The first day I came into the office, there was just this one desk in the back, so I sat down and opened up the book and I saw what we'd said in our Faith in Action proposal—that transportation was an issue but that we'd also visit people in their homes and help with meal preparation; that we'd have fifty volunteers by the end of the first year; and that we'd help a hundred people."

"Did you know this when you took the job?"

Michael shrugged. "More or less."

Today, six years later, Michael said that about a 150 people volunteered for the program over the course of the year, serving upward of three hundred people on a one-to-one basis. "Each week we're helping between fifty and sixty people. Right now, for instance, we're taking five people either to or from dialysis anywhere from three to six times a week, and the dialysis treatment center is up in Ellsworth [about twenty miles north of Bar Harbor]. We deliver meals to about ten or twelve people every day. And we do have people visiting people. But transportation is probably 60 percent of it."

Setting up the rides could be complicated, he said. You generally knew when somebody had to be at the doctor's because you knew what time their appointment was. But there was no way to know how long they'd be there. "Some days it might take only fifteen minutes. Other days it might take two or three hours. So what do you tell the volunteer? It can drive you crazy." But despite the stress, he clearly enjoyed it. And he knew every street, every hairdresser, and every doctor's office within a thirty-mile radius.

When I asked Michael how involved the congregations were, he acknowledged that by and large, the churches weren't as involved as they could be. Some remained active, contributing both volunteers and money, but others had scaled back or dropped out.

"Does it really matter?" I asked him. "After all, your Robert Wood Johnson grant ended almost five years ago. And you're called Island Connections—not Faith in Action. So is this really still Faith in Action, or has it evolved into something else?"

Michael thought for a moment before answering. "Maybe a little," he acknowledged. "But you know, one of our biggest volunteers in the program is from the Baha'i faith. Of course, it's a very small congregation. But he definitely does this as a way of living out his faith. In fact, maybe you should talk to him while you're here."

"Sure."

"Because what I think is special about Island Connections is that there *is* this faith piece in it. Being nongovernmental is *very* important, and so is being more than just a social *service* agency. I mean, social service agencies—they're caring, too, but in a different way."

"You mean because they're paid professionals?"

"Right. I mean, having this spiritual faith—it's something that maybe we're underutilizing, but it's certainly something we should still be involved with. And I say that even though I'm not an especially spiritual person."

I did two more interviews in the meeting room that morning, plus a long one after lunch, which was supposed to be it for the day.

"Well, I've got him," Michael grinned when I walked back into his office after my last interview.

"Got who?"

"Jerry, the Baha'i volunteer I told you about this morning. You said you were interested in talking to him."

"Oh, right."

"He asked if you wouldn't mind meeting him at his house."

"That would be great," I said.

"We'll need to leave right now," Michael added. "He's only got until four o'clock."

Jerry

I followed Michael's bright red Volkswagen Jetta as he barreled north up Route 3. He turned left at a place called Hull's Cove, and a hundred yards up the road, he swerved into the gravel driveway of a large, gray two-story farmhouse. The house was in good shape, with lace curtains in all the windows, freshly painted black shutters, and a nylon American flag flapping from an aluminum pole in the front yard. Bales of straw and half a dozen uncarved pumpkins sat on the front steps, and baskets of yellow apples stood on the front lawn. "Jerry and his wife run a bed and breakfast," Michael told me.

As we started up the front walk, a big sandy-blonde man with a thick walrus mustache, rose-tinted aviator glasses, and a gray velour shirt with a matching gray cap bounded down the front steps to greet us.

"Jerry, this is Paul," Michael said as we shook hands. "Paul, Jerry Keene."

"That's Keene with three e's, like the one in New Hampshire," Jerry said, smiling broadly. "Welcome to our home."

I followed Jerry into the house. He led me into a big old-fashioned farm kitchen, complete with a massive wood-burning stove, where we sat across from each other at a round wooden table strewn with brochures and maps of the area—presumably for the bed and breakfast guests.

"I'm what they call a native of the area," Jerry began.

"A real native?" I laughed. "Everyone else I've met so far here in Bar Harbor has been from somewhere else."

"Well, I was born in downtown Bar Harbor in 1954," he chuckled. "And both my parents are from Maine. So I think that does make me a real native.

"We have four children," he went on. "And we're about to adopt another, which is kind of neat. My wife and I have been together twenty-three years. And on our *twentieth* anniversary—as a surprise—I took her to Haifa, you know, where the world center is for the Baha'i faith." He was beaming.

I asked Jerry how he had gotten involved with Island Connections.

"I'd been a Baha'i for a couple of years before Island Connections got started," he said. "So when it started I was really interested. Because a very big part of the Baha'i faith is thinking of others before your own needs—and looking for ways to help others in need. And so I immediately got hold of Michael, and it has been just a wonderful experience."

"What do you do?"

"What I do primarily is I give people rides. For a while, I would visit people—just to be with them, you know—but right now it's mostly giving people rides. And it has just been wonderful," he repeated. "There's that old saying about how you give and you get so much more in return. And it really is true, you know."

I asked Jerry if he had any examples that he could share with me.

"Well," he said, "there's Steve. Steve used to be a big scrapping guy, bigger than me. And always in good shape—a good athlete. He loved to play golf, and he was a good basketball player. Loved sports. But he's always had diabetes, and it turned into a very progressive form of diabetes. And so he wound up having a kidney transplant, and his legs removed, and now his hands are being removed, piece by piece.

"So for years I've been giving him rides from the dialysis center to his home. But the fact is, he's taught me more about life—and about what's important in life—than almost anybody I've ever met. Because the man has gone through *fifty-seven* major surgeries. He was told by his doctor five years ago that if he ever wanted to just give up, 'Just come to the hospital, and we'll put you in a room. We just won't give you dialysis, and you'll go to sleep.' That was something like forty surgeries back, okay?

"All that agony and everything else, and when I went and got him this morning, he's still joking and laughing. We go and have lunch together, because he's very, very thirsty when he gets off the dialysis machine—and he's always hungry. So we just stop at McDonald's or somewhere and get something quick, and we eat together on the way back to his house."

Jerry went on rapidly, the words pouring out. "But, you know, he's just a remarkable individual whom I really wouldn't have gotten to know on a personal level if it wasn't for Island Connections. Because before, it was just in passing. We'd meet each other at football games because our sons both played football—this kind of thing. But to truly get to *know* this individual, not just as a wonderful person but as a *strong* person. . .

"*Now* when people tell me, 'I've got a splitting headache,' I just . . . Or myself: I stub my toe or I feel miserable some day, and I just think of my friend Steve. He told me a long time ago, 'On one of my good days, most people would want to end it. On my *good* days.' Yet he can still smile and enjoy his family, so it's *that* kind of gift that's absolutely priceless to me."

"Right."

"And, you know, he was just given a prognosis by his doctor that his heart is fading now. He's got a thickening of a major valve in his heart. The doctor gives him between six months and four years."

"How old *is* he?"

"Oh, I guess he might be four or five years older than me," Jerry said. "He might be fifty-five to fifty-seven, something like that. Probably only weighs about a 130 now because he's got no legs. And if he gets a scratch on his hands, he usually loses that section because of the circulation being so poor. He's going blind. He has cancer removed from his face about every two or three months—they have to take the tumors off his face. And yet the guy just keeps right on plugging."

Jerry leaned toward me, his face intense.

"The thing that I *really* admire about him is . . . Well, you know, there are a lot of people coming into dialysis that are just not sticking to the regimen—drinking just so many fluids, and all that—and *they're* coming in on their own two feet. They've got their legs, and perfect hands. Steve would give anything in the world for that. And yet these guys are killing themselves. They're slowly just killing themselves, and they'll die very soon—even though they're on dialysis and they're going through the system. Because they're not truly taking care of themselves.

"But this guy takes care of himself. He makes sure he only drinks so much, he watches his diet—he does his *best*," Jerry said, slapping the table. "And that kind of attitude—that kind of scrappiness—is absolutely priceless."

I nodded.

"And," Jerry added, "he's a lot of fun. He's just a real funny guy."

"So do you guys spend time together besides the rides?"

"Oh, sure. Like this summer, every once in a while I'd call him and I'd say, 'You wanna go to lunch?' And I'd take him to his favorite burger place. Or like his kids aren't playing basketball in high school anymore, but my son is starting his freshman year. So I just asked Steve last week if he'd be interested in going to some of the games. And he says, 'Call me whenever you're gonna go.' So we'll probably do that this winter."

"It's terrific that you're able to do that."

"Well, it's really a blessing for me. A lot of times when we're busy in August and we're feeding forty people, my wife will say to me, 'You know, it's okay if you miss a day.' But it really isn't—because, you see, the ride is only part of it. It's that relationship that we have with each other."

Jerry paused.

"He has a very strong anxiety. For example, with some of my rides, if I needed to go in and get something at Wal-Mart, I could do that. But with Steve, I can't—because he has a real anxiety about being left in the car unattended. Because he doesn't know what's going to happen. So he's comfortable with me. Whereas with new people coming in out of the blue to pick him up, it would be hard. And also," Jerry added somberly, "with the news that he's not going to be with us very much longer, each day is precious."

I asked Jerry to say a little more about the link between his faith and his involvement with Island Connections.

"Well, part of the Baha'i faith is that every moment of our lives, we can make a difference in humanity," he said. "And, you know, that's very empowering. If you're loving and caring and kind and give a smile, you can help someone's whole attitude and touch their soul on a positive level, so to speak. Of course, the bad edge of that sword is that if you backbite or if you're negative or mean to an individual, you touch that individual's soul in a negative way. And so, really, the only reason that we're here on this earth is to love one another and to help one another. That's really what it's all about."

Jerry's eyes almost seemed to glow. "You can have all the money in the world. You can have all the power on earth. But you're only here for the blink of an eye. And when you go to the next world, the only thing that you're ever going to take with you is the relationships that you've made on this earth. If you've been loving and kind on this earth, those relationships come with you."

I asked Jerry if he had grown up Baha'i.

"No," he said. "I was baptized in the Episcopal church. And though I believed in Christ and loved Christ, I was never really living a spiritual life. But at a very young age, when I was four years old, I was in a situation where I discovered prejudice—in a very painful, negative way."

"What happened?"

"There was a new shopping center opening in Ellsworth, and our parents took us to the grand opening," he said. "There was a Native American family in front of us, with three beautiful little kids. We waited out there for over an hour, with a big line behind us. And just before they were getting ready to open the door, this pickup truck pulls into the parking lot and these guys get out of the truck. They come running over, and they start pushing the Native Americans out of the way, saying: 'Get back on the reservation, you so-and-so's.' Just the most painful . . . "

Jerry stopped and took a deep breath. "And at four years old, I remember tears coming down from my eyes. It was like a knife was in my heart. These kids crying. And to really *feel* prejudice—and to *know,* instantly, that it was so *wrong.*"

Jerry choked up.

"And so all my life," he said, "the whole time I was growing up, I hated prejudices. But I never dreamed that there was a whole form of religion out there that is about ending prejudices. It's their life's work. You know, it's the oneness of all people and the oneness of all religions."

PART THREE

DEEP SOUTH

SOUTHBOUND

ALMOST AS SOON as I got home from Maine, I started planning the next leg of my exploration of Faith in Action: a two-week trip through the South, including New Orleans, one of my favorite cities. But when I finally did manage to track down the woman who was listed on the Web site as the Faith in Action director in New Orleans, she told me—apologetically—not to bother: there really was no more program. There *had* been while they'd still had the grant money from the Robert Wood Johnson Foundation, she said. But that was all used up now, and it was hard raising new money in this economy, and, well, you understand. It was the same story a little farther east over in Mobile, Alabama, where Faith in Action had funded a program to support people with AIDS.

This was discouraging. We had known from the outset when we were putting Faith in Action together that not all the programs we started with these small seed grants would be sustained after the money was gone—but, after all, wasn't this the Bible Belt? Surely, if Faith in Action was going to take root anywhere, shouldn't it be here?

But gradually, after long hours on the phone, I was able to map out a two-week itinerary that would take me deep into the South. Flying from Newark to Memphis, I would pick up another rental car and drive down to West Helena, Arkansas, a few miles west of the Mississippi River; then southeast across Mississippi to the town of Morton, just east of Jackson; and then down to Petal, a suburb of Hattiesburg in the southeastern corner of Mississippi. From there I would turn west and drive to Mandeville, Louisiana, across Lake Pontchartrain from New Orleans; then up to New Roads, just below Louisiana's elbow. After that, I would head up to Shreveport, in the northwest corner of the state, swinging northeast from there to Pine Bluff, Arkansas. And then from Pine Bluff back up to Memphis. This was sort of a clockwise loop from Memphis to the New Orleans region and back again, with enough time to allow for a few detours here and there, including a weekend in the New Orleans area.

So on a bitterly cold Monday morning—January 19, 2004—I boarded the 5:25 A.M. train at our local New Jersey Transit station to begin the second leg of my travels. Susie had driven me to the station, and as she slowly made her way down our snow-covered street, we could hear the thick crust of ice crunching under the car tires like broken glass. I was taking the train as far as the Newark Liberty Airport, where I was booked on the 9:05 flight to Memphis.

While it wasn't quite as cold in Memphis as it had been in New Jersey, at twenty-four degrees it wasn't exactly Miami Beach either. At least, though, it wasn't overcast. We hadn't seen much of the sun in New Jersey recently, and it felt good on my face as I pulled out of the Avis lot onto the highway.

I didn't need to be in West Helena until that night, since my visit there wasn't scheduled to start until the next morning. And I figured that it would take me only a couple of hours to drive down there, which meant that I could spend the afternoon in Memphis.

It turned out to be an interesting day to be in Memphis, because January 19 was Martin Luther King Day, and it was right here in Memphis, on April 4, 1968, while standing on the second-story balcony of the Lorraine Motel on Mulberry Street, that Dr. King had been assassinated. And so after a first-rate barbecue pork sandwich at the Bar-B-Q Shop on Madison Avenue ("Home of the Original Dancing Pigs Bar-B-Que Sauce"), I decided to drive down to the Lorraine Motel, which had been transformed into the National Civil Rights Museum.

The nearest parking place I could find was six blocks away. Big modern tour buses, lumbering school buses, ancient church buses, and cars from as far away as Illinois, Texas, and Georgia jammed the surrounding streets. And there was a long line of people waiting to get in.

A lot of the people waiting in line with me were young black families— parents who had brought their kids to show them what Martin Luther King Day was really all about. And in spite of the long wait in the cold, the kids were remarkably well behaved. They seemed to know that this was a special place where you didn't fool around.

The exhibit was worth the wait. Seeing the original Greensboro lunch counter where the sit-ins had started, the charred remains of one of the fire-bombed Greyhound Freedom Rider buses, and, at the end of the exhibit, the room where Martin Luther King had lived the last few moments of his life before he was gunned down was a powerful reminder of what had happened not so long ago in this part of the country.

In Maine, apart from Jerry Keene's harrowing childhood memory of the incident at the shopping center with the Native American family, race had never come up. Here in the South, it was everywhere.

I wanted to get to West Helena before dark, so after a quick detour past the old STAX recording studio where Otis Redding and Sam and Dave had made some of the most amazing records ever, I headed down McLemore past the Friendly Food Market ("Join Us for the True Bourbon"), the Memphis Baptist Ministerial Association, Lovell's Magic Touch Shoe Shine Parlor, and the C&L Carwash ("Fifty Cents"), and turned south onto Highway 61. A few miles before the Mississippi state line, I passed a billboard with a hand stretching out between prison bars that warned NO DEALS: DO THE CRIME—DO ALL THE TIME.

Suddenly all the traffic came to a halt. There seemed to be an accident up ahead. First an ambulance passed me on the shoulder, then another, and then the Action News van.

Time to bail out.

I turned onto a nearby side street and gradually made my way around the traffic, which was blocked in both directions. When I finally did get back onto Highway 61, I was in the Magnolia State.

It was a clear, beautiful evening. There had been a few billboards for the Tunica casinos back in Memphis, but now they were coming fast and furious: $100,000 BLACK-JACK TOURNAMENT AT THE GRAND CASINO . . . WILD HOLD 'EM STUD ONLY AT BALLY'S . . . CATFISH DINNERS JUST $5.99. . . .

By this time, the hills of Tennessee had vanished, and the land around me had flattened out completely: endless cotton fields on both sides of the highway, stretching to the horizon and beyond, and nothing but a few lone trees here and there and the occasional pawnshop. The sky out here was huge.

By the time I reached the turnoff onto Highway 49, the sun had fallen below the horizon and the sky had gone from flamingo pink to a deep violet. A sign said it was ten miles to the Isle of Capri Casino, which was just this side of where Highway 49 crossed the Mississippi River to Helena.

As I drove west toward the river, the cotton fields on my left were totally black—except where the standing water between the cotton rows caught the dying glow of the sunset. The result was a weird pattern of fiery purple stripes reflected against the blackness. You didn't see sunsets like this in New Jersey.

With a population of 8,689, West Helena was no Memphis. But it did have a Taco Bell, a Sonic, a Subway, a KFC, a Pizza Hut, and a Wal-Mart. It also had the Best Western motel where I had made my reservation for the next two nights, and my room was ready, waiting, and clean. I checked in, ate too much at a family-run Mexican restaurant just up the road, started reading *As I Lay Dying,* and fell asleep minutes later in the middle of one of Faulkner's interminable sentences.

WEST HELENA, ARKANSAS

THE NEXT DAY WAS another beauty—cold, clear, sunny, not a cloud in the sky. I wasn't scheduled to meet with Eddie Mae Martin, the Faith in Action project director in West Helena, until 10:30, so I had time to take a look around and maybe find a place to have breakfast. Turning left out of the Best Western parking lot, I headed toward town where most of the businesses seemed to be—a couple of funeral homes, a pawnshop, the Plaza Barbershop ("Human Hair Wigs"), the Pay-Day Money Store ("Cash Advances Up to $500"), Twin City Liquor—but no place for breakfast.

Then as I turned around and headed back toward the motel, I spotted Nicole's Café. Nicole's seemed to be where locals went—at least the white male locals. Even though two-thirds of West Helena's population was black and 55 percent was female, everyone in Nicole's that morning— myself included—was a white male. They were considerably quieter than the guys at Fred and Pete's Deli back home in New Jersey, some of them reading their morning papers, others laconically exchanging the latest local news.

"I hear Henry's subdividing his property again."

"That right?"

"And Jimmy's back from up North."

"That right?"

"That's what I hear."

Eddie Mae

Eddie Mae Martin's office was at the Phillips County Department of Human Services just outside of town on the 49 Bypass.

"You're here to see *who*?" the young woman at the front desk asked me.

"Eddie Mae Martin," I repeated as clearly as I could.

"Oh," she said, "you mean Miss *Martin*."

I thought that was what I'd said, but it seemed that my accent, which I hadn't realized that I had, was a problem.

She picked up the phone and punched in three numbers.

"Miss Martin? Somebody here to see you." She held her hand over the phone. "What did you say your name was?"

"Paul," I said, not wanting her to have to wrestle with my last name. "Just tell her Paul is here for the interview."

"It's Mister Paul," she said into the phone. "He's here to be interviewed . . . All right, I'll tell him."

She hung up the phone. "You can go on in," she told me. "Just go through this door here and make a right turn and that'll be her office, right there in front of you."

Eddie Mae, a big woman who looked every inch the nurse that she was, welcomed me to her office, apologized for the mess, and then apologized that she hadn't been able to get in touch with all of the people she'd wanted me to have a chance to talk to, including a family whose son was in a wheelchair.

"What with the holiday," she said—meaning Martin Luther King Day—"and then my sister got bit and I had to take her to the hospital. But I can give you the phone number, and you can call her at about five this evening. The name is Lula Jones, and you can just explain that you understand that Faith in Action provided the wheelchair ramp for Kevin and you just wanted to talk to her about it. And I'm pretty sure she will. I just never got a chance to catch up with her."

Eddie Mae gave me the phone number.

"You see, we serve the elderly *and* the handicapped. And even though Kevin's only seventeen, he's had a stroke. And so he's in a wheelchair, and his family needed a wheelchair ramp at the house for when he got out of the hospital in Little Rock. So we did that for them."

The other client Eddie Mae wanted me to talk to was Gracie, an elderly woman she *had* gotten in touch with, and Gracie had agreed to meet with me some time today. I just needed to give her a call before I went over to her house so that she would know to expect me.

And then there was Gracie's volunteer, Miss Owens, who had also agreed to talk with me. But, again, I needed to give her a call to set up a time that would be convenient for her and to get the directions to her home.

Finally, there was Eddie Mae's board. "Two of my board members are already here: Chris Taylor and Connie Huff," she said. "They work right here in the building, so you can talk to them when we get done talking.

But the ministers—they're a lot harder to catch up with. In fact, I'm still trying to catch up with them, because I'm trying to have a board meeting next Friday, so I'm going to have to mail out letters to them, I guess. Like I've got one board member—he's a minister, but he also runs a Sonic drive-in restaurant and some other businesses—*and* the food pantry. So he's hard to keep up with."

As a matter of fact, Eddie Mae said, she was a board member herself. She was just running the program "because of a situation that occurred here": the lack of a director.

"So like I told you on the telephone," she went on, "right now we don't have a lot of people that we serve that are ongoing. Like one lady we helped to get a walker—so once we did that, that was it. And then two other people we helped with getting medicines, because they didn't have Medicaid. And then we had another elderly lady, she was washing clothes and linens on her knees because she didn't have a washing machine. Well, we were able to get a washing machine donated to us so we provided that to her.

"But right now we just have Gracie that we're serving on an ongoing basis, and one other lady—she's a schoolteacher who had a car accident and broke her leg. One of our volunteers has been running errands for her. But she's kind of private, so she's not going to agree to an interview."

"Sure," I said. "I understand that."

I was also beginning to understand that there wasn't much of a program here—at least not in terms of people who were getting ongoing help. And it didn't look as if I was going to have a lot of people to interview, either: just Eddie Mae, the two board members who also worked here at DHS, Gracie, Miss Owens, and maybe Lula Jones.

I asked Eddie Mae whether they'd been able to serve more people when they had still had their director.

"Well, you see, that was the problem with the director," she said. "We didn't have any records of serving anybody. We've done more since she left. You know, we've got a thrift store with a couple of volunteers, and that's how we've been able to get funds to help people out. And then people donate things too—like the washing machine I was telling you about. And we got a refrigerator and a stove."

"So the money that you got from the Robert Wood Johnson Foundation—the twenty-five thousand dollars—that's all been used up?"

Eddie Mae nodded. "That was all used up before she left."

"You mean just paying her?"

"Exactly. And that's why we terminated her—because we were under the impression that things were being done. And then we come to find out that she was just being paid a salary, using money that shouldn't have been used, you know."

I asked Eddie Mae whether she had been involved with the grant from the beginning.

"Almost from the beginning," she said. "At first, I was kind of reluctant to get involved, because I'm on a lot of other boards too. I'm on the Minority Health Commission, and I also had a youth group that I was doing at my church." That was on top of her job here at DHS as the field supervisor for a home nursing program for the elderly that covered twenty-three counties.

I asked Eddie Mae how she had become involved with Faith in Action.

"Well," she said, "this was something they presented to me. They said, you know, that there was a lot of racial disharmony in the county and that the economic situation was bad and a lot of elderly people needed help. You see, we have no public transportation—unless you have Medicaid. And we had a lot of people who didn't qualify for Medicaid because they were ten or fifteen dollars over, so they couldn't get transportation unless they paid for it. And there were a lot of people who couldn't buy medicines because they didn't have a Medicaid card and the medications were so high.

"Now as a nurse, I had the knowledge of the drug companies and how to get some of the medicines for people who didn't meet the criteria for Medicaid. So I shared that information with the people who were bringing this Faith in Action program together, and at that point they asked me, 'Why don't you just serve on the board?' And I told them, 'I don't want to, but I will.'"

She laughed.

"But also," she added, "the board was a way of bringing the races together. Because it was an interracial board, and we felt that we could serve the entire community if it was made up of people that were like what the community was like. You know, if the board was all white, it might make the other race feel like, 'Well, they're not going to serve *me*.' So we just felt that it should be interracial and interdenominational—which meant all denominations."

"How many congregations did you get?"

"Let's see. We have Faith Outreach, which is a mixed congregation; we have the Church of the Living God; we have my church, the Church of Deliverance; then we have the Catholic church and the Baptist church and the Assembly of God. So I guess we have all the major churches. And we have two radio ministers on the board—one's black and one is white."

"Are the volunteers also interracial?"

"That's right."

I asked Eddie Mae whether the racial disharmony she had mentioned had been improving.

"I can't say that it's worse, but I can't say that it's . . ." She stopped and reflected. "Well, maybe it's a *little* bit better."

"In what way?"

"We don't have the fighting and bickering the way we used to between the races. But," she added, "now we have it in the powers that be. I think most of the people in the *community* have figured out that we need to work together in order to grow. But the powers that be are still wanting to be in control. Even when blacks get into a position of power, it becomes a power struggle. Instead of working together to make it better, it's like, 'You were there at one point in time, and you did this to me. Now I'm going to pay you back,' rather than saying, 'It didn't work when it was done that way, so let's forget about the past and see what we can do to make it better.'"

Eddie Mae sighed. "Now, this is just my opinion. I'm just speaking for myself. But that's what I feel is what's going on."

"But you're still optimistic?"

"I am," she said emphatically. "I feel like if you can get some open-minded people in leadership positions, then I think the attitudes of the majority of people will change."

She frowned. "So far, though, we haven't been able to do that. Like the mayor, for example. Even though he's black, we're having some conflicts because I disagree with him on some of the things he's doing. Because it's more of a *power* struggle than really working for the benefit of the community.

"You know," she said fiercely, "sometimes it's better to be at peace than to try to put your opinion over, because you're just going to give a bad picture of the entire community. It's just like the council and the mayor. Well, people see that as the *community*. And then all the negative stuff makes the newspaper, so when people read about the community, they think it's the worst community in the world. They think, 'They just hate each other and they're always fighting'—which is not the case. *Everybody* is not fighting. It's the people in public office that are fighting."

Changing the subject, I asked Eddie Mae about the community.

"Very few jobs," she said. "People are having to leave this community to go other places for work."

"What kind of work is there?"

"Well, people work at Wal-Mart. Some of them work at the local stores. The people that have any medical training work at the hospital—and some of them work over here at DHS, which is government jobs. Besides that . . . "

"What about agriculture?"

"A few work in agriculture. But you know, now it's become so sophisticated until the manpower that's needed is much less than it was in the past. The tractors and the other machines, they're all computerized now. You have a few farmers that are still left here, but the farmhands and the farms where people could get work . . ."

"They're not here anymore?"

"That's right. You have a few chemical plants where people work at, but besides that, it's the convenience stores and the casinos."

She sighed heavily.

I turned the conversation back to Faith in Action.

"It seems like you're the one that's keeping Faith in Action going," I said. "Even though the money's been used up and the director's gone, you're sort of the acting director, aren't you?"

"Right," she said. "And the board of directors. At first, we just contributed our personal money in order to keep things going. And then we opened the thrift store, which has given us some additional money to keep it going."

Eddie Mae told me that she probably spent between four and six hours a week, most of it after hours, arranging the services, supervising the volunteers, and so on. But she was hoping, with the help of her fellow board members, to raise enough money from local businesses to be able to hire someone on a part-time basis who could begin to take over and build up the program. "There's so much that needs to be done, but I just don't have the time."

"Why do you do it at all? I mean on top of all your other responsibilities."

"Because I have lived in this community all my life," she said. "And I really feel that this community can be a very positive place. It has the potential to improve to where it should be. And I'm the kind of person . . . I feel like you can't just sit back and identify the problem if you're not trying to do anything to address it."

"Why not?"

"Because that's my Christian belief," Eddie Mae declared. "If you really care and you want to see change . . . Faith without works is dead. You've got to put work into it. And you serve God through serving other people—all my life I've felt this way. Not only that, but I grew up without a mother. My mother died when I was five years old. And my father had Parkinson's disease, which meant he was limited. So somebody had to give to me. Had it not been for somebody helping me . . ." Her voice trailed off.

"And who did that for you?" I asked.

"People in the community. Different people. You see, I was raised by an aunt who was an alcoholic, but there were other people in the community who inspired me to keep at it. There was hope, you see."

"Was this through the church?"

"Partly through the church—and also just neighbors, you know." Eddie Mae smiled. "The lady across the street, she would always encourage me. She would encourage me to go to Sunday school and to church. She would encourage me to stay in school and to do my homework. So with that encouragement . . ."

She blinked several times, fighting back tears. "You know, if somebody hadn't reached out to me, I could have been an alcoholic."

"And instead you're an RN."

"That's right," she said proudly. "Instead, I'm an RN."

Eddie Mae walked me down the hall to another office, where she introduced me to Chris Taylor and Connie Huff, her two fellow board members at the Department of Human Services.

I had been dismayed by Eddie Mae's initial description of their Faith in Action program; there hardly seemed to be a program at all. But as she'd described some of the things that they had done despite the loss of funds—and, more than that, as it had become apparent how deep her feelings about her community ran—I had begun to take heart and to think that maybe, just maybe, this phoenix could still rise from the ashes.

But clearly Chris and Connie didn't agree.

"I don't see this particular group as going anywhere," Connie said bluntly. "Because it's basically made up of Eddie Mae Martin, Chris, and myself—and maybe one or two others that we could call on."

"Why do you think that is? What's the problem?"

"Everyone's got a lot of their own responsibilities, and they can't really participate. They may have the desire, but they don't have the time or the energy to put into it like it really needs."

It was clear that both women were still bitter about the original director. In fact, they didn't want to talk about her. "We don't even like to hear her name," Connie said.

Although they both thought highly of Eddie Mae, neither was optimistic that she would be able to resurrect the program.

"We *have* helped some people with emergencies and things like that," Chris said, "so it's done *some* good."

"But we don't get the participation," Connie sighed. "Just a lot of promises."

As I left the building, I wasn't sure what to think. My conversation with Chris and Connie had been somewhere between a cold shower and an ice bath. On the other hand, Eddie Mae didn't strike me as a quitter.

I reminded myself that we had known from the start when we were putting Faith in Action together that not every seed would germinate and not every flower would bloom. Still, when I thought about my earlier calls to the defunct programs in New Orleans and Mobile, I was beginning to wonder whether anything could grow in this southern soil. Certainly I hadn't run into anything like this in Maine.

I recalled a conversation that I'd had with Margaret Mahoney, the retired president of the Commonwealth Fund in New York City. Margaret, a southerner born and raised in Nashville, had warned me that she didn't think Faith in Action would ever take root in the South. Why not? Because, she said, there wasn't a sense of community in the South—at least not like there was in New England or in the Midwest. There wasn't the same tradition of people in a community helping one another out.

Yet what about all those people "in the community" who had reached out to Eddie Mae when she was growing up? Or was that only within the black community—a community that itself had been through a lot of changes since the days of Eddie Mae's childhood?

Hopefully, some of the other programs that I would be visiting during the next two weeks would be in better shape than the one here in West Helena. Because it was already clear, less than twenty-four hours into my trip, that if there was any place in America that desperately needed what Faith in Action had to offer, this was it.

Gracie

"Did you have any trouble finding my house?" Gracie asked after I'd come in and introduced myself.

"Well, I wasn't sure if you were on East Park or West."

"East," she said. "They know me at the post office. Sometimes I'll get something that has West Park on the address, and they know to put East on it."

Gracie was in the front room of her house, ensconced in a recliner across from the television. She had turned the sound off when I came in, but she'd left the picture on. It looked like a soap opera.

She wore a dingy checkered robe and had an oxygen tube at her nose. An aluminum cane leaned against the small table beside her chair, and on the table were two Bibles and a telephone. The room was fairly dark, with a couple of pictures on the walls and what looked like a handwritten proclamation that began with the words, "To Grandma."

"How long have you lived here?" I asked her.

"In this house, about twenty-three years," Gracie said. "I've been here in Helena since 1953. That's a long time."

"Sure is," I said. "How old are you now?"

"Seventy-nine."

"And where are you from originally?"

"Earle."

"Earle," I said knowingly. "Uh-huh."

"Do you know where that is?" Gracie was sharp: she knew that I didn't have a clue.

"No, I don't," I admitted.

"Well, it's about a two-hour drive north from here."

"And what brought you to Helena?" I asked.

"My husband. He had worked for Mr. Black in the termite business when we was in Earle. Then we moved on to the other side of Memphis—he worked in a candy factory there. But we found out that Mr. Black had died, and so my husband came down here to see Mrs. Black. She wanted him to come down here and take over the business. But I didn't want to move—I had two little boys—so we stayed in Tennessee for I don't know how many weeks, and he drove back and forth. Then finally I gave in and we moved down here."

In West Helena, Gracie had become a waitress. I asked her where she had worked.

"Just about all the restaurants around here," she said. "Never did work at the Holiday Inn, though."

I asked her how often she got out of the house.

"I haven't been out no farther than the front porch in several months," she replied. "Well, I did go to the doctor once, but that's the only thing."

"Do you have any family still living here?"

"I have a son and a daughter-in-law that live about three and a half blocks from here, but I don't really see them that often. He's a truck driver, and he goes back and forth to Memphis every day. He calls me maybe once a week."

"And you get along with him?"

"Oh, yeah, we get along fine."

"Sometimes people don't," I said.

"Well, I guess that's like my older son," she chuckled. "He says I'm too mean to die. I don't know where my older son is. He calls me every once in a while, but he won't tell me where he lives. He called me the other day. He's a truck driver too, like my younger son, but he drives long distance. I believe he said he was calling from someplace outside Cincinnati. He said it was zero degrees, and even though he was wearing a jacket and a coat on top of that, he said it was like he wasn't wearing nothing at all. On account of the wind, I guess."

"I take it your husband's no longer living."

"I don't have a husband," she said flatly. "I've been married three times, and all of them are dead."

"I'm sorry to hear that," I murmured.

"The first one, we just couldn't make it," Gracie said. "We was together a year and two weeks. My next one, we was together twenty-nine years. He died of heart trouble. And three years later I married again—and then he died of cancer. I nursed him for four years before he died."

"So how long have you been on your own?"

"He died in '88."

"So you've been on your own for fifteen years now?"

"Uh-huh," she said. "And I've had some hard times, but then I've had some pretty good times, too."

Before going any further, I decided to tell Gracie about my book project and about the purpose of Faith in Action.

"I want to tell you, it's good that you all are doing that," she said. "There was a lady that came to see me—she's been here twice. But my church don't . . ." She paused. "Well, my pastor as good as told me he didn't think there was anything wrong with me."

I asked Gracie about the lady from Faith in Action who had been over to see her. At first, she couldn't remember her name.

"Was it a Miss Owens?" I asked her.

"That's right. Evelyn Owens."

"And she's been here to see you twice?"

"That's right. We just sit and visit. She's real nice."

"I'm glad," I said, "because I'll be meeting with her this afternoon."

"And have you been to see Connie Brandon?" she asked.

"Who's Connie Brandon?"

"She lives over on Second Street. She's a bad diabetic, and she's an invalid. And she gets so lonesome—just like myself."

"Do you talk to her?"

"Every once in a while I do."

"You call her up on the telephone?"

"Uh-huh. Lately she's been real bad. She's likely to lose a toe. Or she did lose it—I don't remember now."

"When did you talk to her last?"

"She called me yesterday morning, and we talked a little while. She's a real talker, like myself. You get that way when you're by yourself, I guess. Anyway, when she wants to talk, she wants to talk. You don't have a chance to say a word."

"It's great that you call her," I said.

"I call her every once in a while, you know, just to check on her and see how she's doing. I believe the Bible speaks about it. The Lord wants us to take care of one another, and so I try and help people out."

"That's great."

"I was helping a family over in Helena. He's in bad shape—and she is too. A very small woman. Wears about a seven. And they had it pretty hard. I called them the day before yesterday, I think it was, and I asked her about their finances. Her daddy had made a sewing box—it's kind of like a little chair. It's real nice. I've seen some of them in books. And she started out wanting about ninety dollars for it, because it's antique, really. So they put it on the radio for, I think, forty dollars. And so I called her and I said, 'If my daddy had made that, I wouldn't sell it for no amount of money.' You see, I'd bought a whole lot of stuff from her. That's the reason I called. In fact, I bought too much from them, trying to help them, you see. And so I asked her why she was selling it. She said her husband has heart trouble and he takes ten different kinds of medicines. And she said they're just trying to get the money to buy the medicines."

"What a shame," I murmured.

"It's a real shame," she said angrily.

I asked Gracie what kind of health problems she had herself.

"I have osteoporosis real bad," she said. "My spine is terrible; I can't stand up but a few minutes at a time. I have bronchial asthma real bad and emphysema pretty bad. And congestive heart failure."

"Sounds like you've got a lot of things going on."

"Yeah. But with prayer and all, I've been doing all right. I pray a lot. Like I told my son—he's had that angioplasty for his heart—he told me a couple of weeks ago how his heart was bothering him all the time. And of course you know how you pray for your kids every day anyway, but he said he was going to see the heart doctor on the thirteenth. And so I said, 'Well, now, that's something special I can pray for.'

"So I started praying for his heart, and a few days after that I said, 'Son, is your heart still bothering you?' And he said, 'You know, it hasn't bothered me at all.' And I asked him again Saturday if his heart was bothering him, and he said, 'It doesn't bother me anymore.' I said, 'Well, it might be because I've been praying so hard for you.' He said, 'I thought you prayed all the time for me anyhow.' And I said, 'I do, but usually I just pray for your safety—and this time I was praying for your heart.'"

I asked Gracie whether she had any grandchildren.

"Sure do."

"Tell me about them," I said.

"I'm proud of them."

"You are?"

She laughed. "Yes, I am. I got one grandson that lives up in Jonesboro. He lived with me for more than five years. He's married now, he's got a little girl."

"So you're a great-grandmother?"

"I'm almost eighty years old, you know," she said. "I'm a great-grandmother several times. I've got two great-grandchildren that live right down here. I've got a grandson and his wife."

"They live right here in West Helena?"

"Just down the street. Like the other night, we didn't have any electricity, and they came down to check on me. He had to go back to the house to get a battery to put in that oxygen machine, but he got it all fixed up for me."

I asked Gracie how often she saw her grandson.

"Well," she said, "he don't volunteer to come down, but if I need him, I can call him. And he's got a son that's sixteen and a girl that's fourteen."

"Those are your great-grandchildren?"

"That's right."

"And do they ever come by?"

"Oh yes. And my grandson and my great-grandson, they've both been saved recently. They've been working at the church, and they're real happy about it."

"Now I want to ask *you* something," Gracie said.

"Sure."

"Do you believe in guardian angels?"

"Yes I do," I said.

"Do you believe you can see one?"

"Do I believe I can see one?" I asked, smiling. "Sometimes."

"A year ago today," Gracie said, "I saw mine." She was dead serious.

"Tell me about it," I said.

"I had been having terrible pains, so I went to the doctor, and he gave me some strong pain pills. So I took them like I was supposed to, and it got to where when I'd get up in the morning, in a little while I'd be sitting here, and I'd doze to sleep."

"Right."

"Well, I did that particular morning, and when I woke up, I noticed there was something over there in that corner, and it didn't look right. First I thought my eyes were playing a trick on me, because I kept looking and looking—and then I figured out it was a woman, standing there warming her hands. And I looked around, and I knew I hadn't unlocked the door, so I said, 'Who are you?' She was looking at me, and I said it again: 'Who are you?' She didn't say anything. So I said, 'How did you get in here?' She still didn't say anything, but she was looking at me all the time. And I thought: she knows how to get in the house without unlocking the doors. You know, that's what I thought. And by that time, I was almost screaming at her. And I said, 'Come here!' And she took three or four steps toward me—and then stopped and stared at me." She paused dramatically. "And disappeared like *that*."

"Wow."

"I just never saw anything like it," Gracie said.

"No, I guess not," I agreed. "So what did she look like?"

"She had on a green skirt and a button-down shirt and green hat to match."

"Did she look like anybody you'd ever seen before?"

"No. And I'm going to tell you why—it didn't even dawn on me at that time. She was black-headed, and her hair—the way it was, you could see the part, and then it came down kind of like this." Gracie moved her hand lightly across her face. "It didn't even dawn on me that I wasn't seeing eyes, nose, and mouth—because I wasn't. And then after it was all over and she disappeared, I just sat here stunned. Just absolutely stunned. I didn't know whether to be scared or what to think."

"Well, that's quite a story."

"It's a true one," she said firmly.

"I understand."

"My pastor didn't believe I saw it. He just didn't believe it. In fact, he said he didn't believe anything. And I said, 'Well, if you don't believe anything, there's no point in me telling you about it.'"

I asked Gracie whether she watched a lot of television.

"I keep it on mostly for noise," she replied. "A lot of times I'm reading or doing something else when it's on. Now it's a mess here, but I've been down for nearly twelve years. That couch is my bed," she added, gesturing toward an old green sofa beside her chair that had a couple of pillows and an afghan spread across it.

"So you don't have to go far."

"Well," she said, "that's because the blacks are kind of bad around here. I've had to run some of them away from the door. And if I hadn't, they would've probably tried to break in. In fact, one night someone tried to break in."

"What did you do?"

"I didn't do anything at that time, because evidently they saw the police or something. It sounded like there was two or three of them. The police, they've chased them through my yard more than one time. One time they shot four times, right there in front of the air-conditioner."

"The police did?"

"They sure did. They shot at someone."

"Are there break-ins in the other houses around here?"

"Oh yes. It was in the paper the other day that the criminals was bad about breaking in and stealing things."

I asked Gracie whether she knew her neighbors.

"Well," she said, pointing out the window toward the house next door, "these right here, I was glad to find out they was white. But I found out later they was dopeheads. She don't have anything to do with me. But that's all right. If they're dealing with dope, I'd just as soon people didn't see them coming in and out of my house. Over there, one of them's an invalid. They're white people. I see them going in and out over there. But other than that, it's basically a black neighborhood."

"And you don't have anything to do with your black neighbors?"

"Well, the one across the street, she's real nice," Gracie said. "She's come over a few times to check on me. And, you know, I'll call her. Or sometimes she'll call me if she wants to borrow something. Sometimes I've got something I want to give her."

"What's her name?"

"Bernice," Gracie said. "She stays in the house pretty near all the time."

Gracie rocked back and forth in her recliner, watching a silent credit card commercial on the television screen behind me.

"So, Gracie," I said after a pause, "tell me what your day is like. What time do you get up in the morning?"

"Oh, eight-thirty or nine. Sometimes ten, if I want to sleep in. I'll tell you, I've been depressed. I went to the doctor, and he gave me some tablets. But, shoot, they didn't help anything."

"Okay, so after you get up . . ."

"I'll usually watch *The Price Is Right*."

"You like that one?"

"Yes, I do," she said with enthusiasm. "And then I'll watch a soap opera, *The Young and the Restless*. I usually watch that. After that, I'll watch the news—just long enough to get the headlines and the weather. And then I'm through. The rest of it is just noise."

And then what?

"Well, I use the telephone a lot."

"Who do you call?"

"I've got an ex-daughter-in-law in Parkdale. She's got the same things wrong with her as me, only her heart is real bad. And she's paralyzed. She's in real bad shape. So I call her a lot. And I've got a brother-in-law in Trumann—he's ninety-four years old. I call him. My brother—he's the captain of a boat, but he lives at home. And I've got a cousin over in Mississippi, he's in bad shape—he's got heart trouble. And then I call people around here who are down like myself. I check on them and see how they're doing."

"So you've got a whole list of people you call," I said. "Family and friends."

"Uh-huh."

"That's good."

"Well," she said, "people around here don't call *me*. There's not but one or two people that ever call me. But I call them anyway and see how they're doing. And they're always friendly when I call."

"Now you say Evelyn Owens comes over to see you ."

"She's been here twice."

"Is there anybody else who comes over to visit?"

Gracie shook her head.

"She's it?"

"I can't think of nobody else."

Ready to wrap up the interview and starting to get up, I said, "It sounds to me like you've had quite a life, Gracie."

"I haven't told you the *bad* part of my life," she laughed, in what I could see was an obvious ploy to extend my visit. "I've had a *terrible* time in my life."

"Well, then," I said, sitting back down, "tell me about it."

"Well. . ." She wasn't sure where to start.

"Now you told me that your first marriage didn't work out," I prompted her.

"That's right," she said. "And he was the best of the three. But he didn't like to work much. He wanted to stay in the house with his parents all the time. I was only nineteen then, but I had to do the washing for all their family and work in the fields too."

"This was back in Earle?"

"Back in Earle."

"Tell me about Earle," I said. "What kind of town is Earle?"

"It was a good, clean little town," Gracie said. "But they say it's rotten now. They say the blacks have taken over. I remember when you could buy just about anything you wanted in Earle: nails, staples, lumber, all kinds of stuff. But they say you can't even buy a nail in Earle now."

"Is that right?"

"Not even a nail," she repeated. "My son and his wife carried me up there one time, and we drove through. It just looked like a dump."

"That's a shame," I said. "But tell me what it was like when you were growing up. Where did you live? Was it on a farm?"

"I lived in the country, and we worked in the fields. Worked hard."

"What kind of farm was it?"

"It was just raising cotton . . . and corn, you know."

"So did you pick cotton?"

"I chopped cotton, picked cotton. Sure did."

"Hard work," I said.

"It *is* hard work," she agreed. "But back then we appreciated everything we got. It wasn't like it is now: 'I don't want this, I don't want that.' We got so little, you see."

"Well, you grew up during the Depression, right?"

"That's right," she said. "And back then it seemed like Christmas would never get here. We got a little fruit, maybe a little gift. My mother would do some baking. *That* was Christmas to us. And it was a good Christmas."

"Sure."

"And it wasn't just our family. It was everybody. Everybody was like that. We didn't have electricity out there, so we couldn't have a tree. And I remember one time my little brother and me, we went and picked out a little old branch and we wrapped it in tinfoil—and that was our Christmas tree." She chuckled. "Sounds like the Waltons, don't it?"

"And how far did you get in school, Gracie?"

"I went through the fifth grade. Then my mother got crippled, and I had to take over."

"When you were in the fifth grade?"

"Twelve years old. The doctors never did know what was wrong with her, but she couldn't walk. She was on crutches for six years, and her nerves was so bad she lost most of her hair. I had to take over the cooking."

"That's a lot of responsibility," I said.

"My daddy and my oldest brother, they'd fuss about the food when I first learned to cook. Oh, they'd get mad, and I'd cry. They'd say it wasn't cooked right. But, foot, I was just a kid—I was just learning. I had a hard time of it."

"I believe it," I said. "That's a lot of responsibility for someone twelve years old. And you were working out in the fields too?"

"Oh, yes."

"And then what happened? You said you got married when you were nineteen, right?"

"That's right," Gracie said. "It was hard on me during my first marriage, having to wash for everybody on the washboard. All those men, you know: my husband and his daddy and two brothers and a nephew. Besides the sheets and towels and everything, you know."

"That's an awful lot of work," I said.

"It *was* a lot of work. I'd stay out in the fields on Thursday and wash on Friday morning—and iron—and then I'd go back in the fields Friday evening. That was hard. And he wanted to live right there with them. But it got to where we just wasn't getting along at all. So that was it, really."

She rocked quietly in her chair, remembering.

"And then what did you do?"

"Then I married again."

"So was it with your second husband that you moved here?"

"That's right. And I think he married me on the rebound. He wasn't good to me at all. He stepped out on me. And he didn't take a lot of time for me and the boys. It seemed like all them years it was just me, Stan, and Johnny. He would never come to their birthday parties or anything. And, well, he was an alcoholic.

"He died in 1975, and I married another man three years later. Boy, that was one. . ." Gracie paused, and a look of pain crossed her face. "I was actually scared of him. He would steal stuff from me. I would do things—sell crochet and babysit for money—and I'd have to hide the money from him because he'd steal it from me. And he was making over six hundred dollars a week! He worked down at the chemical plant. He was a welder. And he made *good* money. But then he would steal *my* money."

"And then you took care of him when he got sick?"

"I took care of him. But I told him, I said, 'I'm going to treat you good, so if you die before I do, I won't have a bad conscience.' And I didn't. Because I knew I'd done everything for him that I could. There was times I had to lift him out of the bathtub and set him on the commode and dry him off and dress him. And he had family here. He had two sons and their wives that lived right here. And do you know, they wouldn't hardly come over and see him to see how he was doing, or call to see if we needed anything."

"So you were on your own."

"That's right. And I'd have to get somebody to take me to the grocery store the times that I could leave him for a little while. It was just . . ." She broke off.

"It didn't work out either, did it?"

"No, it sure didn't," she said. "And there was times that I would pray that the Lord would let me die to get out of it. But it looked like it wouldn't happen, so I said, 'If you won't let me die, then let *him* die.'"

"And that *did* happen," I said.

"That *did* happen," Gracie said. "So I went back to the church, and I thanked the Lord. And then I finished paying for this house. I know it don't look like much—it's gone down a lot—but I finished paying for it by babysitting and selling crochet and doing what I had to do."

"So you've got your own place."

"That's right. It's paid for. And I even had siding put on it. Never missed a payment," she said proudly.

Evelyn

Evelyn's home was on a two-lane highway across from a big open field a few miles outside of town and was very much like the other houses that lined the road: a trim one-story ranch with a small Ford parked in the driveway. A flag decal on the rear bumper said, "Standing Tall."

We sat in the living room, which was as neat and trim as the exterior of the house. In fact, Evelyn herself was neat and trim in appearance, calm and soft-spoken in conversation. I told her that I had just come from a long visit with Gracie and that Gracie had told me how much she appreciated her visits.

"I've got to get back over there," Evelyn said, a little embarrassed. "I've only been to see her twice."

"When did you start?"

"Eddie Mae called me probably about the first of December, so then I called Miss Gracie and I asked her what would be a good time. She told me that she had an aide on Tuesdays and Thursdays, but she said Mondays would be good."

"And what do you do when you go over there?"

"I had signed up for Bible reading, because I enjoy the Bible and Bible studies. But the first time I went over there, with my sister, we just got acquainted, really. It was about an hour and a half, and she seemed to enjoy it."

"You brought your sister?"

"She likes to come along," Evelyn said. "But she doesn't say much. Mostly she just sits there quietly and listens."

I nodded.

"Anyway," she continued, "Miss Gracie mentioned that she'd like to have some candied fruit from Wal-Mart, and I said, 'Well, I'll go get it for you.' So I went out and got that and brought it back to her. She wanted to do a fruitcake for Christmas."

She shifted in her chair. "I had *intended* to go each week, and so the next week we went back again. This time we went for about an hour—and *sort* of got off on the wrong foot."

"How so?"

"I was telling her that I have Sky Angel. I don't know if you've ever heard of it, but it's a satellite station that when it started was all religious programming, but now it also has a lot of what they call family stuff on it. So I was telling her that twenty-four hours a day, you could get preaching or teaching or gospel music—and I mentioned Oral Roberts."

She grimaced, and continued, "Now, during the first visit, she had told me she didn't like my pastor. She had told me a story about him from way back yonder. He had come into a restaurant where she was working—him and a bunch of church people—and he just kept making demands. You know, 'If you could get me just one more piece of cornbread, I'll leave you a good tip.' And when he left, she said he left her a quarter. Well, that's so unlike him, because he always tips good. He will worry the heck out of you, like he's wanting special service, but then he'll leave a good tip.

"But, anyway, Miss Gracie had already told me she didn't like him, and so when I went back the second time, I apologized for him. I had told him about it, and he'd offered to go and talk to her, but I told him it wouldn't do any good. And then when I mentioned Oral Roberts"—Evelyn sighed—"oh, she just got kind of adamant."

"She's not an Oral Roberts fan?"

"She said, 'I don't like him.' Well, it *was* a founded thing, because a couple of people—one was her sister who died of cancer and I can't remember who the other one was—they'd been really sick, and they felt that if they could just get to Oral Roberts, they'd be healed. And they were *not* healed. And it left them bitter—and it left her worse. So, I mean . . ." Evelyn sighed again.

"Anyhow, I believe she got to feeling bad afterward, because she called me up and she said, 'Oh, someone really bragged on you last night.' And I said, 'Really?' She said, 'Yes, they said you was a fine woman.' And I said, 'Well, praise the Lord that *someone* thinks I'm a good woman.' She said, 'Well, now, don't you think the Good Lord thinks you're a good woman?' And I said, 'Well, I trust that He does.' But I think she was trying to make amends."

"Sounds like it."

"But then she hasn't called me anymore. She was calling me maybe two or three times a week, and then I called her the other day. And I said, 'Miss Gracie, did you have a good Christmas?' And she said, 'By *myself*?'"

"Oh, no."

"I said, 'You're kidding.' And she said, 'No, I am *not*.' She told me she had cooked a ham and about all the trouble that she had gone to trying to fix something because she thought that her grandson was coming. Well, she wound up eating by herself. They had a big dinner down at the son's house, but they didn't come and get her. Now she said it's very hard for her to get out—which I'm sure it is, with the oxygen and all. But it hurt her feelings so bad. And when she called over there and said something, they had already eaten dinner. And they said, 'Well, we'll bring you something.' And she said, 'I don't want *food*.'"

Evelyn looked up sorrowfully.

"I just felt so bad."

The weak winter sun was already low in the sky by the time I pulled out of Evelyn's driveway an hour later. A couple of stray dogs trotted silently along the edge of the road, and the stop sign at the end of the road was riddled with bullet holes.

After dinner at a roadside barbecue joint, I went back to the Best Western and called Lula Jones to see if she would be willing to talk to me that evening. The poor woman sounded as if she were in the middle of a war zone. I could hear a bunch of kids laughing and yelling in the background and what sounded like *The Simpsons* turned up full blast.

Well, yes, she would have been happy to talk to me if she had known about it ahead of time, but she'd just gotten home from work and she was still fixing supper. She was very sorry, but she just wouldn't have time to meet with me tonight. Yes, she knew about Faith in Action—they were the ones that had come in and built the ramp for Kevin, which had definitely been a big help to them. Maybe the next time I was in town, if I could call ahead of time.

So that was that.

No more interviews, tonight or tomorrow.

I had planned to be in West Helena for two full days of interviews, leaving the next afternoon for Jackson, Mississippi, but now there was no point in hanging around.

MORTON, MISSISSIPPI

I SPENT THE NEXT DAY, Wednesday, driving south along the Mississippi River to Natchez, a beautiful town that I had always been curious about, and then drove up the Natchez Trace to a Red Roof Inn east of Jackson, since there were no motels at all listed for Morton in my Triple A Guide. Thursday morning, after breakfast at a bustling Waffle House, I took I-20 east toward Morton, straight into the blinding sunrise.

It was twenty-seven degrees, and there was frost on everything. I turned off at Exit 77 and turned right onto Highway 80, which took me straight into Morton. On the outskirts of town, I noticed a small Peavey electronics plant that looked as if it had been closed down. Then, up ahead, beside the railroad track right in the middle of Morton, I saw what looked like a much bigger plant—almost like a small oil refinery. Only instead of the typical squat storage tanks that you'd see at a refinery, this plant had three towering aluminum silos, each topped with a conical lid. As I approached the plant, I saw the traffic light that Sister Nona Meyerhofer, the Faith in Action project director in Morton, had told me to watch out for. "Make a right turn the block before the traffic light," she'd told me. "You'll be on East Fourth Avenue. We're number 110. You can't miss it."

Number 110 turned out to be a one-story brick building with a forest-green awning and a big sign: EXCEL COMMUNITY AND LEARNING CENTER. One thing that made it easy to find, apart from the big sign, was that the town itself was so small. According to my atlas, its total population was 3,482.

Sister Camilla

Although Sister Nona was the project director, she had scheduled my first meeting of the day with her predecessor, Sister Camilla Hemann. A deceptively cherubic middle-aged woman with white hair, glasses, and a peach-colored cardigan sweater, Sister Camilla shook hands with a firm grip and led me into the kitchen, where we sat across from each other at a plain wooden table.

"So," she said, looking me straight in the eye, "how can I help you?" There was no nonsense about Sister Camilla—that was immediately clear.

Born and raised in a large family in northeastern Iowa near the Minnesota line, she had grown up on a farm, gone to nursing school, and joined a convent at age twenty-one. Until moving to Morton six years ago, she had spent pretty much her entire life in the Midwest.

"So how did you wind up here?" I asked her.

"We're the Sisters of St. Francis out of Dubuque," she said. "And every four years we meet and decide what it is we're going to do for the next four years. In December of 1996, we'd met and decided that we would go to two new places where it was sister-scarce and multicultural. One place would be in Iowa, and the other place would be somewhere else. Our leadership team chose Morton."

"Why Morton?"

"When we first came here to look around in the mid-1990s, we went to the city hall and looked at the census. And we saw that in 1990, the population here was about 49 percent white and 51 percent black. But by the mid-1990s, the chicken plant was recruiting very actively from the Latin American countries to come here to work."

"Is that the big plant down the street?"

"That's right. Scott County is very heavy with chicken plants. So, anyway, there were lots of Hispanics moving in, and they've just increased a whole lot since we've been here. So that made it multicultural, and that's how we got here."

When Sister Camilla and her colleague Sister Terry arrived in Morton in the summer of 1997, they'd had no jobs and no real plan—just a mission statement to work with the poor and try to form "a multicultural community." As it happened, about two years earlier, the Junior Auxiliary had done a study to try to find out what some of the community's unmet needs were, and one of the needs at the top of the list was "the elderly in their homes that don't have anybody to help them." Based on that finding, a small local organization called the We Care Mission had applied for and gotten a Faith in Action grant to address the problem.

But We Care had no one to run its program, and so Sister Camilla and Sister Terry took the job as codirectors for about two years—at which point Sister Nona, who had recently joined them from Iowa, took over the program. By that time, Sister Terry had become increasingly involved in her work with Morton's growing Hispanic population, while Sister Camilla, drawing on her nursing background, had become active in hospice work.

I asked Sister Camilla how they'd initially gotten the program off the ground.

"We started from zero," she replied. "Today we have volunteers from about fourteen or fifteen churches. They told us at the first church where we spoke—the Church of the King—that they thought we were pretty courageous. And we thought about this ourselves. You know, we're in the Bible belt of the country, and here we were, a group of Catholic nuns coming in from Iowa."

"Did you run into any actual hostility?"

"I wouldn't say hostility, no. In fact, through this program, we've received some of the best friendships that we could ever have."

"Tell me about the community," I said. "What's here besides the chicken plant?"

"That's it," Sister Camilla said flatly.

"That's *it*?"

"We had International Paper here, about three miles out of town, but they went out about two years ago. They're still doing a lot of logging, but I'm not sure where they go with all these big semis full of logs. And then we have something like twenty-eight freight trains that stop through here every day. A lot of them are carrying lumber too."

I asked her about the Peavey building that I'd seen on the way into town.

"Oh," she said, "they went out too."

"So would you say this is a poor town?"

"It's poor."

"What about crime? Is crime an issue here?"

"Yes," she said. "Drugs."

"Really? You've got drugs here?"

She nodded. "Between here and Forest—that's the county seat, just up the road—there are lots of murders."

"Is that right?" I said, incredulous.

"I mean for an area this size," she said.

"And this is all drug related?"

"Drugs, robberies. We've had a number of Hispanics murdered here. A lot of them are undocumented, so they don't bank. And so if it's payday, they know they've got money with them. So they're watched and . . ." Sister Camilla shook her head sadly.

Just then, a tall, angular woman with short brown hair, glasses, black pants, and a gray checkered top stepped into the kitchen. "Good morning," she said, giving me a warm smile as she shook my hand. "You must be Paul. I'm Sister Nona. I hope I'm not interrupting."

"Not at all," I said. "We've just finished."

Sister Camilla was obviously relieved to hear that. She had to get to work.

Sister Nona told me that my next interview was scheduled for nine o'clock at the Methodist church just down the street. As we walked over to the church together, I asked Sister Nona for a quick update on the program. She said that the hospital donated the meals and that right now she had fifty-seven volunteers who delivered meals every day to ten people. Of course, not everybody delivered every day. That would be too much. That was why they needed all the volunteers: they had to take turns.

I thought, Only ten people? Then again, I thought as the two of us walked up the church steps, that's ten people who would otherwise go hungry.

Alice

"Pastor Burris has been kind enough to lend you the use of his conference room today for all your interviews," Sister Nona explained as he and I shook hands. "I'm afraid we need all the space at the Center for our classes. And besides, it does get a little noisy."

Thanking Pastor Burris for his generosity, I quickly followed Sister Nona down the hall into the conference room. As usual, there was a conference table in the middle of the room and an American flag in the corner. The cinderblock walls were painted white, and on one wall was a large poster of a shepherd that read, "Where others see a Shepherd, God may see a King." An electric coffee pot and a stack of Styrofoam cups stood at one end of the conference table, and a slim, middle-aged woman in a floral blouse was fixing herself a cup as Sister Nona and I walked in.

"Paul, this is Alice Harris," Sister Nona announced. "I'm sorry we're running a little late this morning, Alice."

"That's quite all right, Sister," Alice said. "I was just fixing myself a cup of coffee. Would you like me to fix you a cup?" she added, turning to me.

I declined.

As Sister Nona slipped out, I asked Alice whether she would mind if I taped our conversation so that if I did quote her in the book, it would be accurate.

"Just be sure you get my southern drawl," she said.

"Do you live here in Morton?" I asked her.

"South of Morton," she replied. "A little community called Pulaski. We have a post office, but that's all."

I asked her how she had become involved with Faith in Action.

"I'm a member of the Morton Homemakers Volunteer Club," she said. "We do a lot of work with charities and so forth."

Alice said that she had joined Homemakers six or seven years ago and that the club had started to get involved with Faith in Action a year later. About a dozen of the club members participated, she said. "We usually go in pairs, and we take seven days a month. So I deliver ten meals one day each month. Some days I take a partner, and if my partner can't go, my husband jumps in and comes with me."

"Why do you like to have a partner with you? To keep you company?"

"Well," she said, a little hesitant, "in some areas for safety reasons."

"Is that right? Have you ever had a problem?"

"I've never had a problem, and I don't know of anybody who has. But, of course, we want to be cautious."

I asked Alice to describe how the meal delivery worked.

"Well, we knock on the door, and they usually have their doors locked. And some of them, you know, it takes them a while to get to the door. I usually call out and say, 'This is Alice! I have your lunch!' so that they won't think it's someone else."

"Do you ever have a chance to actually talk to any of them?"

"Oh, yes, we always try to talk a little. We can't stay as long as some of them would like. *Some* of them we're the only person they see in the day, I would imagine."

I asked her to tell me about some of the people she'd gotten to know.

"I think everybody loves Miss Helen," she said. "Every time you go to her house, Miss Helen has some type of floral arrangement fixed for the person driving the car and for the one delivering the meal. It may be an elephant ear with a lily attached to it. She has lots of pretty flowers in her yard, so she does that."

"She lives alone?"

"Far as I know. And then we've had some couples where we'd deliver to the husband and to the wife. They would both be unable to prepare a meal. And we have some of both races—some black and some white. Just whoever is on the list that has a need. And when a position opens up, there are several waiting to get on the list."

I asked Alice whether there was anyone besides Miss Helen whom she wanted to tell me about.

"Well, we had Miss Addie that passed away," she said, taking a sip from her coffee. "I loved her. She was just always so thankful. You know, when you'd come in the door, she'd start praising you for being there and doing what you're doing. So I think sometimes we get as much out of it as the recipient does.

"You know," Alice reflected, "you sort of get comfortable in your own little world, and you don't realize that the need's there. You're sitting at home in your little house where you have everything you need, and we've had people that were in just bad situations. People that lived in trailers that were poorly heated—or not heated at all. Just really bad situations.

"Thank goodness most of those have been helped in different ways. I know one that went into the nursing home. She was living in a bad situation—an old trailer. And then there was another one that lived in an old house where part of the floor was missing, part of the roof was missing. And the church here, I believe it was, got it started to buy her a trailer. So she's in a warm place now. I think they really had to talk to her to get her to give up her old house. She'd lived there forever, you know. And so it was a big decision for her."

"Do you still deliver meals to her?"

"Oh, yes."

"And is she happy in her new trailer?"

"She is," Alice said, smiling. "She truly is."

Sister Nona

I spoke with a Baptist minister and two more volunteers—a librarian and the wife of an IRS attorney—before Sister Nona came back bearing sandwiches and iced tea for lunch. We had a few minutes to ourselves before my next interview, so she agreed to use the time to tell me a little bit about her own background. "Go ahead and eat, and I'll talk," she said.

As I picked up my sandwich, she pulled the Pearlcorder across the table toward her. "This is Sister Nona," she began, talking directly into the recorder, "and I grew up in a little farm town that is actually the same as Sister Camilla Hemann's."

"You lived in the same town?"

"Stacyville, Iowa," she said. "Actually, we're cousins."

"No kidding!"

"It's up close to Mason City in Iowa—the cold section up near the Minnesota border. I came from a big family. My twin and I are number twelve and thirteen. Actually, only eleven survived—two died in childbirth. But we were the youngest in a big farm family, and so everybody had their chores.

"My dad had four sisters who were religious sisters. They'd been in a community—the same one as I am—for many, many years. Then one of my sisters who was seven years older than I am joined the convent. And we used to pray that we would know what God wants us to do—'But please don't let it be to be a sister.' But you know how God zaps you and says, 'No, that's for you.'"

"So when did you realize that you were going to become a sister after all?"

"Right out of high school. I remember that it was March, and the priest gave a talk about the requirements. And we thought, 'My gosh, this fits me.' You know, if you have the health and the desire to help people, then you should go. It was like, 'I don't want to, but I should.' I think that was God's way of just saying, 'You've got to give it a try.' And it's been right for me. Last summer, my twin and I celebrated fifty years in the convent."

"Fifty years?"

"Our jubilee," Sister Nona said with quiet pride. "It was a great celebration."

"So tell me, once you became a sister, what did you do?"

"I was always in education. I mean, when we went, we didn't start out wanting to be teachers, but in that day and age, if you had college—and we did our college during our novitiate—then you did teaching. So I've been a teacher in elementary school, and a principal, and then I was in the central office both in Sioux City and in Dubuque."

"These were Catholic schools?"

"Right."

"And were you in Iowa the whole time?"

"No," she said. "I was in Illinois two different times—but I guess that's it: Illinois and Iowa. And mostly Iowa."

"So this is the first time you're in a place that doesn't start with the letter I?"

"And that isn't 99 percent Catholic," Sister Nona laughed.

Sister Nona went on to tell me the story that I had already heard from Sister Camilla about how the Sisters of St. Francis had decided to work in Morton, starting with Sister Camilla and Sister Terry, and followed two years later—when they realized that they needed someone with teaching experience—by Sister Nona. "They were asking for someone to apply, and I don't think they'd gotten a lot of response, for whatever reasons. Then, about March, I got this call: 'Would you consider?' And you know, a personal call does a lot. Well, I knew I was at the point where I was almost sixty-five, and so I thought, 'If I'm ever going to do anything besides this central office, I need to make a move now.' So I said that I would go and take a look. And from the beginning it just felt so right. I wanted to serve people and I wanted to help the poor, and I still had the health and the vitality to do it. So I did."

"And no regrets?"

"Oh no," she said. "I can't believe how quickly five years went by. Now we've got to be looking to see who'll be doing this when we're not here."

Miss Helen

Later that afternoon, after I'd done several more interviews, Sister Nona returned, slightly out of breath and wearing a baby blue windbreaker. She was running a little late and had rushed back from the Excel Center, trying to keep me on schedule. "I thought you might like to go for a ride and meet Miss Helen," she said. "She's one of the ladies that we serve."

"The one who hands out the flowers?"

"That's her," Sister Nona said. "I think you'll like her."

The sky was an even deeper blue than it had been that morning, and although the sun was still out in full force, the air seemed colder than before. As we drove out of the downtown area and wound our way past the bleached fields, dried scrub, and battered mobile homes that surrounded Morton, Sister Nona filled me in on Faith in Action's current finances. Among other things, I learned that Sister Nona herself, as the current Faith in Action director, was being paid fifty dollars a month for her time. "That's based on the minimum wage," she explained, without complaint.

And how, I thought.

Gradually the road started to narrow and the blacktop began to give way. Minutes later, we pulled up to a big two-story house with a beat-up old mobile home nestled in the weeds beside it. "This is it," Sister Nona said, nodding toward the mobile home.

"You're kidding."

"Afraid not," she said.

It was quite a place. Some of the weeds, I discovered, were actually the dormant remnants of last summer's garden—but not just *any* garden. This was a kind of phantasmagorical display garden, its bare trees and bushes festooned with bright green plastic Sprite bottles, shiny red Coke cans, colored plastic bags, and faded baseball caps. In the midst of it all sat an enormous white enamel bathtub.

Sister Nona and I made our way through the weeds and started up the plywood ramp that led to the front door of Miss Helen's mobile home.

There were wooden railings on either side of the ramp draped with small rugs and bits of carpeting—presumably to protect your hands from splinters.

Sister Nona knocked loudly, and almost immediately the thin aluminum door swung open, revealing a small elderly woman with a wizened face and a halo of snow-white hair. Her face lit up with a brilliant smile when she saw Sister Nona, but what really impressed me was her voice: an extraordinarily high-pitched soprano that sounded almost like the keening of a bird, laced with a warm southern drawl.

"Why, Sister Nona," she said. "What a nice surprise!"

"Hello, Helen," Sister Nona said. "I've brought somebody to meet you."

"Miss Helen, how are you?" I said. "My name's Paul."

"Miss White came over," Miss Helen said as we shook hands. "She's going to get her toenails done."

"Oh, okay," Sister Nona said, sounding a little disappointed that there was someone else already here. "You were a hairdresser at one time, I understand."

"That's right," Miss Helen said brightly. "Now will you be coming in?"

"You're sure it's all right?" I asked, not wanting to intrude on a pedicure.

"Of course," she said. "Just hold the dog while we get in."

I picked up a small mongrel dog that must have followed us up the ramp so that Miss Helen and Sister Nona could get inside, but when I put it back down to go in myself, the dog slipped inside with me.

"You can't stay in here because you're too bad," Miss Helen scolded the dog. "You can't control her," she told us with a laugh. "She's still a puppy and she chews up everything."

"Oh, we don't want that," Sister Nona said.

"Maybe she's fixing to get a pedicure too," Miss White joked from across the room where she was waiting patiently in a recliner covered with blankets and pillows.

Miss Helen's mobile home was as wild on the inside as her garden was on the outside: a bewildering jumble of old wooden chairs, tea tables, lamps, rag rugs, rag dolls, hand-quilted cushions, American flags, Christmas tree ornaments, brightly striped towels, footstools, and clocks of every description—including a tall wooden grandfather clock that loomed over the chaos like Big Ben over London. I was amazed that Miss Helen could get through it all without tripping. Stepping carefully, I went over and introduced myself to Miss White.

Miss White nodded and gave me her limp hand. She must have been at least as old as Miss Helen, and her pallid skin was almost as white as her hair and the thin cardigan sweater she was wearing.

I took a seat on a rocking chair beside Miss White, and Miss Helen came and sat on a low stool beside Miss White's feet so that she could work while she talked to me. She had a small table at her side with various pedicure implements on it and a goose-neck desk lamp aimed at Miss White's feet.

"Where did you say you're from?" Miss Helen asked me.

"New Jersey."

"My goodness!" Miss Helen exclaimed.

"You're used to cold weather then," Miss White chimed in.

I asked Miss Helen whether she would mind if I took another picture of her while she was working on Miss White's nails. "You're working so hard," I said.

"Oh," she laughed. "I'm eighty-five, so I guess I should be retired."

"She's eighty-five, and I'm ninety," Miss White said.

A sharp whistle suddenly sounded from the kitchen. I thought it was a tea kettle, but it was the phone.

"Could you get it?" Miss Helen called to Sister Nona. "And take a message, please."

Sister Nona stepped over a footstool and reached for the phone, said something I couldn't hear, and then hung up.

"They hung up when it wasn't you," she told Miss Helen.

"I'm glad I didn't try," Miss Helen said. "It takes me so long to get to the phone that I just can't get there."

"And then it's somebody you don't want to talk to any way," I said. "Somebody that wants to sell you something."

"That's for sure," Miss Helen said. "They call at night, usually at six o'clock."

"That's right," Miss White agreed.

"So, Miss Helen," I said, "tell me about Faith in Action."

"Well, it's a wonderful program," she said. "I tell you, I look forward to it every day. They come, and I just look forward to seeing them. And they serve such good meals. I'm just so glad to be on it, I could shout!"

"Don't let me stop you," I said.

We all laughed.

"And you know, I don't really like to cook for just one person," Miss Helen added. "Especially in my condition."

"What do you mean, your condition? You look like you're in pretty good shape."

"At my age, I'm supposed to be in a rocking chair," Miss Helen chuckled.

"Instead, she'll be out there picking flowers almost every day," Sister Nona said. "You'll find her outside even when the weather is awful."

"I was outside digging my garlic this morning," Miss Helen acknowledged.

"Digging *what*?" Miss White demanded.

"Garlic," Miss Helen repeated loudly. "I like it better than onions. And besides, I can't grow onions too well."

"This toe over here needs a little more," Miss White said, leaning forward and pointing at her foot.

"This one?"

"That's right. It still feels a little rough."

"And then they deliver on Christmas too," Miss Helen said, looking up at me. "She fell down the steps at one place—didn't you?" she said, turning back to Sister Nona.

"It was frosty," Sister Nona said. "Just like it would be back in Iowa. No broken bones, but I was pretty bruised up. And I still have a little bit of a lump on my right side."

"You need a ramp like I've got," Miss Helen said. "I got to where I just couldn't get up the steps, and my dog couldn't get up either. I used to have a dog," she explained to me, "but somebody stole my dog. Now I always get the runaways over here."

"The ones that need to be fed," Sister Nona said.

"And I don't feed them because I don't have dog food," Miss Helen said. "So I'll give them a chicken bone or something. I had chicken skins today, so I imagine that's what that puppy was anxious for."

"Before you lived here, you had a fire, right?" Sister Nona asked.

"Right," Miss Helen said. "It burned my house and everything in it. I just had what I had on my back. No insurance."

"How long ago was that?" I asked her.

"I've been here about five years. I came here to live with my son—you know, he lived next door. He was fifty-five, but he died. I've just had so many shocks. The preacher even said I could be remorsed, but I'm not. As a Baptist, I try not to be."

"Do you get to church?" Sister Nona asked.

"I get to church every Sunday if I can," Miss Helen said.

"How do you get there?" I asked.

"Well, I used to drive, but I quit driving after that old man that was eighty-five ran over those people—I got nervous about it. And my grandson wasn't here, so I called my daughter-in-law. Her car was over there, but she didn't answer the phone. And sometimes she doesn't . . ."

Miss Helen stopped in midsentence.

"Does your daughter-in-law still live here?" I asked.

"You mean in that house?"

I nodded.

"Well, she works, and so . . ." Miss Helen paused again. "Monday night my heat went off. I didn't look at my heat. I think it was on five. And I didn't dream it was empty, because it hadn't been but two or three weeks since I'd had it filled. But it's just been running so much 'til my heat went off at midnight. So I put my cap on." She laughed. "Put all my clothes on. . . ."

"Did you call anybody?" Sister Nona asked.

"No, I just got all my covers and crawled under them. It was the coldest night of the year, and they didn't get here 'til twelve o'clock to turn my heat back on."

"Twelve o'clock the next day?" I asked.

"The next day. My heat's done that before on account of the gauge not working, but this time it was out of gas."

"And there wasn't anybody you could call when that happened?"

"Well, I didn't want to. I just wanted to get into bed and get warm."

"Would your daughter-in-law come if you called?" Sister Nona asked.

"No," Miss Helen said. "She didn't even answer the phone when I called on Sunday. But I think she felt guilty. She called me on Monday to see if I was all right. I told her about it, and she said she'd spent the night with a friend—so she wasn't even over there. So I can't depend on her since my son died. And one of my grandsons is in Afghanistan, so I can't depend on him, either."

"Do you have any other grandsons in the area?" I asked.

"I do have one, but he's in the hospital. He's not well. But," she said, brightening, "when the man came to bring me my lunch today, he said, 'Well, it won't be long until spring.' And I told him, 'I sure hope so, because it's been such a cold winter.'"

"It sure has," Miss White agreed.

PETAL, MISSISSIPPI

THE NIGHT I LEFT Morton, I stayed at the Baymont Inn in Hattiesburg, and the next morning was delighted to find an IHOP just down the street where a friendly waitress brought me a double order of Swedish pancakes and a pot of coffee. A group of college girls at the next table was in a state of high anxiety because they had just locked themselves out of their big silver Explorer, and they positively had to get to biology by eight o'clock because today was the big exam. Feeling less chivalrous than I probably should have—and imagining that I would undoubtedly set off a howling car alarm if I did try to pry a wire coat hanger through the window—I stuck with my pancakes. Besides, I had to get to Petal, the suburb of Hattiesburg where Sylvia Forster, the local Faith in Action director, had her office.

It was yet another beautiful winter morning, with just a few stray clouds scattered across the brilliant blue sky, and as I headed back out Highway 49 toward the 1142 bypass, I drove past the University of Southern Mississippi's massive football stadium, emblazoned with a fierce golden eagle. Once on the bypass, I stayed in the left-hand lane, crossed the Leaf River Bridge, got on 42 East, and crossed the railroad tracks into what Sylvia had described on the phone as "the center of Petal—not to be confused with the Center of the Universe." I turned right at the Subway onto South Main and kept going until I spotted the sign for the Petal Discount Grocery on my left. There was also a sign for Petal Beauty Supply and a small roadside sign indicating that the "Grandparents as Parents Group" would be meeting on January 29 at 6:30.

Sylvia's office—that is, I assumed it was her office—was in a small storefront catty-corner from the Petal Discount Grocery with the words PETAL ASSOCIATION FOR FAMILIES stenciled across its plate-glass window in large white letters. There were all kinds of posters behind the window: "McGruff and Me" with a picture of the famous crime-fighting dog; "Grandparents: You're Not Alone" with hand-drawn smiling red hearts; a bumper sticker that read, "Turn Off TV, Not Life."

Sylvia

I stepped inside and spotted one of the familiar blue and orange Faith in Action posters taped to the wall. And at the other end of the room, sitting at a desk piled high with all kinds of files, letters, books, and papers, was a woman I assumed must be Sylvia—if for no other reason than the fact that she was on the phone. She looked about my age, her brown-blond hair cut short, and wearing blue jeans, a blue turtleneck, and a man's wristwatch with a black plastic watchband.

She waved hello, and while she continued her phone conversation in rapid-fire bursts, I wandered around the office, reading the many signs, posters, calendars, letters, and newspaper clippings that were plastered all over the walls. With cardboard boxes, videotapes, brochures, and books piled everywhere, and with old wooden chairs, tables, desks, and open file cabinets having turned the office into a formidable obstacle course, it looked almost as if Sylvia had brought Miss Helen in from Morton to do her interior decorating.

One item in particular that caught my eye, hanging amid the posters of kids and old folks, was a Ph.D. diploma from the University of Massachusetts with Sylvia's name on it. How on earth, I wondered, did a Ph.D. from UMass. wind up running a Faith in Action program in Petal, Mississippi?

"So," she said, slamming down the phone, "did you want any coffee?"

"No, thanks. I just had."

"All right," she said. "Now tell me how this usually works since I haven't really done one of these before."

I laughed. "You haven't *done* one of these?"

"No," she said. "Like yesterday I just got done with the United Way, where I had to talk to them about why I need six-*thousand*-nine-hundred-and-sixty dollars. I mean, good grief!"

In less than thirty seconds, I liked her.

"Now I've got a whole bunch of people lined up for you," she said, plunging ahead. "I've got a caregiver, a care receiver, a coalition partner . . ."

"Great!" I said. "That's what I need. Plus I need to talk to you."

"Right," she said. "But it's been busy. My dog had to get her teeth cleaned this morning, so I had to get her there at 7:30. And then I'm working on this big conference, which is a week from today."

"Okay," I said. "But what's the schedule for today?"

She rummaged around the bottomless pile of papers on her desk until she extracted a sheet of yellow loose-leaf with some notes scribbled on it in pencil. "Here it is. At 10:30, we're supposed to see . . ." She stopped. "Now how does this work? I have all these people. I have their addresses. Do I go along with you to try to get you there?"

"No."

"Really?" she said hopefully.

"As long as you give me directions," I said. "After all, I found *you*."

"I guess," she said. "Anyhow, Mark is going to be at his home, and I'll have to give you that address. Arlena Lymon is going to be at *her* home. Kim Breland will be at my office at about 5:15 because she works."

"Okay," I said, without a clue who any of these people were.

"Kathy Masters is a professor of nursing. We're interacting with them in a community partnership, and she wants to take you to lunch at Chesterfield's. And then Jenell—I called her a couple of days ago, and I said, 'Now, Jenell, are you going to remember that I talked to you?' Maybe she will; maybe she won't. And then I've got this other woman— Ozzie Powell. I did *not* get in touch with her. Anyhow, these are two different people that are both care receivers, but they receive different things. Ozzie Powell had her leg cut off because she has diabetes, so we cut her grass. Even though she has a daughter caring for her, the daughter is sixty-one and has heart trouble. And Ozzie Powell's eighty-something. But I couldn't raise her—on the phone, I mean, not from the dead."

"Right," I laughed.

"And Jenell is a stroke victim, and she gets friendly visiting and grocery shopping. So those are two quite different cases—and that's why I did that."

"Good."

"Laurie Risher is a coalition member," Sylvia went on. "And through her we're interacting with at-risk youth, involving them in Faith in Action. Tomorrow we're doing a huge Angel Food Box Ministry where they deliver the meals to the homebound."

The phone rang.

"Sorry," she said. "I have no help today, so I'm going to have to answer it."

"By all means."

Since she wasn't exactly soft-spoken, I couldn't help overhearing Sylvia telling whoever it was that she was talking to on the phone in no uncertain terms how unhappy she was with a prominent expert on Alzheimer's who had been scheduled as the featured speaker at next week's conference but who had apparently forgotten all about it and made other plans.

Fortunately, she calmed down as soon as she got off the phone, and we spent the next twenty minutes trying to finalize my schedule for the day— a process that required several more phone calls, including a long one with Ozzie Powell about Sylvia's efforts to find her a new hospital bed. Finally, though, my schedule was set and I could begin the interview.

"So," I started, "what's your doctorate in?"

"Biology," she said.

"And where did you grow up?"

"Chicago."

"And what kind of family was it? Big family? Small family?"

"I had parents who got married late," Sylvia said. "My mother was forty-one when I was an infant. Later I said to her, 'Ma, you didn't get genetic testing?' And in her great wisdom she said, 'Why? You turned out okay.' And then of course I had children late too—but I *did* get genetic testing.

"Anyhow my father was always ill—constantly. And it was a very weird religious family. My father was an Orthodox Jew who didn't practice, and my mother was a Lutheran who was turned off to the church. So we were raised sort of . . ."

"Faith *out* of action?"

"That's right," Sylvia laughed. "But we'd tested it all out. My sister and I had tried the synagogue and all that. And really, we were a solid family— did a lot of stuff together. Put a high priority on education."

"Was volunteering a part of your growing up?"

"Never."

"And in what part of Chicago did you grow up?"

"Central," she said. "First it was Polish immigrant, then it turned Hispanic—and then it just got wild. I left for a number of years to go to school. I did an undergraduate and a master's in biology at the University of Illinois in Chicago, and then I went on and got a doctorate at the University of Massachusetts in Amherst."

"Why UMass?"

"Because they offered me money. And the guy was in my specialty, which was palynology"—the study of mold spores. "So I did specialized work with him for a year and a half, and then I wrote my own grant from the National Science Foundation. After UMass, I found an institution— the Field Museum [in Chicago]—to take me, and I did research for twelve years, first at the Field Museum and then at DePaul University.

"In the meantime, in graduate school, I'd met my husband, who was finishing his doctorate in political theory—and that was not a big job market either. But he eventually finished up and became interested in social work. And so he was pursuing a master's in social work and also a master's in sort of theology-slash-philosophy.

"In the meantime," Sylvia continued, "we had young children. And he also worked in a residential group home with kids—Puerto Rican girls. A wonderful, wonderful man. You could not ask for a better husband. Just a real caring person. He was raised very Catholic. I went to church for maybe twenty years myself before I said, 'You know, maybe it's time I become a Catholic.' Even though I do still have some reservations about Catholicism and everything. My father would just absolutely roll over, being an Orthodox Jew."

"So did you become a Catholic?"

"Yeah, I went through it all and became a Catholic. My kids are baptized, and they're christened, and that's fine. I mean some of the things Jesus says are a lot better than the Old Testament, where they're always cutting off heads. A lot of head cutting. So I don't know. Probably deep down, I might be a Baha'i or something. I have to say, it really doesn't matter who you are. But the Faith in Action—I have not a clue how I got that. You know, we were very liberal—so then we end up in Petal, where there's like four of us who think that way in the entire town. But we always talked about social justice back then. When we were in graduate school, we were part of the unionization for graduate students. We were involved in antisexism, antiracism—all of that."

She grinned. "Anyhow, then we had kids, and I refused to have them in day care, so I set up a lab in my home. I actually had a lab downstairs where I did all kinds of work, and that went on for a few years. But research money was becoming increasingly difficult to get, and so I ended up adjunct teaching."

"Now where were you at this point?"

"This was in Chicago—when I was working with the Field Museum. Then I took my grant to DePaul, which is a Catholic university. And I did some research there, and I did an adjunct there. But the adjunct pay was so pathetic—it was like thirteen hundred dollars. So I took to developing a home-based program, tutoring and working with kids."

From mold spores to kids?

"Now, you had no training in that field, right?"

"No," she said. "But I'd read a lot. And my husband—I talked to him every day, and he was working in residential care."

"Okay," I said. "I was just wondering if I'd missed something along the way."

"No, no, no," she laughed. "But I did a lot of reading—stuff on token economies. And tutoring—well, I *knew* how to teach."

In the meantime, Sylvia had also decided to home-school her two children. "They were just too smart for school. I mean, I don't want to sound . . . But school was going to stunt their little growth. So I did that for two years. I think that's where I got all these gray hairs."

Finally, to top things off, Sylvia was also caring for her elderly mother.

"Had your father passed away?" I asked.

"Oh, yes," she said. "He passed away at sixty-one. But my mother was okay until she got degenerative macular disease and she couldn't see. She gradually went blind. Plus she smoked for sixty-two years."

"And she was living with you?"

"For twelve years. But during that time, she became gradually more and more incapacitated, and had it not been for us, she would have been dead. Because she'd turn up the gas, couldn't see it, and it would fill up the place. She could not see to plug things in. And she never *ever* accommodated herself to that situation.

"Of course, she never complained, and she was great with the kids. But she smoked, and then she got chronic obstructive pulmonary disease. And that was just very limiting. She couldn't do anything. So I took care of her completely. I mean, she didn't just lie around in the bed; she wasn't homebound. But everything had to be done for her. If she wanted to get to an activity, I would have to drive her. If she wanted . . ."

"So you know what it's like," I interrupted. "What some of these family caregivers are dealing with."

"Oh, I do," Sylvia said. "And, look, she was an ideal patient. When she died—she died here five years ago when she got cancer of the pancreas—I cared for her at home until she died. And she never complained. She had a very high pain threshold, and she didn't take morphine until two weeks before she died."

"So tell me, Sylvia," I said, "how *did* you wind up in Petal?"

"Actually, the reason we moved here from Chicago is that we have an aging mother-in-law who lives in New Orleans, and we could see that sooner or later she was going to be needing care too—just like my mother. So my husband started looking for an academic position that was near New Orleans—and USM [University of Southern Mississippi] came open. That was in 1994."

"So he's at the university?"

"Right."

"And how about this?" I asked, waving my arm around the room. "How did you get all of this started?"

"When we first came down here," she said, "I operated a retail educational business. I sold materials for teachers, and I did trainings for early childhood education. I did all kinds of things while working out of my home. I don't think I made enough money to live on. In fact, I don't think I've ever made enough money to live on. But these are things that I've chosen to do. I could have gone into some retail place and sold cell phones, but that's not what I wanted to do. And anyhow, my husband was over at the university trying to get tenure, so he was working full time."

She took a breath.

"Anyhow, we'd been talking about my doing not-for-profit work, and when I was at the Field Museum, I'd written proposals to the National Science Foundation, so how different could it be? I really didn't start out with the idea of a grant, but in 1999, a place came open in the center of town, and my husband said, 'You know, it's now or never. You've just got to do it. Even if we have to take money out for rent, if you want a shop—if you want a place—this is the time.'

"And I said, 'Oh, my God, are you *sure*?' Well, I did it. I went for incorporation. I learned how to become a tax-exempt nonprofit organization. And then I got started by enrolling kids in CHIP—you know, the Children's Health Insurance Program. And I said, 'Wow, there are a lot of grandparents taking care of these kids.' I became familiar with the law that said that they could sign up their grandkids—they didn't know that. And my very first CHIP case now is also in our Food Box program. So I became what *I* considered—and I still *am*—an expert on CHIP."

"No kidding."

"In 1999, we only had five hundred kids in all of Mississippi signed up for CHIP. And it went to thousands because there was a real push on it. So that was actually quite successful. Of course, now our governor wants to cut Medicaid because there are too many kids on the CHIP program."

"The state giveth, the state taketh away," I said.

"But anyhow, I saw there was a real need," Sylvia went on. "Because every time I signed someone up who was a grandparent, they would burst into tears. They were just like, 'Oh, my God,' you know. And I said to myself, 'These people need help.' I'd never run a support group—never been *in* a support group—but I said, 'I think they need someone to talk to.' So I did a little reading on support groups, and then I just went ahead and started one. I went through the schools, got my first people, and it's just taken off."

I remembered the sign I'd just seen out front announcing the upcoming "Grandparents as Parents" meeting.

Sylvia went on to describe blow by blow how she had gotten a grant from the Brookdale Foundation to support her work with the grandparents, followed by a contract under the National Family Caregivers Act, which had just been renewed. "I've been working since September without any money," she said, counting off on her fingers: "September, October, November, December, January—five months without getting paid."

But meanwhile, she said, she had come across Faith in Action.

"It came up as a link on something else," she said. "And I looked at it, and I said, 'Faith in Action. This is *it*.' Because in the meantime I'd been coming in contact with more and more elderly people, and I realized that most of these people were completely impoverished and in terrible shape—especially in Mississippi. In fact, 50 percent of the people here over age sixty-five are disabled and live below the poverty line. That's a high number.

"And then I was meeting more and more blacks. Because I was in early childhood, and so I was going to black day care. I go everywhere—which is unusual, because most whites don't go to black day cares, and they don't have black associates. I go to black day cares and black churches. I go everywhere, so I know all those people. But it takes a long time. You know, I don't talk like a southerner."

"Oh, really?" I said.

She laughed.

"Anyhow, it takes a while. If you're a Yankee, it's still there. If you're white, it's still there. You know," she added, "Petal has one of the only Ku Klux Klans in the state of Mississippi, so no blacks want to come into Petal."

"Is that right?"

"And our group is mixed. We're the only black and white group. It's wonderful."

"When you say 'your group' . . ."

"I mean our grandparents' support group. And of course Faith in Action is mixed too. That's white and black—although everybody's poor."

"Now, when you say mixed," I asked, "do you mean the recipients or the volunteers?"

"Oh, I don't have any black volunteers. No, wait, I do have one black volunteer. The problem is that a lot of the churches are real tough to break into. They're the hardest nut to crack. The big churches are arrogant—they've got all the programs covered. And the poor black churches, or the smaller black churches, they don't know where the hell they are—and they're always looking to see what they can get. Is there any money in it from you guys? I mean, that's just there."

"But you managed to get some clergy?"

"Oh, yes."

"How did you get them?"

"I went up and talked to them."

I asked Sylvia how many congregations had gotten involved in Faith in Action so far.

"Let's see," she said. "There's Trinity Episcopal, and there's Petal Presbyterian, and there's Mt. Olive Baptist, which is black Baptist—and which we're going to have to retalk about because the woman never shows up, and we can't have anyone in the coalition who never shows up. And we've got Church of the Ascension, which is Methodist; and then we've got Sacred Heart, which is Catholic."

"So you've got five congregations, which is pretty good," I said.

"And we're going to hook up with the Hattiesburg Community Church—and with Rivers of Light, which is fundamentalist."

"*That's* not easy to do," I said.

"No," Sylvia agreed. "It's not easy."

Miss Ozzie

Armed with a detailed local map that Sylvia had marked up for me, I found and interviewed Jenell Chambliss, who lived in a well-maintained senior housing complex in Hattiesburg, had lunch with Kathy Masters from the nursing school at a busy restaurant near the stadium, and then headed to the south side of Hattiesburg to interview Miss Ozzie Powell.

Miss Ozzie lived in a small, dark brown house on May Street, a short street that actually ran from White Street to Martin Luther King Street. It seemed that just about every town I'd visited here in the South during the past week had a street or a boulevard or an avenue named after Dr. King—but always in the poor section of town. This one was no exception. While some of the homes, including Miss Ozzie's, were still in good shape and were well maintained, others were boarded up, their paint peeled off and their lawns long since gone to seed.

I parked in front of Miss Ozzie's house, walked up the plywood wheelchair ramp that had been built over the front steps, and rang the doorbell.

"Come on in!" a woman's hoarse voice called from inside. "Come on back here."

I pushed the door open and followed the voice through the living room into the kitchen. An elderly woman with iron-gray hair and wearing a pink sweater over a pale blue dress sat in a wheelchair by a table shelling pecans. Her right leg was missing.

"Miss Ozzie?"

"Come on in," she growled pleasantly. "When I'm not doing anything, I like to crack pecans."

"My wife does that too," I said. "And she makes a great pecan pie."

"Well, I ain't a good cook now," she said, "but I still like to crack 'em. Or sometimes I get busy with them green beans. I just like to keep busy. Wherever there's a will, there's a way, ain't it?"

"That's true," I said.

A television was turned up high in the next room. I wondered whether anybody was watching it or whether Miss Ozzie just kept it on for company. There was a small white Honda parked in the driveway, so maybe Miss Ozzie's daughter was in the house somewhere.

"So, Miss Ozzie," I said, "let me tell you a little bit about who I am and what I'm doing. My name is Paul, and I'm writing a book about the Faith in Action program. Now do you know about the Faith in Action program?"

"Oh, yes," she said. "I can recommend it."

She listened patiently while I ran through my spiel, steadily cracking pecan after pecan and nodding politely as I rambled on. "So," I said in closing, "I was eager to come and meet you and to talk to you and to find out a little bit about you—what your life has been like, what your life is like these days, and how something like Faith in Action fits into your life."

"You know what?" she said. "Before I go any further, I want to thank God for sending you by here to ask me that. Because I've been here in Hattiesburg all my life."

I asked her how old she was.

"I'm eighty-two years old. I was raised right across the street from the church."

"Right here in this neighborhood?"

"All my life," she whispered. "And let me tell you one more thing," she added, returning to her normal voice. "Whatever the Lord has for you in your life, you'll get it. It's the Lord that's sending you through here right now and that has us talking like this. The Lord has it already planned out. If He's got anything for you—*whichever* way He's got it for you—you just watch Him. And I can't help but telling you this, because it's in my heart."

"I appreciate that," I said. "Now, Miss Ozzie, you said that you were born and raised in this neighborhood."

"I was born right over there on the corner of Rosa Avenue and John Street. There was a little old house there, and that's where I was born."

I had passed that corner on my way to her house. It was just a block away.

"And did you have any brothers or sisters?"

"I had seven brothers, and there was six sisters. So my mama had thirteen children. But now all of them is dead but me." She gave me a sad smile. "Most of my brothers and sisters was born in Alabama. But before she married, my mama moved to Hattiesburg from Alabama. And she had my brother and me born in Hattiesburg."

"So you and your brother were the youngest."

"That's right. But my brother was younger than me."

"So you weren't the baby."

"No," she laughed. "*He* was the baby."

Miss Ozzie said that after a while, the family had moved to another house, right across from the church on Fredna Avenue, which was one block south of where she lived now. Then, when she got married, her husband bought this house, and she had lived here ever since. "He was a minister," she said. "He's dead now. He died about ten years ago. Now, he was raised in a little town called Mount Olive, Mississippi."

"But he moved here?"

"Well, he moved down here to Hattiesburg when he was a young man, and he worked around at different jobs. And then for many years after we were married, he worked at Hercules [a pulp and paper plant owned by the Hercules chemical company]. And that's when he passed. He passed while he was working at Hercules. He was there about ten years . . . going on eleven years."

"And did you have children?"

"Yes, I have one daughter," she said, and called out, "Carolyn!"

A middle-aged woman quietly entered from the living room.

"Oh, hi!" I said, shaking hands. "It's nice to meet you."

"Nice to meet you," she murmured.

Now that I knew that Carolyn was not in the room with the television, I asked her whether it would be all right if we turned down the volume. It was hard for me to hear some of what Miss Ozzie was saying over the used car salesmen.

"I can turn it off," Miss Ozzie said, picking up a remote control from behind the bag of pecans and snapping it off.

"So, Miss Ozzie," I asked, "did you go to school here in the neighborhood?"

"Um-hm," she said. "Right over there. It used to be called Sixteenth Section. Now it's called . . . What's it called, Carolyn?"

"Mary Bethune," Carolyn called out. She had gone back out to the living room, but obviously she could still hear our conversation.

"And how much school did you get?" I asked Miss Ozzie.

"I got to the eleventh grade," she said. "That's when I stopped."

"And what was your best subject in school?"

"Well, now, you know what? None of 'em was my best, but I used to love to read. But now if you asked me some of the things that I used to read about, I don't remember 'em like I used to."

"Do you still read now?"

"Yes, but I don't read as much now."

"What do like to read?"

"I read the Bible mostly. And then I got a lot of books in there," she said, nodding toward the living room. "But now I ain't telling you I've read them all. But I read books, and I read my Sunday school lessons."

I asked Miss Ozzie whether she was still able to get to church.

"Oh, yes," she said. "So as I can praise Him. You know the reason I can praise Him so? I have tell you this. Because He looked way down in life—now, I didn't know it, but He did—at the America we got down here. And He knew these days was coming. The Lord knows it. He put me right here in this place where I'm at right now."

"Right."

"And you know what? It's a joy for me to wake up on a Sunday morning, and my daughter to carry me to Sunday school—and I'm at the church until two o'clock. And if my daughter can't carry me over, I ain't got to do nothing but put this old chair out front and wave, and somebody'll come over here from the church to carry me over."

"So they'll come pick you up?"

"Yes."

"And what church do you go to?"

"Antioch Baptist. Reginald Wood is my pastor."

"Have you been going there a long time?"

"All my life."

In fact, she said, she could remember when Reginald's grandfather had been the pastor at Antioch a long time ago. "But to me, Reginald will tell us what it is the Lord wants," she said. "He'll tell it to us. Whether we want to hear it or we don't, I got one of them preachers that will tell you what the Lord tells him. And I love that, because the Spirit don't lead you no way wrong."

"That's right," I murmured.

"That's the way I am about it," Miss Ozzie declared, "and I thank the Lord for letting me be able to stay here. And that's why I'm telling you that the Lord knew these days was going to come."

I felt as if I were in church myself.

"So, Miss Ozzie," I said, "have you seen a lot of changes here in Hattiesburg since you were a child?"

"Yes, I have."

"Tell me about some of the changes."

"Well, I'll tell you," she said. "I had an old mother; she was a good old Christian working lady. She worked in the church, and she worked in the fields, and she did what there was for her to do. And she learned us how to work. And I'll tell you, I come along when there was cotton trucks come through this corner." She laughed. "It don't look like it now, but there used to be cotton trucks that come, and we would have to get up on one of them cotton trucks every morning and go pick cotton."

"Is that right?"

"I didn't pick a whole lot of cotton, but she expected you to go. You went, and you picked what you could."

"How old were you?"

"I will tell you the truth, that was when I like ten or twelve. Because when we were young, they would catch the young children to pick cotton. Used to be trucks coming through here around three or four o'clock in the morning. If you didn't catch the one, you got another."

"And what did you get paid for a day's work?"

Miss Ozzie laughed. "Sometimes you wouldn't get fifty cents out of it. They didn't pay you much in them days."

"That must've been hard work," I said.

"It was," she said. "But you had to. You didn't play because sometimes your mama was there, and she could pick three or four rows at a time and keep you coming right along with her. And I'm telling you the truth. That's the way it was."

"So you finished the eleventh grade," I said. "What did you do after that?"

"Well, I'll tell you what, I worked homes—like people'd want somebody to keep the children. You know, there used to be the president of William Carey College—Doctor Holcomb. I used to keep his children. I used to work for Doctor Holcomb and his daughter, because his daughter had a son. And I was a nurse, you know. I'd nurse and keep the children for them for years. And then after that, I got married, and I got a job in the cleaning shop."

"And what kind of work did you do at the cleaning shop?"

"Silk finishing. That's what made my most work—doing silk finishing."

"What is that like? What do you do?"

"At this time it was doing dresses," Miss Ozzie said.

"Ironing," Carolyn called from the living room.

"That's right," Miss Ozzie said. "Because them silk dresses couldn't go to the presses. They had to be done by hand. Or sometimes it was tablecloths that had to be done by hand. That's the kind of work it was. And I did that for years until my mother got sick."

"You took care of your mother?"

"That's right. She lay sick here for a long time. She had her own house, but she moved here when she got sick. And that's when I stopped working.

"But she was always a lady that liked to work, you know. Or she'd be helping over at the church—anything she could do. She was that kind of a lady. She didn't play. And when it come time for *you* to play a little bit, she'd let you play a while. But you didn't just play all the time."

Once again I asked Miss Ozzie to tell me about some of the changes that she had seen in Hattiesburg over the years. I knew that Hattiesburg had been in the thick of the civil rights struggle back in the 1960s, and I was curious to know what effect, if any, that tumultuous period had had on her life.

"Mister," she said, "I'll tell you the truth. To me, it's just like a mystery what the changes is now to what I've seen then. Because back then, you had to show respect to your elders, whosoever they was. And my mother used to train us how whatever you do, wherever you work, you do your best. And I always say, if I don't know it, it ain't because my mother didn't try to teach it to us."

"And you don't think it's that way anymore?"

"Well, now, you know what? I'm looking at today's world, and if you want me to tell you *my* feelings, I feel like the Lord's got a blessing coming for today's world. I feel like that if they're trained in the right direction, it's going to be different with *these* children than it was. They're not dumb, but they're not like children when we come along. Because, see, when *we* come along, we didn't know things like these children can know now. These children now can learn anything that you want to learn 'em, and so you've got to be careful in how you train 'em—you know what I mean?"

"That they learn the right thing," I answered.

"That's right!" Miss Ozzie exclaimed. "The Lord is trying to tell us: 'Whatever you teach 'em, be sure and teach 'em right.'"

"Sure."

"And one more thing," she said. "At the time when I was coming along, anybody that was older would tell you what was right—and you'd respect them. In them days, you couldn't come home and fib over what the older peoples told you—because your mother wouldn't listen to you telling about how the old people did. They told you you've got to *mind* what the older peoples told you."

"And it's not that way anymore?"

"You know, I'm looking at these children, and I see children that's smart. I look at the television and I can't hardly tell you what double-u, double-u, double-u is, but you catch a little-bitty child—and they can do it!" She laughed. "So I feel things is going to be better. If we stay with the Lord, and he guides and directs us, it's going to be a better day."

"So Miss Ozzie," I said, "how do you spend your day?"

"When I was coming up?"

"No, I mean now. Now that you're here at home, how do you spend your days?"

"You know how I spend my days? Mister," she said, "if there's a little something I can do, then I do it."

"You mean like the pecans."

"Oh, shoot, I can do *that*. But I also clean up my room as good as I can. And I can shine shoes. I told them ladies over at the church, 'You all might be busy and don't have time to shine 'em. Bring your shoe polish and bring 'em around here. I'm sitting in this chair, and I can shine 'em.' And I do.

"But you see," she added, lowering her voice—maybe so that Carolyn wouldn't hear—"the man that come over here, he said that maybe I need to get up out of the chair. But I don't know. I feel like I don't want to fall. The little things I can do, I try to do that. But the Lord might not want me to fall. And if I fall, I might get broke up worse than I already am. And then I might have to have somebody to pick me up and to do the things that I can't do for myself."

This brought us back to Faith in Action.

"Tell me, Miss Ozzie," I said, "what does Faith in Action do for you now?"

"You know what? I want to tell you just like it is," she said, her voice still almost a whisper. "All my life coming up, I've never seen faith in action like I see it today. Because you know," she chuckled, "in those days, colored people did the working for the whites. In them days, if you would go to the whites, you had to go through the back—you know that. And whatever *you had to do, it was always you doing it for them*. I never seen faith in action then like I'm seeing it today. And that's one of the things that astonished me when this little lady come out here and mowed my yard."

"Right."

"I told her and I told the Lord," Miss Ozzie said, her voice rising with excitement, "nothing but a God is doing them kind of things. Because I've seen the time when if anybody was to do that, we was the ones that'd do it. But that little girl, she come here with much courage and much wanting to do it. And it look like to me that's how I pitch that little lady—that nothing but a God had that little lady come out here and show me that God is at work."

I was thrilled. Here was the answer to my question about the changes in Hattiesburg—but in a way that I had never for a moment imagined.

"Do you know her name?" I asked. "The lady who mows your yard?"

"Carolyn!" she called out. "What's her name?"

Carolyn didn't answer right away.

"I know she's a nice little lady," Miss Ozzie continued. "Every time she come here, she comes in and talks with me and encourages me—and I encourage her. And she'd have her little son . . ."

"Kim!" Carolyn called from the living room. "Kim Breland!"

"Oh, okay," I said. The name sounded familiar. "I think I'm going to meet her later on today." I checked my schedule. "Yup, here it is. Five o'clock over at Sylvia's office."

"Anyways, I tell her how nice her little boy is," Miss Ozzie continued. "And I will tell her how she's starting him out right while he's young. He's got a little tractor. and he follows right behind her when she's cutting the grass." She paused. "I'll tell you the truth: it's a mystery to see how the Lord works," she said, shaking her head. "But He do work that way, don't He?"

Kim

Kim Breland, the young woman who cut the grass for Miss Ozzie, was waiting for me with her son, Drew, when I got back to Sylvia's office a few minutes after five.

Although Drew was ten years old, Kim looked almost young enough to be a high school senior. She wore a raspberry-colored sweater with black and white stripes, blue jeans, and a slim gold chain around her neck.

"I met Miss Ozzie this afternoon," I told Kim after we had settled ourselves in the conference room where Sylvia and I had talked that morning. "We had a wonderful conversation. And she thinks the world of you."

"We think the world of her," Kim said. "She is a loving lady, she really is."

"So, Kim," I said, "are you originally from Hattiesburg?"

"Originally," she said in a deep Mississippi accent, "I'm from Brooklyn."

"*Brooklyn?*"

"Brooklyn, Mississippi," she explained with a laugh. "It's about seventeen miles south of Hattiesburg."

"Tell me about Brooklyn, Mississippi."

"Oh, well, we don't have much. There's a post office, a couple of stores, a railroad track, a gas station—that's just about it."

"Did you grow up there?"

"I did."

"'Til you were how old?"

"Let's see, I left there when I graduated high school. Well, actually, I left there in '88. I graduated high school in '87, and at that point I went on to junior college. My first year of junior college I lived at home, but then after that I moved into the dorm in '88. And I've been gone ever since."

After finishing school, she said, she had moved to Hattiesburg for a year. "I worked for a civil engineer for a year doing his drafting—that's what I do for a living. Then after a year I came to Petal, where I worked for a land surveyor, and I've stayed with him for over thirteen years."

"And somewhere along the line you met your husband?"

"That was way back along the line," she said, taking a breath. "Because I've been divorced for about ten years. It's just me and my little boy. It's been me and him since he was nine months old."

"That's a lot to deal with."

"It's quite a bit," she agreed. "But, you know, going through things like that, it teaches you compassion. And there's lots of things that you go through during your life and you think, Why is this happening? But one thing is that it does teach you compassion—how to care about people who are not necessarily going through the same things that you are, but they have their own things that they're going through. And they feel pain from those things as well, you know."

"Say a little more about that," I said. "Because people often say that— that going through hard times teaches you compassion."

"It does," Kim said.

"But how?"

"Because you would like at some point for somebody—for somebody to just give you a hug—at some time when there is nobody there, you know. It's very, very alone sometimes. Here you are; you're by yourself. All these bills that you've got to pay when you're trying to make ends meet. And then emotional problems and how you deal with those kinds of things"

"And then you've got a nine month old," I said.

"Right. And then I also went through an illness. I had Ménière's syndrome. I don't know if you've heard anything about that. It's a inner ear thing where I would have dizzy spells for hours. I couldn't even see to get through a door—and I had a baby. So I tried to deal with that from when Drew was one year old. And then I had the surgery, which fixed that."

"It sounds like terrible disease," I said.

"It's horrible," she agreed. "But, see, God's blessed me, though. There's always been a step up, every year. It's kind of snowballed: things get better and better and better. But never forget where you came from to begin with.

"But the thing is, when you're left alone, a lot of times other people have their own families," Kim continued, the words bubbling out now. "So you don't always have somebody there who can hug you. So any time you can give that back . . ." She paused, trying to find the right words. "Because, you know, if you see someone suffering, I just feel that that's the same thing they're going through."

"Sure."

"You'd give anything for a hug sometimes. Or just a kind word. Or *some* kind of assistance. You know, something. I know that when I was sick, I would get so sick there'd be nothing that I could do."

"And did nobody help you during that time?"

"Very little," Kim said, without a trace of self-pity. "Very little. I pretty much had it on my own. And I don't want anyone to ever feel that."

"Has faith always been an important part of your life?" I asked her.

"It has," Kim said. "Since I was about eleven or twelve. But, you know, *then* you don't really know a whole lot about it. You go through high school and you've got all these crazy things going on, you know. I worked through high school. I've worked since I was fourteen years old—a full-time job. Go to work and go to school, you know. And then when you have spare time, you do things with your friends. So I got away from church. But then when I got into college, I could feel Him pulling me back. So in my life, it's just been up and down, you know.

"But through it all, I always know that He's there. I always know that what I have is because of Him and what He's given me. And so I know that that's what I need to do. There's no question about it. He made me the kind of person that I am because there's work here to be done."

I asked Kim whether she had any brothers or sisters.

"I have one brother," she said. "He's older than I am."

"Is he still in the area?"

"He is. He still lives at home. He has some . . . disabilities."

"And are your parents both living?"

"They are," she said. "But they've been separated for about seven years now."

"Oh, so they were going through changes too."

"They were," Kim said. "So it was kind of hard on them—and that's just a whole nother story, you know, because they were going through things of their own, with hard feelings on all sides."

"So you were kind of out in the cold," I said.

She nodded.

"Well, you sure are resilient to get through all of that."

"You have to be," she said. "Because if you let yourself, it can get you down."

"Oh, I'm sure it can get you down," I said. "The question is, how do you get back up?"

"That's right. But you just have to push it back. You just have to forget about it and find something else. And that's another thing," she quickly added. "I have found that one of the releases for some of the things that I've felt was that if you help someone else, you think less of your own problems. It kind of lightens up your situation, and it makes it better. Because you don't focus so much on your own problems—unless, of course, it's something serious that you have to take care of."

I asked Kim to tell me about her volunteer work. "Did you do any volunteering before you got involved with Faith in Action?"

"Not in an organization," she said. "I did things for people as I saw fit. But about a year ago—maybe a little further—I wanted to find a place. And right now, I don't have a whole lot of time because I work a job and a half."

"A job and a half?"

"I draw people's house plans out of my home. So there are times when I work seven days a week."

"So you're self-employed part time, and then you're still drafting full time?"

"Right. And then I've got Drew, and I've got the house that's got to be kept up. But there are times that I do have, and that's where I need to put me—that's where I need to put in some of my time."

"So how did you connect with Faith in Action?"

"I knew Sylvia before, because my little boy went to Young Einsteins Day Care, and she had brought some learning materials in. But it was about a year and a half ago that my little boy brought home a little pamphlet, and I saw on the back, 'Petal Association for Families,' and I thought, 'Gosh. That's really something that I'd love to do.' So I called the number, and I asked Sylvia what it was that she did. And she explained everything that she did, and she thought that maybe I was looking for services. But then I asked her was she in any need of volunteers, and she was like, 'Yes! Yes! Yes!'"

We both laughed.

"So that's how that happened," Kim said.

"And so how long have you been cutting grass for Miss Ozzie?"

"We just worked for her this summer. And then when the grass stopped growing, we haven't done a whole lot lately."

I asked Kim whether, after she'd cut Miss Ozzie's grass, she had also visited with her.

"I did," she said. "And she loves to talk. And Drew would go in and talk to her. She has so much emotion, you know. And she'll start to cry at different things. So we talk to her and her daughter. They're both very, very friendly."

"Had you ever known anybody like Miss Ozzie before?"

"I have," Kim said. "Growing up in a small town—and, of course, it's an older town—so there's lots of older people. And being there all your life, you pretty much get to know all of them. And when they're at that age, they all have disabilities and different things. So as a child, you know, you're riding your bicycle and you say hello, and you stop and you visit while they're in the yard. So. yes, I have known people like Miss Ozzie."

"Well, I think it's wonderful what you're doing. I just hope you're able to keep doing it."

"Oh, absolutely," she said.

After Kim and Drew left, I talked to Sylvia for another hour, but finally, at seven o'clock, I said good-bye. I was hungry, I wanted to find a place to eat, and I still had to drive to my motel outside New Orleans more than a hundred miles away. Unfortunately, the restaurant that Sylvia had recommended was packed, with at least a forty-minute wait, so I went back to the IHOP where I'd had breakfast twelve hours earlier.

An hour later, as I sailed through the night down I-59 toward New Orleans, I suddenly heard a loud snap and saw a small crack in the windshield on the passenger side. My first thought was, *Oh my God, a bullet hole!* And I remembered what Sylvia had said about the Ku Klux Klan. But moments later I saw a big dump truck up ahead of me, bits of loose gravel spilling out behind it and dancing on the highway like hail. I started laughing and couldn't stop.

NEW ROADS, LOUISIANA

IT WAS A FEW MINUTES after three o'clock Monday afternoon when I merged onto I-12 and headed west out of Mandeville toward New Roads. I'd spent the weekend in New Orleans and the bayou, and had just finished my visit to the Faith in Action program in Mandeville, talking with some of the residents in an assisted living facility. Dark gray stratus clouds were piled high on the horizon, but the low winter sun had burned enough of a hole through them that I had to pull my visor all the way down.

Eventually I picked up Highway 61 on the eastern edge of Baton Rouge—the same Highway 61 that I'd taken a week earlier from Memphis south into Mississippi. Judging from the map, it looked as if I could head north up Highway 61 as far as St. Francisville—probably less than an hour's drive—and then cross what appeared to be a bridge over the Mississippi and follow a small county road for about another ten miles down to New Roads.

Here on the outskirts of Baton Rouge, it was all business: Crawfish City . . . Roadrunner Gasoline . . . Pizza Hut . . . Big A's Carwash . . . Baton Rouge Scrap Metal . . . a Deltech chemical plant . . . a big Georgia-Pacific paper mill. Incredibly, according to the intermittent street signs, this stretch of Highway 61 had been declared a scenic highway. But it was at least another five miles before the seemingly endless stream of roadside blight gradually began to give way to open country.

By then, it was after five o'clock and the sun was slipping rapidly toward the horizon. I could sense the Mississippi River itself somewhere off to my left, although I couldn't actually see it yet. Unlike the delta, the land here was hilly, and there were a lot of trees. But the sunset was just as spectacular, its rays radiating up through the low clouds and into the empty blue void above.

When I got to St. Francisville, there was a small sign that said "Ferry." I kept going, looking for a sign for the bridge, but when I didn't find it, I turned around and turned off at the ferry sign, figuring that the bridge must be down by the ferry.

But there was no bridge, just some concrete barriers where the road ended about thirty yards from the river, divided by a passageway just wide enough for a car to get through. A black metal arch over the passageway with a sign hanging from it read, "Bon Voyage." Far out on the river, I could see a low black boat with a single light silhouetted against the water. Probably the ferry.

There was a graffiti-covered bench off to the side with a hand-painted sign beside it that said that the ferry left on the hour and the half-hour, which meant that I had a twenty-minute wait. The sunset by this time was a deep gold, and with the light breeze coming off the river, it was a moment of pure peace.

The ferry left at six, its motor thrumming somewhere far below the deck as it backed away from the landing. As we slipped farther from the shore, the breeze picked up. I stood by the railing and took a deep breath, tasting the cool dampness of the evening air.

The last few embers of the sunset were still glowing along the horizon on the far shore, where three tall stacks stood in a row against the deep blue sky, each with an aerial warning light blinking in a steady pulse from its summit. A lone barge was slowly making its way around the bend in the river below us, and for a moment I wished that I could stay right where I was for the rest of my life.

The next morning was Tuesday, January 27, and according to the digital sign in front of the Regions Bank building down the street, the temperature matched the date: 27 degrees. The sky was a deep rich blue, and my breath was frosting from the cold as I took my suitcase back out to the car.

On the next block was a big brownstone church with a white plastic banner strung between two metal poles on the front lawn. The banner, which included a bright red Coca-Cola logo, proclaimed: "Catholic Pointe Coupee Celebrates 100 Years of Catholic Education, 1904–2004: Founded by Sisters of St. Joseph."

Pointe Coupee? Had I somehow gotten the name of the town wrong— or had I missed the turnoff to New Roads last night and wound up in the wrong town?

Twenty minutes later I ordered breakfast, and the man behind the counter at McDonald's patiently explained to me that "Pointe Coupee" was actually the name of the parish in which the town of New Roads was located.

"So I'm in Pointe Coupee Parish?"

"That's right," he said. "And you're also in New Roads. You want hash browns with that? It's only a penny more with the special."

"No, thanks."

Gail

Gail Hurst, who ran the Faith in Action program in New Roads, was the director of an organization called HOPE Ministry of Pointe Coupee, located in an unassuming one-story brick building just behind the fire station. HOPE, I learned, stood for Helping Other People Everyday.

Soft-spoken and disarmingly gentle, Gail nevertheless radiated energy and enthusiasm. Moreover, as I watched her in action and talked with the many people she had called in for me to interview over the course of the day, it became clear that her enthusiasm was contagious. Everybody raved about her. Some even said that through the work of HOPE Ministry, Gail Hurst was transforming the entire community.

I got a taste of how she operated right away. After introducing myself, I asked Gail how much time she had to talk with me before I started my other interviews.

"I'll give you thirty minutes," she said. "We have a schedule for the rest of the morning; then we have a luncheon; and then we have a break until it's time for us to go to the women's group meeting that I have to speak with."

"Okay, great. And so what time do you think we'll be done?"

"Well, we should be done by 2:30."

"That's good," I said. "Because I've got to get up to Shreveport."

"Unless you'd like to say hello to my governing body," she added sweetly.

"And what time is that?" I asked cautiously. The people in Shreveport had estimated that it would take me at least four hours to drive up there from New Roads.

"The governing body's meeting starts at five o'clock. I'd just like for you to be introduced to them so that they can understand that all this that we're doing is part of a bigger national program. They really like the program and everything that we do for the community, but they need to know something about the depth of how this really got started."

"Sure," I said. "I'd be delighted."

"Oh, wonderful," she said. And then she added with a grin, "You're already on the agenda."

I began my interview with Gail by asking her how she had become involved in Faith in Action herself.

"Faith in Action," she sighed. "Well, I've always been involved in my community, and I first heard of Faith in Action through HOPE Ministry of Pointe Coupee because they kept having articles in the *Banner* when they first originated in 1995. And they asked anyone in the community who wanted to get involved to come on in. I would read the articles and I would always think, 'Oh, I want to get involved with that.' But then I was so busy, I never did make one of the meetings."

One day, though, she did. She had been active in a youth group at her church, and from time to time she came across kids who had disabilities that she didn't know much about, like autism. And it turned out that one Saturday, HOPE Ministry was bringing someone in to speak on the subject of autism at the First Baptist Church. Gail and a friend who had seen the announcement in the *Banner* decided to go.

"So we got down there and sat down," she recalled. "And here came one of the persons who was already involved with HOPE Ministry and sat right next to us. She introduced herself, and we introduced ourselves, and then we started talking. And she started talking about the organization and how they had filed for a grant with the Robert Wood Johnson Foundation for Faith in Action.

"They had gotten the money, and now they needed someone to direct the organization. So she looks right at me and she says, 'Golly, you say how much you love this community. It seems like you'd be a good person for this. Why don't you come to the meeting?' And my friend says, 'Yes, you'd do well with that.' She tells the woman, 'Gail is always volunteering for this and for that.' So I'm like 'Robert Wood Johnson . . . Faith in Action. . .' Trying to decide, you know.

"And so finally I went to the meeting, and the woman was so happy to see me. But it was something that I was interested in because of the volunteer part of the community and the church part. You know, you have all those parts that your values connect with. That's what really got me."

I asked Gail whether she had had a job at that time.

"I did," she said. "I was working for Maison Blanche department stores as a customer service rep. And I had just stopped working for an insurance company where I'd been selling life insurance for nineteen years."

"So you were in transition."

"You talk about transition," she said. "My husband had passed a few years before, and so I was like, 'What'll I do now?' I didn't want to be the director, but they said, 'Just fill out the application.' So I did. But I never thought they would choose me. I didn't think I would be any good."

I asked Gail if she was from New Roads originally.

"Born and raised here," she said, smiling. "Educated here. My parents were born and raised here. We're a family of eleven children, and I'm the middle child. So that's why it's so easy for me to do things. The older ones say, 'I'm too big,' and the younger ones say, 'I'm too little.' So Mama says, 'Gail, will you do it?' And I always did." She laughed.

I asked her how many congregations were involved in her Faith in Action coalition.

"Fourteen," she replied. "Nine that are really steady and that never miss. They're our pledging churches—all the major churches—and they support us for anything extra that we might need. The others come in on an annual basis, and we understand that, because they're small."

When I told her how impressed I was by that—how, in other communities, some of the big churches had said that they were "already doing it" and therefore didn't feel the need to join a Faith in Action coalition—she laughed.

"That's just why they did it here," she said. "The pastors were all writing checks, but they didn't have the time or the staff to investigate and to find out the full story. People may call and say, 'Look, I need some food,' but it may be that the house needs cleaning, or they may need somebody to transport them to the doctor. They may need a prescription filled that's sitting on the dresser but that the card didn't pay for. So when you go there for one thing, there are so many other things. That's why we try to get the whole story—whatever it might be."

Gail said that currently they were serving about 750 families with sixty-five volunteers. "Now when you talk about families, you've got to break that down too," she cautioned. "Because in any one family, you may have two or three people that you have to work with."

The coalition's financial support, she said, came first of all from the churches—but also from local industry, including BP-Amoco and Reliable Oil and Gas; from a local foundation; from the United Way; from Wal-Mart; and from a lot of private individuals.

I was impressed. "So you've managed to turn that twenty-five-thousand-dollar Faith in Action grant into something big."

"It's something the community needs," Gail said. "It's the backbone of the community now. The people you'll talk to today at the governing body, they will tell you. Because they are there to serve the people. And when they get a complex situation with one of their constituents that they can't handle, they have to call us—and they have. You know, one of them had not seen a certain constituent on the street for a while, and he just happened to stop by. The man had had surgery and was laying in a bed and couldn't get up. And the landlord was trying to evict him.

"So what do you do? I remember the man on the governing body coming to me and saying, 'Miz Hurst, you've got to do something for him. He can't be evicted. He's got health problems.' So you've got to help him with his rent. And then you have to get bandages because he couldn't even afford to get the bandages. The Medicaid card was paying for the medications, but the card doesn't pay for the bandages. It doesn't pay for the gloves—and if you don't have the gloves, it'll get infected. It's so many of these little things that you couldn't even imagine unless you were a volunteer and you got to know these people."

Along with her sixty-five volunteers, Gail now had a staff of six. "When I started, it was just me. And next week, on February third, it'll be six years since I've been doing this."

"So do you enjoy it?"

"Oh, do I ever. And sometimes, when I look at all of the needs in this parish and all of the things we have to do, I wonder: How did people ever make it before?"

Gail went on to talk about all of the partnerships that HOPE Ministry had formed over the years—with the Salvation Army, with Pointe Coupee Good Neighbors, with Saint Vincent de Paul, with the Sheriff's Department—and about the many donations that they had received: the phones came from the First Baptist Church, the computers from BP-Amoco, and a local philanthropist had recently given a hundred thousand dollars toward a permanent endowment fund that would help to sustain HOPE Ministry for the long haul.

I was blown away.

"We built the organization on the background of what Faith in Action had given us," Gail said. "We still use the books. In fact, I've got a stack of them," she laughed, pointing at some of the familiar Faith in Action manuals piled on the edge of her cluttered desk. "We always go back to the books. But then you have to start designing it to fit the needs of the parish."

I asked Gail, who was African American, whether race had been a challenge in putting the coalition together.

"On race relations, we're making little bitty steps," she said. "Because now you hear people talking about the needs of *people*. You hear them talking about the needs of *our* community—including the poor as well. You don't have a whole group of people designing government for just the rich.

"You have even the government thinking about the poor. We have a very compassionate president of the governing body now. The guy's in his forties, a white male—a very compassionate man. And there's not anything that I would call him for that he wouldn't do what he could to help. Like utilities is one thing. They can be cut off, and they do not know who is in the house. So one day, they cut off the utilities of a lady with no legs."

"Oh, no."

"Well, you can't blame the utility company. She gave her son the money to pay her utility, and he used it on drugs. She had no way of knowing that. She can't read, and he brings her a receipt from two months back. So she thinks her bill is paid. But they go ahead and cut the utility, and so the lady next door calls me and says, 'The utilities are cut off. And she don't have any gas and tonight is getting cold.' Well, *I* can call the president of the governing body on his cell phone. Now you know he respects people that he gives his cell phone number to. And he can get the order—whatever time it is—and they'll put it back on. Because he knows that I would not call him unless there was a need."

"You must very proud, Gail."

"I'm proud of this community," she said emphatically. "The people here, they can actually work together. And they're beginning to see the need. I'm not pushing anything on them. But we're educating them. And the pastors—along with the readings, along with the Gospels—the people can see that they're living it. I see it when I go to church. I can see that they're living it—and they're going to do more. As it grows, they're going to do more."

I checked my watch. Not surprisingly, Gail and I had talked considerably longer than the thirty minutes that she had said she would give me when we'd started. It didn't particularly worry me, though, until she handed me the neatly typed schedule for the day. According to the schedule, I was supposed to interview *eleven* people before lunch—and that didn't include the hour or so that I'd just spent interviewing Gail, which had already put me more than half an hour behind schedule.

Billy and Zina

"And what is your name?" I asked the man in the wheelchair. He had a full beard and looked about my age—early fifties—wearing a green windbreaker and a faded camouflage cap that said "Real Men Hunt." A woman with sallow skin and glasses had come in with him and was sitting quietly on a chair against the wall behind him.

"Billy Henry," he replied.

"And you've been getting help from the program?" I asked him.

"For the last six, seven years," he said in a thick backcountry drawl. "Like I say, I worked on a farm all my life. I got taken with a disease that I was born with—though I didn't know it. I was paralyzed from the waist down and couldn't work anymore. And like I say, I needed a ramp, and Gail helped me with the ramp. And sometimes with the utility bills and all when I couldn't pay 'em. Because I'm on a fixed income. Any way she could help me, Gail helped me."

"And how did you connect with HOPE Ministry? Did they find you, or did you find them?"

"Oh," Billy said, "I had an old piece of a ramp, and I fell off of it on my wheelchair, and it got broken. And this police jury woman come around because it was around election time, so I asked her for some help. Really, I asked her for some gravel, because I had mud all around my ramp, and it wouldn't hold. So then she contacted Gail, and the next morning Gail was out there. She could see what I needed, and from there it went on."

"And that was about six years ago?"

"How long has it been?" he asked the woman, turning in his chair. "About seven years?"

"Gail's always been there," the woman said. "She'll just drop by or call without us even asking."

"I'm sorry," I said. "I didn't get your name."

"Zina Henry," she said.

His wife, I thought. Or maybe his sister.

"Like I say," Billy said, "Zina's got a bad back problem. And then when she can't afford to go to the doctor or to get the medicine, I'll call Gail, and Gail'll try to get the best help she can get for us. But the people I worked for all my life, they kind of put me out of their house after all this happened. So I got another house. And then just this past year, Gail got me *another* house and built me another ramp. The house is old, so they put me some insulation in it, between them and AARP. They put some old rugs in the house for me. Got it livable. It's not the best, but it keeps the rain off, you know."

"So tell me a little about your life," I said. "Were you born here?"

"I was born right here in New Roads. In the old St. Joseph Hospital. I got one brother and two sisters—one deceased sister."

"And what about your parents?"

"Well, my dad died when I was four years old."

"So you were raised by your mother?"

"By my mother. She was very sickly. She passed away when I was—what? Sixteen years old?"

"That's right," Zina said.

"So I was raised by her and my grandmother," Billy continued. "Grew up and worked in the hayfields and the cotton fields when I was a kid. I graduated from school in '72 . . ."

"So you finished high school?" I interrupted.

"In '72," he said. "And then from there I went to work in farming. That's all I've done for thirty years."

I asked him what kind of farming he had done.

"Soybeans and grain farming. Like I say, I've done that all my life. I had no easy life. The little bit I had, I had to work for it, you know. Nobody put it on a silver platter. And her and me, we raised three kids."

"And how old are your kids now?"

"I got a daughter that's . . ."

"She's what?" Zina said. "Almost twenty-nine?"

"Twenty-eight," Billy said. "We got three grandkids by her. And I got a son that's twenty-five, and he's got another one of our grandkids—a grandson. And our baby's twenty-one. They're all married, and they all still live here in the parish. Well," he corrected himself, "my oldest lives in Breaux Bridge, down in St. Martin Parish."

"But you get to see your grandchildren," I said.

"Oh, yeah," Billy said. "The grandson, he's there every day. My oldest daughter, like I say, they come about twice a month. It's kind of hard for us to go down there in my old car. You can ride around in it, but you can't trust it. If you could walk or something, then it'd be all right. But if you get on that interstate and you get broke down, you know . . ."

"Have you had that happen to you?"

"Oh yeah," he said, laughing bitterly.

"Quite a few times," Zina said.

"Like the Christmas before last it went out on us," Billy said. "We'd spent a ton of money on it, and the motor went out. My kids gave me another car—well, they bought it for me. And what was it? Christmas Eve again this year?"

"Yup," Zina said.

"I told her, I said, 'Let's go get the things we need in town because tomorrow everything's going to be closed.' And you know what had happened last year—it did the same thing this year."

"It broke down again?"

"The other car did the same thing," he said. "It quit on us."

"On Christmas Eve?"

"Christmas Eve."

"So you were what? Stuck on the highway?"

"Out on the highway," Billy said. "The year before last, it was during that sugar cane season with all them big trucks out. It was storming, pouring down rain, and them cane trucks wasn't paying us no mind. It like to turn me over into the False River trying to get out of the car."

"So what happened? How did you get out of there?"

"My daughter and my daughter-in-law. They come, and I was sitting on the edge of that riverbank. One was trying to hold the wheelchair while the other one drug me—cut ruts about that deep in that mud on the side of that riverbank with me in that wheelchair."

"How did they find you?"

"My neighbor that used to live by me, he seen me by the side of the road. He was going to work, and he stopped and he had his cell phone."

Billy told me that his everyday life was a mixed bag. "Some days it's good," he said, "and some days it's bad."

"Tell me about a good day," I said.

"Well, on a good day I don't hurt too much. Like I say, most of the time I get up about 7:30—maybe a little bit before that. I piddle around two or three hours, you know, just this and that. And then I got to go lay down because my back goes to hurtin'."

"That's a good day?"

"Well, then I'll get up in a little while and play around. I got an old four-wheeler. I can get around on it. So I'll go in the woods, and I'll hunt a little bit."

"On a four-wheeler?"

"Off the four-wheeler. That's right."

"What do you hunt?"

"Deer. Deer and squirrel. Well, anything, you know. I mean, as long as I can sit on that four-wheeler. I got a back I built for it, and a table on the front that I can prop up on, you know. Because my balance is real bad."

I nodded.

"I go lay down for a little while and get up. Then I go lay down again and get up—because after a while in this wheelchair, your tail hurts, you know. And she can tell you, lately I get in that bed at night and I might sleep for thirty minutes. Then I twist and I turn. I mean, when I get my legs comfortable, my shoulders hurt. Then my back."

"Has the pain gotten worse over the years? Or is it pretty much the same?"

"Well, I had surgery. When they found out what I had, they gave me surgery. So I've got the feeling back in my legs but no motion. So I can't stand on 'em or nothing like that. And the pain . . . it's a nagging pain. I take a couple of Tylenol, and she'll rub it, and that eases it up, you know. But some days it don't, so I got some muscle relaxants. I took them for the first three years after my surgery—but then I had to wean myself off of them things. Actually, I try to not take them. Because that medicine is just so expensive, we can't afford it. I've got Medicare and Medicaid, but it don't pay for my medicine.

"And *she* takes a lot more medicines than I do," he added.

"And what do you take medicine for?" I asked Zina.

"I have lupus," she said.

I asked Zina to come join us at the table because she was clearly as much a part of the story as Billy.

"She takes a bunch of medicines," Billy said.

"And I take Paxil," she said.

Paxil, I knew, is an antidepressant.

"And does HOPE Ministry help you with the medicines?" I asked.

"She helps us as much as she can," Billy said. "But I mean, I can't depend on them for everything."

"I hate to ask too," Zina said.

"You know, when we're in a bind and we've got to have it, I'll call Gail," Billy said. "But other people need help too. A lot of people in this parish need help."

I asked Billy and Zina how long they had been married.

"Forever," Zina laughed.

"It's going to be twenty-nine years in June," Billy said.

"And how did you meet?"

"In the barroom," Billy said.

"I'm from Shreveport," Zina explained. "My mother's godparents used to own a little bar and café down here, and so we came down here—my mother and I. And he walked in one day. He made a nasty remark to me, and I had to throw a beer at him."

"You're kidding!"

"He's been apologizing ever since," she said.

"Twenty-nine years," Billy chuckled.

Miss Ethel

"In here, Miss Ethel!"

It was Gail, coming through the door with a frail elderly woman in tow. The woman wore a handmade gold-colored knit cap and a big white cloth winter coat buttoned up to her neck. Shoulder-length white hair, dry as straw, framed her face. "Miss Ethel has a hearing problem," Gail explained as she handed me a yellow legal pad. "So she's going to write down a lot of things."

Gail helped her into a chair and left.

"Good morning, Miss Ethel," I shouted, passing the pad and a pencil across the table to her. "It's nice to meet you."

Miss Ethel picked up the pencil, wrote on the pad, and passed it back to me. Her handwriting was better than mine: I'M DEAF. YOU WILL HAVE TO WRITE DOWN WHAT YOU WANT TO ASK ME.

I picked up the pencil. It looked as though this might be even harder going than my interview with Doug Barker back in Concord. THANK YOU FOR COMING IN THIS MORNING, I wrote. I AM WRITING A BOOK ABOUT HOPE MINISTRY AND OTHER PROGRAMS LIKE IT. HOW OLD ARE YOU?

I passed the pad back to her, she read it, thought for a moment, and then wrote: 75.

DO YOU LIVE ALONE? I wrote, and passed the pad back.

This time it took her a while to write her response. I HAD TO ASK MY GRANDSON I RAISED + HIS WIFE TO COME TO LIVE WITH ME BECAUSE ALL MY FAMILY DIED. MY MOTHER + FATHER THE SAME YEAR. MY SON WITH HODGKINS CANCER 6 MONTHS LATER.

"You've had a very hard time," I said, looking up.

"I hear very little," she said in a faint voice that was cracked with age.

"You hear very little?"

"Yeah," she said. "You see, the doctor gave me a hearing aid that was very expensive. And since I wasn't hearing, about seven months ago I went back to him where I'd been going in Lafayette. But the one in Baton Rouge who I always did go to, he said that I needed a new mold. I went to him—I got the receipt. Paid him all that money for a new mold, and I'm still not hearing."

I was having a little trouble following her. But at least it seemed that we would be able to communicate enough that I wouldn't have to conduct the entire interview on paper.

"I figure that it's just like Mr. J. P. Jewel, a lawyer friend of ours, told me," Miss Ethel went on. "He said if we're deaf, eventually we ain't going to hear no more. And I figure that's true. I've been reading about that."

"How long have you been deaf?" I asked her.

No response.

I repeated my question, louder this time.

"Maybe twenty years," she said after a long pause.

"That's a long time," I said, keeping my voice loud. "And Miss Ethel, *how* has Gail helped you?"

"Yes, uh-huh."

"How has Gail helped you?"

"I don't know what I'd do if it wasn't for her."

"Say a little more about that."

"Well, the priests used to help," she replied slowly. "But, you see, now everybody turns all their money over to one place—that's here. And Gail's been doing that. I've been knowing Gail since she was a little baby. So she really has helped me with food. She's helped me when I needed diabetic strips, and she's helped me with my light. And with my medicine."

"Medicine too?"

"But I try to buy it myself," Miss Ethel said. "Because they can't constantly help the same person, you see."

"Did you grow up here?" I asked her, then repeated: "Are you from here?"

"Yeah, I'm from here."

"Have you seen a lot of changes here?"

"With HOPE?"

"With New Roads. With the community."

"With the community?"

"Right."

"Yes," Miss Ethel said, smiling for the first time. "Things have really changed. Things is much better than it used to be."

"In what way?"

"People is much more friendly than they used to be. If you ask a favor—even if they don't know you . . . Like one day I was walking up to town to go to the drugstore and I saw a lady at the post office, and I asked her would she give me a ride. I knew her casually, but she said, 'Sure!' I remember there was a time people wouldn't do that.

"And then I called different people to come and go to the grocery with me. And they're willing to come—white and black."

"White and black?"

"Well, I've nursed mostly all the whites in New Roads that were ever nursed—or nursed their children, you know. Babysat 'em. Stayed with 'em all weekend if they had to go out someplace. So I know all the whites. I can go to almost any one of 'em and tell my problems to 'em. They would not turn me down. Because they know I've worked for 'em. Or if it's a young one like you, then usually I've worked for their mother and father."

"Tell me about your life now," I said.

"Well, I'm really sick now. I'm a diabetic. My heart's not so good. And I have motion sickness now. The motion sickness came about from an inner ear infection—and the medicines don't help the inner ear infection. But I have medicine for the motion sickness. All I have to do is take it an hour before I leave home. If I don't, sometimes I get dizzy, and then they have to rush me to the hospital. I get so dizzy that I'm about to pass out. And then if my sugar gets too low, I can get dizzy from that too."

There was a knock at the door. It was Gail. "Miss Ethel," she said in a loud voice, "it's time for us to go on over to the luncheon." She turned to me. "We're going to take Miss Ethel over there now," she said. "But there's some people here from BP-Amoco that have been very good to HOPE Ministry that I'd like you to meet before you go."

The *Pointe Coupee Banner*

After the luncheon and several more interviews, I met with a tired-looking man by the name of Tommy Comeaux. Tommy, who wore a full moustache, faded jeans, and a checked flannel work shirt, handed me his card and slumped back in his seat. According to his card, Tommy was the editor/reporter for the *Pointe Coupee Banner,* the local weekly.

"You're the editor and the reporter?" I asked.

"Actually, my title is pretty much editor-reporter-photographer-and-anything-else-that-has-anything-whatsoever-to-do-with-the-news. So there's no question about who gets the best assignment. It's got to be me."

Tommy was from Baton Rouge, but he said that New Roads had turned out to be a perfect match for him. People here had been very accepting of him, and it was close enough to Baton Rouge that he could still continue to live there, commuting back and forth.

"So tell me about HOPE Ministry," I said.

"I don't know how long you've been up here or who you've talked to," Tommy said. "But I'm sure that their recurring comment has got to be how impressed everybody is with how well Gail manages—in a community that is somewhat divided—to unite people for a common goal and to help the folks who are in need."

No one, I said, had been quite that explicit.

"Well," he said, "as an outsider, maybe it's easier for me to see divisions here that they may either be in denial of or they've put blinders on so they just don't see it."

"Are we talking race? Religion? Class?"

"There are divisions here along all kinds of lines," Tommy replied. "There are social divisions, there are racial divisions. I mean, I've never been in a more legally segregated community in my life."

"Is that right?"

"And I was born and raised in southern Louisiana," he added with a grin.

I asked Tommy if he could give me an example.

He nodded. "Like the school system here, by and large, is legally segregated. Probably 95 percent of the white kids are going to private schools, while 95 percent of the black students are going to the public schools. And that's a real problem when it comes to the school budget."

Not all that different from the urban schools in New Jersey, I thought.

"And there are lots of other divisions," Tommy continued, tapping his pen on the table. "I mean, there are the haves and the have-nots that don't seem to mix. Old-line New Roads families that don't let outsiders in."

"But you were saying that you think HOPE Ministry is making some inroads."

"That's right," Tommy said, pulling himself up in his chair. "And I think in large part it's due to Gail's personality."

"How so?"

"Because Gail makes it quite apparent that what she does, she is doing for the good of the people. Gail Hurst is not doing what she does for the good of Gail Hurst or for any personal interest that she has. She does it because it's the right thing to do. And that comes across to anybody whose path she ever crosses. Couple that with the fact that she's a very bright, cheerful person who people enjoy being around—and the fact that she's incredibly persuasive."

"You're telling me," I chuckled, recalling how deftly she had talked me into meeting with her governing board.

Then I brought up something that had been bothering me. "Tommy, let me ask you a cynical question since, after all, you're in the newspaper business."

He grinned.

"You know," I said, "somebody could look at this and say, 'This is a wonderful thing, but maybe the reason that people support Gail—especially the powers that be—is because this is kind of a way of keeping a lid on things. You know, she meets enough needs—not enough to really solve the problem, but enough to keep the pot from boiling over. And so if they invest in her and in HOPE Ministry, then maybe they won't have to face the real problems. How would you respond to that?"

"I think that there may be some truth in that," Tommy conceded. "But I also think that there is a large contingency of the people here who want HOPE Ministry and what it's doing to truly be successful and to continue to unite the parish to solve some of these problems."

"Some of the real problems?"

He nodded. "Look," he said firmly. "I've been up here long enough now to realize that there are some very hard-working, very genuine people who are doing some very positive things in this parish. I think Gail is just a part of that, and I think that she provides kind of a conduit to all of the facets. Because she gets along with everybody." He paused. "You know, I'm not even sure that Gail sees race. I'm not sure she even sees the color of a person's face when she talks to them. And that's contagious."

SHREVEPORT, LOUISIANA

"YOU'RE AMAZING TO FIND US!" Mack McCarter boomed as he shook my hand the next morning in his office in downtown Shreveport. He was lean and relaxed in blue jeans and a navy turtleneck.

Ten years earlier, Mack, an ordained minister, had used one of the early Faith in Action grants to help him put together an ambitious, long-term communitywide campaign that was explicitly intended to heal the racial divisions in Shreveport. In other words, the gradual improvements in race relations that Gail Hurst and her colleagues at HOPE Ministry were beginning to see as a by-product of their work in New Roads had been Mack's explicit goal in Shreveport from the outset. I had long been curious to see how Mack's program was working out.

"I'm delighted to be here after all these years," I said.

Mack led me down the hall. The walls were lined with framed local newspaper stories with headlines: PLAN REBUILDS CITY A BLOCK AT A TIME . . . LEARNING THE LESSONS OF RESPECT FIRST STEP IN CONQUERING RACISM . . . PLAN OFFERS SAFE HOUSES FOR NEIGHBORHOODS . . . CHANGE STARTS IN THE STREET WHERE YOU LIVE.

We stepped into a conference room with a big whiteboard on the wall covered with mysterious diagrams and philosophical-sounding phrases written in blue and black and red markers, with arrows and dotted lines running from one to the other like tangled vines.

For the next two hours, Mack told me his story: how he had gone from his childhood in the segregated Shreveport of the 1940s and 1950s, where he had earned the reputation of being "the lover of another race, although of course it was a little cruder than that," to Texas Christian University and the seminary, where he had learned about liberation theology and had started thinking about the need to change the structures of society. He had then gone from the seminary to a small town in the West Texas Panhandle, where he headed up his first congregation and started trying to put some of his ideas about social justice into practice.

He chuckled: "You know, Watergate is happening, and I'm up there preaching all these social action sermons—that Nixon is guilty, that we've got to bus, et cetera. And all these farmers and cowboys are looking at me like, 'Who *is* this?' I mean, they were wonderful folks and wonderfully patient, but you know, they're like, 'Who *is* this idiot? We want to hear about God and Jesus!'"

In the mid-1970s, after transferring to another congregation in another small West Texas town, Mack met his intellectual hero, a Quaker philosopher and theologian by the name of D. Elton Trueblood. Trueblood encouraged him to keep going after his vision of social change and turned him on to new sources of ideas, like Arnold Toynbee's history of civilizations and Lewis Mumford's history of cities. Again, working through the churches, he tried to put some of his ideas into practice, with the same discouraging results.

Finally, one day in 1991, in the midst of his frustration, a boyhood friend from back in Shreveport, who had become a successful local businessman and had been following Mack's career in West Texas, asked him to come back to Shreveport to see whether he could use some of his ideas to help save the city. "If the city goes under, my business goes under with it," his friend told him.

And so, with the financial support of his friend, Mack returned to Shreveport and started putting together a strategy to heal the racial divisions that he believed were at the root of the city's decline. Three years later, he received one of the early Faith in Action grants to help him get his strategy, which he named Community Renewal, off the ground.

"So what did you do?" I asked him.

"We said, 'Okay, we've got three hundred thousand people here. Now how do we come together?' You see, we have so much diversity here—black, white, brown; rich, poor; Catholic, Protestant. And so we said, 'We're going to celebrate diversity. We'll recognize our differences, but we're also going to say what it is that brings us together' because diversity has got to be transcended by a passion for unity. We've been created with a drive for uniqueness, but we've also been created to be brothers and sisters. And so we asked: 'What do we share in common?'"

Mack looked at me meaningfully, but I had no idea.

"We all have the capacity to care," he said, adding, "with precious few exceptions."

"You mean the sociopaths?"

"Right. But, you see, we can lessen their impact if we can increase the pool of caring people. Now, we set out in the beginning thinking that we had to find ways to make people more caring—and then suddenly it dawned on us: they already are. And this was a huge breakthrough. I mean, if God were to look down on Shreveport-Bossier, He'd see 299,000 people who are caring—and only about a thousand who want to hurt people. But the problem is we're invisible.

"You see, one of the reasons that a complex society crumbles is that as the capacity for communication increases, our awareness of that small minority of harmful people really increases, while we don't see this vast invisible majority of caring people. And so the harmful minority dictates our psychological perception of our environment. So anyway, the idea was, How do we make the caring majority visible?

"And so we did a simple thing. We formed the We Care teams. Fill in this card, and write down one caring act each day. You know how hard it is for a caring person to do one caring act a day? To open a door for someone? The fact is that we're constantly caring. But it's the preponderance of caring acts as opposed to criminal acts that is so stunning."

I asked Mack how many people were involved at this point.

"We've got over 10,000 people who have signed," he replied. "And we'll have more than 20,000 before long. So that's the first part of our strategy."

"So you'll only have 280,000 left to go," I said.

"Right," Mack agreed. "And that's no problem. We've just got to make them visible. Now, of course, the culture and the community can collapse even though you've got all these individual caring acts: the *key* is to connect caring people."

And so, along with creating the We Care teams, Community Renewal had started working block by block. "We'd mobilize and train somebody to rebuild friendships on the block where they lived. And we've systematized it by hooking them together: train them, send them out, and then bring them together—so that now we've got an army of over five hundred block leaders. We've got rich, poor, black, white—but they're all doing the same things to try to connect the people on their block to one another. Our motto is, 'We're remaking our city by making friends.'

"And then the most intensive part was: How do we help our brothers and sisters who have been victims of institutionalized racism and who live in neighborhoods that are impoverished and have terribly high crime rates? And the idea there is to train caring people and to move them in.

Instead of sending missionaries to India, we go into our local neighborhoods. That's called our ICU—the Internal Care Unit."

He paused and then continued: "People get in there and they follow a
plan to rebuild caring relationships. And it becomes a matrix for the ontology of the village. We believe that there are eight ontological elements that
have to do with the village life. And if you get a whole village, then you
begin to produce whole human beings."

Ontology, I learned when I returned home to my dictionary, is "the
branch of philosophy that deals with being." At the time, I couldn't help
wondering how Mack's eight ontological elements would play in the
neighborhoods that he was talking about. Then he became more specific.

"For instance, you've got to have a health care delivery system," he
said. "And right now, we're on the verge of a huge breakthrough with the
whole mobile pediatric thing coming into the neighborhoods. Because
we've got an 'airport' where they can now land, and so we've got the res-
ident doctors from LSU Medical School. As a matter of fact, Lloyd Mich-
ener, the chairman of family and community medicine at Duke University,
has come down and he said that this is a huge breakthrough."

In addition to health care, the other ontological elements that Mack listed
were adequate housing, meaningful work, education, leadership development, a common culture, and a means to create a safe environment.

A piece of cake.

Still, thirteen years after returning to Shreveport and ten years after receiving his Faith in Action grant, Mack now had a staff of thirty and an annual
budget of more than $2 million, including a congressional earmark and a
substantial new grant from the Robert Wood Johnson Foundation. According to their latest count, Shreveport Community Renewal now had 1,647
volunteers actively providing services in the community—and that did not
include the roughly ten thousand local residents in the We Care teams.

"So are you still having fun?"

"Oh, God," he laughed as we both stood up and shook hands. "Never
had a harder year in my life than this past year."

Before heading off to a meeting, Mack introduced me to a lean middle-
aged man with a faintly quizzical expression and a neatly trimmed, gray-
ing beard, dressed in jeans and a pale blue dress shirt. "Paul, this is the
dentist I was telling you about: Mike Leonard."

We shook hands.

Mack had indeed mentioned that there was a dentist who had given up
his practice to work with Renewal and that he was shadowing Mack,
which I took to mean that he was Mack's designated successor. Mack also

introduced me to his volunteer coordinator, a young woman by the name of Lynn Bryan, who was to be my chaperone for the remainder of my visit.

Mike

For his interview, Mike and I sat in a small office crowded with black metal filing cabinets and a wall of cardboard boxes. I began by asking him how he had become involved with Community Renewal.

"Let's see," he said. "I guess it was in 1995. Mack came and spoke to the men's group at our church—I go to a little Methodist church in the Highland area. We were trying to get our men's ministry together again, and Mack came and talked to us about Community Renewal. And I can remember sitting there in the group and thinking, What he's talking about makes sense. I mean, it didn't seem terribly complicated—this whole idea of building a relational foundation. It just resonated in my spirit. So I got all of the information and went home and tossed it on my desk—and never looked at it again. And then one day I was jogging by his house and he was walking out of his study. And I tell everybody now: the greatest mistake I ever made was stopping."

I laughed politely.

"But I did," Mike went on. "And he said, 'Leonard, I was thinking about you. I've got a book I want you to read.' So he puts *The Master Plan of Evangelism* in my hands—this little bitty book by Robert Coleman. I wasn't much of a reader at that time, but I said, 'Okay, well, I've got a trip coming up. I'll read it while I'm gone.'

"So I went off on this trip, and while I was on the plane, I read this thing. And I got caught up in the whole process of reading this book about discipleship—you know, Jesus's strategy to teach His disciples and then turn them loose on the rest of the world. But, anyway, when I got back, I called him, like I was supposed to, and he said, 'Did you read the book?' I said, 'Yeah.' So we went and ate breakfast one morning, and he said, 'Would you like to start getting together so we can go through this book and talk a little more about it?' And I said, 'Sure. That'd be great.' So for four years, once a week, we faithfully met at 6:30 A.M. in his study. And it was in that process that God really got a hold on my life."

"Are you from Shreveport originally?" I asked.

"Born and raised in Shreveport," he said. "I came back after dental school and opened up a practice here. And I've been blessed in the success that we've had. It's been a good run for me. I've accomplished just about everything that I've needed to accomplish in my professional career."

"And how old are you, Mike?"

"I was born 1955. So I'm coming up on fifty."

"So you're old enough to remember the segregation here in Shreveport."

"Oh, yeah. I was in the ninth grade when they desegregated the school system. And it was . . . I mean, you talk about an interesting time to be going to school. I can remember a number of times the black guys'd be lined up on one side of the parking lot and the white guys'd be lined up, and the police'd be funneling in there. Nothing really major ever happened, but there was a lot of tension. It was a lot of stress and pressure on all those kids. The thing that I thank my lucky stars for is that I was an athlete. Because as athletes, we were thrown together in ways that the rest of the student body couldn't be thrown together. We had a common cause and a common goal."

"What was your sport?"

"Football. And because of that experience, I got to know these guys as just people. Because up until that point, the only African American folks I'd ever met, really, were housekeepers. I mean, I grew up in a real basic middle-class home. My dad died when I was pretty young. My mother basically raised myself and my brother and sister. So other than that, that was really my only intercultural experience. And then I went to LSU and played football there—and even then, there were very few African American kids on our team. Four or five at the most—out of ninety. Scholarship kids. Anyway, it was an interesting time to be growing up as far as the South goes."

I asked Mike how much he thought race relations had changed here in Shreveport since those days of his youth.

He stroked his beard thoughtfully for a moment before answering. "I don't remember any overt racism," he said.

"Is that right?"

"I don't know if it was just that people in our neighborhood . . . I mean, I'm sure there were some racists out there. Or some well-meaning people out there who just didn't understand—whatever you want to call them. But I just don't recall being exposed to any overt racism. In fact," he said, his face reddening, "when I moved back here to Shreveport and went to work, I probably had more prejudice than I did at any other time of my life. I'd just spent four years down in New Orleans going to dental school, and I probably came back from that experience more prejudiced than I ever was at any other time."

"What happened?" I asked him.

Mike swallowed hard.

"I think, you know, that it was in my ignorance and not understanding," he said, sounding chagrinned. "I was paying taxes, and I thought,

'Look at all these dudes on the dole.' You know, the welfare system looked to be a mess to me. And they kept taxing me and cutting into my ability to make an income—and I just blamed the black man."

"And then what happened?"

"Well, I guess I spent a few years going through that process, until God began to get a hold of my life in 1986. That's when I began to get back into the church deal."

"How did that come about?"

"Up until that point, whatever I'd set my mind to, I'd pretty well accomplished," he said. "I would discipline myself. If I wanted to go to dental school or if I wanted to do athletics—whatever it was—once I'd sunk my teeth into something, I could generally get it done. But then I ran into a little problem with alcohol." He chuckled to himself. "I couldn't quite . . ."

"You couldn't quite lick it on your own?"

"That's right. And so I went through about a three-year process of mostly sobriety—but I had some slips. And then finally, it took. I haven't had a drink since December 5, 1997."

"So go back to Mack now," I said. "You were meeting with him . . ."

"On Thursday mornings at 6:30. And I'm telling you, I was such a mess about my spirituality. I kept trying to be this good Christian kid, but I just couldn't measure up. I kept on repeating the same sins over and over again, and I just couldn't get it together. But then, in this process of discipleship, I finally learned—after about a year and a half—that I was never going to get good enough for God. That it really was his grace and love that had the power to change somebody."

"I guess that must've been kind of liberating," I said.

"It was," Mike said, nodding vigorously. "It was very liberating for me. And it came purely as a result of Mack's patience and God's speaking to me through him. I mean, I cannot tell you . . ." His eyes glowed.

"I mean, every Thursday he would tell me, 'Leonard, don't you know that God just loves you? He just loves you. Period. End of story.' And he just kept rubbing that oil of gladness onto me. He put that crown of beauty on me. And after a while, it finally took."

I asked Mike what impact he thought Community Renewal had had on Shreveport so far. Had anything changed?

He thought for a few moments. "The most exciting thing to me is to see what's happening with what I would call the wealthy or more affluent part of the city and the impoverished—and how the whole relational foundation is being rewoven."

"In what way?"

"Like through the bus tours. We're taking folks on tours—people from the more affluent neighborhoods, and whoever wants, really—to come and see some of the work that we're doing in the neighborhoods. And sometimes we have time to go in and talk to some of the community coordinators, who are the folks we have that live in these impoverished neighborhoods. And I can't think of but just a few that didn't have their minds blown by the work that is going on. Not only that, but also the incredible need for the work to be done.

"It's just like the first time I drove through those neighborhoods. I frankly just wasn't aware of it. You know, you read the newspaper, you turn on the news—you're aware of it in that sense. But unless somebody was sticking a gun in my face and carjacking me in my driveway, I was going to work and playing golf and showing up in church once a week, and then I was *done*. I mean, that's all there was to it. That was my whole concept of life.

"But then discipleship occurred through my friendship with Mack, and I became intimately aware of the need. I mean, there are people I can now call friends that live in Cedar Grove; in Allendale; in Mooretown."

"These are all low-income neighborhoods?"

"Low-income folks that are just salt-of-the-earth, wonderful people. You know, there's not a person that isn't my brother or sister anymore. Because in God's eyes, we're all related, and we're all in the family—this human family and collectivity—and what's hurting the least of us is hurting us all."

"Tell me about some of these folks," I said.

"Well, for instance, Margaret Myles is a seventy-six-year-old lady who lives in Cedar Grove. She has become part of our Adult Renewal Academy, which is a program that began a little over a year ago—and she's going to get her GED. At age seventy-six! She never graduated from high school, and she wants to get her GED. That's the kind of remarkable woman she is. But besides that, every third Thursday of the month, she has a community breakfast at her house. People from all over Cedar Grove come, and some of us folks from Community Renewal come, and she just feeds us."

"How many people does she have at one of these breakfasts?"

"Probably fifteen or twenty. And I mean, it's just a little bitty house. We're sitting all over each other. But we come together, and we pray. That was the whole point of it. And then it just kind of developed into, 'If we're going to pray, we might as well eat.' And Margaret was just so gracious to have us in her home.

"And then there's Rosie Chafford. Rosie Chafford is a lady from Allendale who started a big community garden. Now I remember when Mack first took me out to Allendale. We were eating lunch one day, and he said, 'Leonard, let's go drive through Allendale. I want to show you the property where I think we're going to build the next Friendship House.'"

A Friendship House, I later learned, was part of Mack's concept of the Internal Care Unit: an actual home, located in a high-need neighborhood, that housed a husband and wife who were employed by Community Renewal and worked intensively to rebuild a sense of community within that neighborhood.

"Now, I had lived here my whole life," Mike continued. "And so I'd heard of Allendale, but I didn't have the foggiest idea where it was. So we're driving my car—I had this Lincoln Mark VIII—and we're just driving through this incredibly impoverished neighborhood with these serious shotgun houses, and Mack says, 'Okay, this is the block where we own some property.' And meanwhile there's these two groups of kids—young men, really—standing on either side of the corner, and Mack goes, 'Leonard, don't look around. Don't stop. Just roll through the stop sign.'

"And when we got up there, they were cussing and screaming and hollering at us"—Mike mouthed a string of obscenities—"I mean, they were giving us *everything*. And I'm saying to myself, 'I'm fixing to die.' I mean, I figured they were coming after us, and I was scared."

"Sure."

"And I said, 'Mack, what are we doing coming out to this neighborhood? I don't think we'll ever get anybody to move in here.' But, anyway, to make a long story short, we began a prayer walk in the neighborhood—not me, but the community coordinators. That's what they do on Wednesdays prior to their staff meeting: they canvass the target neighborhood with prayer. And so this one morning we're walking and praying, and there's this lady out in her yard planting flowers and spraying and doing all kinds of stuff.

"So we go, 'Hey! How're you doing?' And we start up a conversation. Her name is Rosie Chafford, and she's just as friendly as she can be. It was just one of those moments, you know. And she was just very thankful for what we were trying to do. So now she's kind of the ringleader out there in Allendale and part of their Adult Care Team.

"And boy, she is smart and she's quick. And we tease each other unmercifully. And you know, she's just been wonderful. I sit back now, and I just go: 'You know, if God hadn't got me, I would have missed all of this.'"

Richard

The next morning, Lynn Bryan, my chaperone, drove me over to King Hardware on Line Avenue, a welcome change from the windowless little office at Community Renewal. It was an independent hardware store that had been in business for something like fifty years despite the competition from Home Depot and Ace. In fact, Lynn said, the store had expanded in recent years under its new owner, Richard Carruth. "And that's who you're going to interview. He's one of our volunteers."

Richard was standing behind the counter when we walked in, a lean, white-haired man dressed in khaki pants and a blue work shirt. Soft-spoken and relaxed, he immediately struck me as completely at ease with himself.

Richard was born in Shreveport in 1946, precisely three years to the day after his sister, his only sibling.

"So," I said, "your mom only had to bake one birthday cake?"

"Not only that, but I was the best birthday present my sister ever got," he replied.

Except for college and thirteen years that he had worked in Houston, Richard had lived in Shreveport all his life. He and his wife had three grown children—two who lived here in Shreveport, the other in Dallas—and four grandchildren, who also lived in Shreveport.

"We're very fortunate," he said.

After high school, Richard had gone to the University of Arkansas and then to Louisiana Tech, where he had graduated with a degree in civil engineering. From there, he had taken a job in the engineering department of a gas company in Shreveport, and four years later he'd been transferred to the Houston office.

"So what brought you back to Shreveport?"

"I got offered a job with another gas company here in Shreveport," he said. "And we really kind of wanted to come back. My daddy wasn't in good health—he was going through some things."

"When was this?"

"This was 1987. So I worked for this other gas company until 1993. And then, in the process of leaving that company . . ." He paused and gave me a grim smile. "Well, you could *say* I left it. I was the senior vice president and chief operating officer of our gas marketing company, and they brought a new man in as part of a deal. And he came in one day and he said, 'Look, I don't really know you very well. But I've got a guy who used to work for me in the company that I came from, so I'm going to bring him in here.'"

"That must've been tough," I said.

"It was a different experience," Richard said dryly. "After twenty-four years to have someone come in one day and say, 'It doesn't have anything to do with your job or what you do or how you do your job or anything. It's just that I've got this other guy, so I'm going to bring him in here.'"

"So how did you deal with that?"

"Myself, I don't think I had any problem with it. You know, there's not anything you can do about it."

"But it's painful."

"Oh, yeah," he agreed. "It's painful. You hear this and you're sitting there at your desk and you say, 'Now I've got to go home and tell my wife what just happened.' And thinking how you're going to do that."

"Right," I said. "And this was totally out of the blue?"

"What he said to me was, 'We'll bring him in, let him see how things operate, and see where we go from there.' So I was around a couple more months after that. And then this guy came in and said, 'Well, the other guy just told me that he told the board last night that you were resigning.' So, you know, it was a shock," Richard said. "It was a very difficult time."

"Had you ever had anything like that happen before?"

"It's funny," he said. "I told someone—I was forty-six at the time, I guess—and I said, 'The worst thing that ever happened to me in my life up until this point was when we lost the state championship football game in my junior year in high school.'"

I started to laugh.

"Were you on the team?" I asked him.

"Yeah."

"So then what did you do?" I asked.

"I wanted to stay in Shreveport," Richard said. "I didn't want to go to Dallas or Houston, where I could have stayed in the oil and gas business. I just didn't want to get back into that environment."

And so he had decided to buy King Hardware.

"It must be a whole new world," I said.

"It is," Richard agreed. "A whole new world."

"Are you enjoying it?"

"I really do. Somebody asked me if it was what I thought it would be. And I guess it is—other than personnel. You know, the people side of it."

"You mean having to deal with your own employees?"

"Well," he said, "I've supervised and had control over departments. But it was a different level of person. All the people I'd dealt with were college-educated, professional white-collar folks. But here in the retail business, the majority of your people may not even have a high school diploma."

"Right."

"And the turnover is just . . . For instance, I had seven people on the payroll, and in the first year, I had twenty-four people fill those jobs. So that's just a whole different ball game."

"But you *are* your own boss now."

"You're your own boss," he agreed. "Well, there's my wife. She works here full time now. She'd been working as a secretary over at the church, but she quit that and came here. So now we both work here full time. And my mother works with us too."

"And you're able to make ends meet?"

"We make a living out of it," he said mildly. "It's six days a week, and sometimes it's ten, twelve hours a day. But we enjoy it. We really do."

Richard had first become aware of Community Renewal around 1996. He remembered, he said, because he had had triple bypass surgery in 1995, and it was not long after that that Tom Harrison, the associate pastor at his church, had started talking to him about it.

"But why did you decide to get involved?" I asked. "I mean, here you had this new business; you were working ten, twelve hours a day, six days a week; you'd just had your triple bypass. Why in heaven's name did you take on something more?"

Richard laughed. "It's just that I like people. I enjoy being around people and doing things with them. And then hearing what Tom was talking about and what Mack was trying to do and the approach that they were taking . . ."

His eyes narrowed. "Because when I'd drive between here and my house, I'd drive through this area that's not really well-to-do," he said softly. "It's where Renewal has one of their homes, in Cedar Grove. You drive through there, and you see the condition of the area, and you know that there's people living in there—and kids—that are there because of nothing that they've done, or for any other reason. And you just feel like if they could just get some help, you know, that they could get out of there. And their life would be better."

I nodded.

"And you know, it's always in your mind," he added. "How can you *do* something? How can you get involved besides just giving money?"

"Well," I said, "some people might drive through the same neighborhood and they might not feel that way. They'd say, 'It's probably their own fault. And besides, there's nothing I can do about it.'"

"Well, I guess I've been brought up to care for people," Richard replied. "Both by my family and by my church. I think the church is a significant part of it. Because that's where it all comes from—through your faith. If you honestly have a strong belief in Christ and in God, you know, that's what God tells us to be. We're servants. And we're to take care of our fellow man and to treat our fellow man with kindness. I mean, it's sort of a cliché, but there but for the grace of God—that could be me walking in those shoes."

He had gotten involved gradually, starting by simply promoting Community Renewal at the store, talking to customers about it, and signing them up to participate in the We Care program. And he'd gone on some of the prayer walks through the neighborhoods—like Cedar Grove— where Renewal was active. But the We Care pins and the prayer walks weren't enough. Richard was looking for something more personal—a way maybe to help at least one person to escape from the streets.

And so last year he had become a mentor.

"I got together with a boy who's a senior this year at Byrd High School— the same high school that I went to," Richard said. "And he plays football. So we had a commonality of interests. And we started getting together, and we've developed a real good relationship. The program asks that you make just one contact a week, either by telephone or whatever."

"What's his name?"

"Ben."

"And how are you helping him? Are you tutoring him?"

"Well, no. You see, Ben lives with his mother and his grandmother. Both of them don't have real good health. Mainly his grandmother has been doing things to try to keep him involved. And he's a good kid. He's been involved in the Community Renewal deal. And my job is to help him to be sure that he gets his education and that he graduates and does whatever else he needs to do after that educational process."

"So do you meet with him, or do you talk by phone?"

"He and I get together every Wednesday morning for breakfast. I go by and pick him up at about 7:15, before school, and we go and eat breakfast together. And we just talk about how school is going, how are the grades going, what's going on. Right now we're working with him on his college entrance and talking about where he's planning to go to school."

"And is he white or black?"

"He's black," Richard said. "A real good kid. He's kind of quiet. He stays at home a lot because of the situation with his mother and his grandmother. And he's already joined the National Guard Reserves. So he'll be going to camp this summer. And then when he gets out of that, he'll be in the reserves and then he'll be looking to go to school in the fall. So that's how he'll get his education paid for."

"And do you look forward to the breakfasts?"

"Oh, yeah. I call him every Tuesday night just to check and be sure."

"And where do you meet for breakfast?"

"Well, we usually either go to Strawn's or to George's Grill. I guess just about every time now, we go to George's. We walk in and the waitress walks up with our coffee and orange juice."

"So she knows you guys."

"Oh yeah," Richard said, smiling. "She knows us."

I asked Richard how he thought things in Shreveport had changed and whether he thought Community Renewal was having any real impact on the city.

"Of course, I grew up in an era of segregation," he said. "Believe it or not, I didn't even know there were black high schools in town. I guess there are still a lot of the same problems, but it's more open now. And you see it everywhere—not just in the black community. It's in the white community as well. Drugs, crime, shootings. . . ." He sighed. "In my line of work—in retail—we see the robberies and the shoplifting. I've chased a guy down the street, which was stupid. But you know, you see a lot more of it in this environment that I'm in now than I used to see sitting on the thirteenth floor of an office building in a coat and tie."

"Sure."

"As for Community Renewal, I believe that what Mack is doing is probably the only way that you've really got a chance of turning things around—through people's one-on-one involvement. I don't think you can do it with just money."

In the car on the way back to Community Renewal, I mentioned to Lynn about Richard and Ben's Wednesday morning breakfasts. She already knew all about it. "You know, neither one of them's terribly talkative," she said. "And so sometimes they'll just sit there and eat together without necessarily saying a lot. And I think that's just great—you know, that they can be that comfortable with each other."

Miss Margaret

At noon, I took the bus tour that Mike Leonard had mentioned through some of the more distressed neighborhoods where Community Renewal had set up its Internal Care Units, and it turned out that my final interview that afternoon was in one of those same neighborhoods, just a few blocks from an area that until recently had been known as cocaine alley.

The interview was with Margaret Myles, the woman Mike had told me about who had gone back for her GED at age seventy-six and who held prayer breakfasts at her house.

"She does the most remarkable, caring things," Lynn told me as she drove us to Margaret's home. "I called her one day and I said, 'Margaret, I want to come by your house during my lunch break and bring you something.' And she said, 'Okay, then I'm going to fix lunch for you.' Well, I got there . . ."—Lynn's voice dropped to a dramatic whisper—". . . and she had a T-bone steak cooked for me. A T-bone steak!"

"Wow."

"And right when I got there, the doorbell rang, and it was the mailman. And the mailman said, 'Miss Margaret, do you have any leftovers today?' And she invites him in and cooks him a T-bone steak too! And then there's the prayer breakfasts. I think she's had as many as nineteen people at one time. The third Thursday of every month, she cooks breakfast for whoever wants to come and pray and eat. And if you're walking down the street and she happens to be in her yard, she'll say, 'Are you doing okay? Do you need something to eat?' I mean, I can call her and ask her to do anything, and I guarantee you, Paul, if it's within her might, she will do it. And she takes care of the elderly people in her neighborhood. They call her the Banana Lady."

"The Banana Lady?"

"She goes to the nursing home to visit folks, and she takes fruit with her. Lots of times, she's got bananas, so now they call her the Banana Lady."

"And she likes that?"

"She does."

As we walked up to her house, Miss Margaret came to the door. A small boy who looked like he was about four years old was holding onto her leg.

"This is your last week with him, isn't it?" Lynn said. "Isn't he going to Shantay's next week?"

"Next week," Miss Margaret nodded.

"And then you'll be a free woman," Lynn said.

"Sure will," Miss Margaret said. "Come on in, come on in."

Miss Margaret had on her We Care pin and was dressed in red pants that matched her red-dyed hair and an oversized royal blue T-shirt with the word "Southern" printed across it in big gold letters. Joyful gospel music welled up from the television.

"Could I turn that down, Miss Margaret?" Lynn asked.

"Oh, sure. You can turn it off."

Lynn scooped up the little boy in her arms. "I'll watch the baby while you two talk," she said. She picked up the fire truck he had been playing with and disappeared into one of the bedrooms with him.

Miss Margaret and I sat on metal folding chairs at a blue card table in the middle of the living room, surrounded by family photographs that covered the walls and just about every inch of available shelf space: school pictures, graduation pictures, wedding pictures, family portraits—some old and faded, others looking as if they had just come back from the developer.

"Looks like you've got quite a family," I said.

"Oh, yes," she smiled. She was the oldest of eight children, she said, and she had eight children of her own—along with, it appeared from the pictures, innumerable grandchildren. Her parents were from rural De Soto Parish, south of Shreveport, and although she was born in Shreveport, she had grown up on a farm in De Soto Parish.

"We raised practically everything that we ate," she said. "A garden, chickens, cows—all of that stuff. I milked cows, churned butter."

"And I heard you learned to cook too," I said. "Lynn says you're an amazing cook."

"I cook pretty good," she acknowledged. "But like I told somebody, I don't brag on my cooking. But then the other day, we were talking about something, and I said, 'Huh. I can do pretty good burning.' So I thought: oh-oh, I said I didn't brag, but I bragged, didn't I?"

I laughed.

"Was your mother a good cook?" I asked.

"My mother died at an early age," Miss Margaret said heavily. "Back when I was young. I wasn't even thirteen years old."

"But you were the oldest," I said. "So did that mean that you had to start taking care of the younger ones?"

"Yes," she said. "I was already learning how to cook, because she was ill before she passed away. So she had to show me how to season whatever it was that I was cooking. I wasn't nothing but a child, but I was being taught."

"Was your father still alive at this point?" I asked Miss Margaret.

"He was still alive," she said. "But I didn't live with my father. He married another. He remarried."

"So did you raise the rest of your family on your own—all your brothers and sisters?"

"I lived part of the time with my mother's sister," Miss Margaret said. "She did part of the raising after my mother passed on."

"And then you came back to Shreveport?"

"That's right. I went to school here in the eighth grade. And I started in the ninth. But then I dropped out of school."

"Because you had to work?"

"That's right. And I started having babies."

She pointed at one of the pictures on the wall. "That's my oldest there. And that's my family there. With my eight children. And that's my husband beside me. He passed away two years ago. My husband and I moved here to this house in 1955. Raised all eight children right here in this house. You see all this wear and tear here?"

I did.

"I lost one of them in September," Miss Margaret said. "The one with the white on. In the middle, standing up there."

"What happened?"

"She passed away. Had a heart attack."

"I'm sorry," I said softly.

She went on to tell me about each of the others. "This boy over here, he works for Bell South. Been with them for thirty years after he finished college in Baton Rouge. And this one—she was a telephone operator. Still is, over at the hospital. But before that, she was with the telephone company for about twenty-seven years."

We talked about her involvement in Community Renewal.

"I love it," she said.

"What is it that you like about it?"

"Fellowship," Miss Margaret replied without hesitation. "We do things, one for the other, you know. Whatever we can do. At least, that's the way I am. I want to be a person that I do whatever I can do for you."

"Where does that come from?" I asked her. "With all the things that you've had to do—raising eight children, working those jobs, taking care of your husband. How do you have the time to even think about doing anything for anybody else?"

She looked up at me and said quietly, "Every morning, before I get out of bed, I say: 'Order my steps in your word, Lord; and let not any iniquity have dominion over me.' That's the Hundred-and-Nineteenth, Number One-Thirty-Three." She paused to let the words sink in. "And it makes me feel like if I walk in His words, His word's not going down. So, you know, I want to do some of the things that I am able to do to please the Lord. And I feel like that's where my source of strength comes from."

PINE BLUFF, ARKANSAS

ABOUT AN HOUR LATER, after Lynn had brought me back to Community Renewal, I was back on the road. It was quarter to five and raining again.

There was no direct route from Shreveport to Pine Bluff, Arkansas, so I decided to go north up US 71 to Texarkana, pick up Interstate 30 there, and then get on US 270 East to Pine Bluff.

Almost immediately after I got out of Shreveport and onto Highway 71, the landscape emptied out. No buildings, no traffic lights—nothing. Just miles and miles of flat empty fields. Not much traffic either.

Every so often, I noticed a small wooden cross by the side of the road—sometimes several crosses clustered together. I used to see them in Florida, marking the places where people had been killed in car accidents. Occasionally somebody had left flowers beside a cross.

There were a few small towns—Dixie, Belcher, Gilliam—but really they were just signs on the road, with maybe a few weathered houses scattered here and there. Mostly the land was empty and bleak. Suddenly a huge cloud of black birds erupted in front of me, filling the dark gray sky just ahead. The rain intensified, hammering at my windshield.

Gradually, as the last of the daylight faded, the land became hillier, and the highway began to twist its way through the hills. I wound up behind two eighteen wheelers and decided to stay behind them rather than risk adding another cross to the roadside.

I had dinner in Texarkana on the Texas state line at a place called Cattlemen's Restaurant, where I treated myself to a T-bone steak—something that I'd been thinking about ever since my visit with Miss Margaret.

While I waited for my steak, I noticed a big group across the room—almost all women—who appeared to be having a company dinner of some kind. Everyone was chattering happily until a woman in a red dress at the head of the table tapped her water glass with a spoon and said that she had a few announcements that she wanted to share with everybody about some "very exciting changes" they were going to be making at the company over the next few weeks.

It was like a big black thunderhead had suddenly blotted out the sun. Nobody said a word as the woman started describing the changes, which of course included cutbacks, and even I—a complete stranger—lost my appetite.

When I woke up in the Comfort Inn on the outskirts of Pine Bluff the next morning, I almost wished that I hadn't included the town in my itinerary. It was the seventh town in less than two weeks, and I was tired, especially after three days of wall-to-wall interviews in New Roads and Shreveport. Moreover, the program here was still just getting off the ground, and Annette Dove, Pine Bluff's Faith in Action director, had warned me when I'd called her that it was "struggling."

Was it going to be another West Helena?

Outside, the sky was still a dismal gray, and the temperature must have dropped at least twenty degrees overnight. A blast of cold wind almost knocked me off my feet as I made my way across the icy motel parking lot to my car. Looking around, I realized that the motel was out in the middle of a big open field with no trees or anything else to shield it from the wind. I later learned that Pine Bluff was in fact perched on the far western edge of the Arkansas side of the Mississippi delta, which explained the flat terrain.

Pine Bluff, it turned out, was also bayou country. Following Annette's directions to her office in town, I crossed Imbeau Bayou and Bartholomew Bayou. A solitary blue heron stood motionless along the edge of Bartholomew Bayou, no doubt miserable in the cold.

I found Annette's office on Second Avenue easily enough, but at first I thought I must have gotten the street address wrong: it was a small frame house with an unfinished front porch and big patches of bare insulation where the siding was missing. Was I supposed to be on Second Street instead of Second Avenue? But I was reading from the directions that she had e-mailed me, so I knew that this had to be it.

The rest of the neighborhood was no great shakes either. A green metal sign just down the street stated, JUVENILE CURFEW HOURS. SUN-THUR 11:00 PM TO 5 AM. FRI-SAT 1:00 AM TO 5:00 AM. DAYTIME CURFEW: NORMAL SCHOOL HOURS.

It was only eight o'clock, so I still had plenty of time for breakfast before meeting Annette at 9:30. I picked a place nearby called Phyllis & Eddie's Family Diner, which promised "Good Food, Good Service, Family Oriented."

In contrast to Nicole's Café in West Helena, where everyone had been white, everyone at Phyllis and Eddie's was black. I ordered the same breakfast that I'd had at Nicole's—ham and eggs, grits, biscuits, and coffee—and it was just as good, especially the biscuits. But the conversation was livelier. First, it was the high school football team:

"Four losing seasons in a row—that's terrible."

"Ain't it though? With eighty-two kids on a team, you'd think you could find eleven of 'em that could play."

"And with more than fifty thousand people living in this town, you'd think you could find one that could coach."

"Amen, brother."

Then it was on to hunting:

"When I was stationed over at Fort Hood in Texas, we used to go out and hunt jack rabbit all the time."

"I like rabbit. I used to have a pet rabbit and I ate it. In fact, I had a pet chicken and I ate that too."

"Come to think of it, I ain't seen your dog around lately neither."

Annette

Annette was waiting for me when I arrived. "Come on in," she said brightly. "Excuse the mess."

Direct in her speech and dressed in a businesslike skirt and sweater outfit with a matching black jacket, Annette struck me as someone who was used to getting things done. We sat down in what she told me was her temporary office: a desk, a phone, a fax machine, a computer, a couple of chairs, and bare white walls. Her permanent office, across the hall, was still being worked on, she said.

"Are you from Pine Bluff?" I asked her.

"Born and raised," she replied. "In fact, this is the neighborhood I grew up in. My mom and dad grew up right across the street. Both of them are deceased now, but they were business owners. I was the rebel child.

"I left home at sixteen and got married—thought I was grown. But I had some problems there. So I went back to work, went to school at night to finish my education, and started teaching."

Annette taught school for the next twelve years and then decided that she wanted to move up into administration. But every time she applied for an administrative position, she was turned down.

"Finally, they had an opening in a program called HIPPY"—Home Instruction for Parents of Preschool Youngsters. "My superintendent asked if I would consider it, and I said, 'No, I don't want that. I want to be a principal.' I was looking at the status of it, you know. And he said, 'Well, I would like for you to try this program.' And he guaranteed me that if I didn't like it, I could come back out. Well, I started working with families, going into homes in the community—and that was my love. I just loved it.

"And you know, the youth director at our church, he worked with a lot of gang members. So my husband and I would just bring them home and work with them at our home and just do different things. And then when I became the youth director, we started programs in the community with the gang members. We got a lot of opposition about bringing so many kids into the church."

"They didn't like these kids?"

"They sure didn't. Anyhow, we traveled around the country. We went and did fundraisers to make sure that they would have an opportunity to get out of town and do some things—trying to keep them off the streets, you know."

I thought of the curfew sign.

"They were really more like my children," Annette said. "They'd call me any time of night if they got into trouble. And my husband—my second husband—he was a parole officer.

"So then," she went on, "I guess it was about four years ago, I've said that it was the Good Lord that told me: 'It's time to go back to your community.' And even though I was doing HIPPY and I was traveling around the country setting up programs for our national office and I loved my job, I told my husband, I said: 'It's time for me to go back to our community and do some things.' And then three years ago, my husband died."

"Oh, no."

"And I told the Lord, 'I can't afford to quit my job now.' It took both of us to live then, and I knew I couldn't. But it just stayed on my heart that it was time to give up my job and go back. So that's what I did. I quit my job, bought this old house—it didn't even have any floors or any walls or anything—and I renovated it."

Along the way, while running a training session for volunteers at a local agency, Annette heard about Faith in Action and applied for a grant.

"It was really kind of strange," she said. "We received a notice that we'd been awarded the grant and that the check had been sent to our treasurer. But he had never opened the mail. So it stayed there about a month. And so when I finally got this letter about the check, I said, 'What check? I never did get a check.' So I called him and asked him, and he said, 'I believe I did receive some mail from Faith in Action.' So he went and opened it, and he said, 'Annette, the check is sitting here—for twenty-five thousand dollars.'" She burst out laughing.

That was just this past July, she said. So she had called a meeting of her board to get everybody behind the program and had held the first training session for her Faith in Action volunteers in August. "We had like eighteen young people at that training," she said. By the end of September, they had started providing services. "Of course, we're not where I know we can be."

"You're just getting started," I said.

"The program that I ran for HIPPY, we served nine hundred families," she said. "As a matter of fact, I had the second-largest program in the United States. So I know how to run a program."

We went over my schedule for the rest of the day, and then Annette gave me a quick tour of the rest of the house. She showed me some pictures of what it had looked like when she'd first bought it—basically, a dilapidated shack.

"You've come a long way," I said.

"A long way," she agreed. "And people have just volunteered and helped and donated their services. So I'm pleased with what we're trying to do in the community. There is such a great need here in Pine Bluff. The poverty is just unbelievable. And it just hurts my heart to see the elderly. You know, trying to walk to the store on their own when they can't hardly walk."

As she took me from room to room, Annette told me how her former employees from HIPPY had bought the carpeting, the bank had donated the furniture, somebody else had donated the windows; somebody had even donated a chandelier. "I told him, 'I don't need a chandelier. I just want to work. But he said, 'No, you need a chandelier.'"

One of the rooms was going to be for the youth coordinator, she said. "He's real good. He's an ex-gang member. I worked with him when I was at the church. He can recruit kids left and right. He also does our meal delivery."

"What's his name?"

"Rodney. You're going to meet him later. He's a nice young man. But he's got diabetes real bad."

"At that age?"

"Um-hm. One day this week I had to go and do the meal delivery because he couldn't get out of the bed. But he's a joy. Knows everybody. And you're going to visit with his mother too. His mother had a leg amputation."

"So diabetes runs in the family?"

"That's right," Annette said. "Can't see, either. I've been working with that situation. But it's just one of those things, you know."

Betty

"So who are we going to see next?" I asked Annette later that morning as we were driving through the neighborhood. I had already interviewed Reverend Breamsey, the enthusiastic chairman of Annette's board and pastor of the First Baptist Dew Drop Church on North Bryant Street, and we'd just finished meeting with Miss Bea, a friendly elderly woman, almost deaf, who was receiving help from the program.

"We're going to see Betty," Annette replied. "Rodney's mother. And I don't know if she's going to be as friendly as Miss Bea."

Annette pulled her car into a dirt driveway between a hopelessly dilapidated house and an almost equally ravaged mobile home. The house had once been painted gray, but most of the paint had long since peeled off. All the windows were shattered—some of them boarded up—and there was junk everywhere: a broken toilet, two rusted lawn mowers, broken chairs, even a faded beach umbrella. The mobile home at least had its windows intact.

"Now let me just tell you a little about the situation before we go in," Annette said as we got out of the car.

"Is she in the trailer or in the house?"

"The trailer. But she's the one I was telling you about earlier that had her leg amputated because of diabetes. She's younger than Miss Bea— probably in her fifties—and Rodney lives with her. He didn't use to live here, but he moved in last week. I had worked out the paperwork so that her daughter would get paid to take care of her. But after we did that—I don't know, there was something between her and the daughter, and the daughter left. So that left Betty here by herself—with her little grandchild. And she's not able . . . Like I told you, she can't really see, so she can't call. . ."

"Because she can't read the numbers to dial?"

"That's right," Annette said. "So that's why Rodney moved in."

"Hey, Betty, it's me," Annette called, opening the front door to the trailer partway. "Can we come in?"

"Sure," said a voice from inside. It was utterly lifeless.

The rusty hinges screamed as Annette pushed the door open the rest of the way and we went inside.

Betty sat listlessly in a wheelchair by the kitchen counter wearing nothing but a faded blue nightgown. Her one foot was bare and her hair was pulled back with a rubber band. Her eyes were half shut, as if she were seriously overmedicated, and there was an open bag of potato chips on the counter in front of her. She seemed to be staring at the big-screen television that dominated the living room area. It was tuned to a cartoon.

"This is Doctor Paul," Annette said.

"Good morning," I said brightly. "How are you?"

She didn't respond.

"Betty," Annette said, "he just wants to ask you a few questions about some of the things we've done with you, if that's okay."

Again she didn't respond.

"So Betty, how are you feeling today?" I asked her.

Not a word.

"Yesterday you told me you weren't feeling too good," Annette said after a moment. "You doing any better today?"

"A little," Betty muttered.

"So Betty," I said, still trying to proceed as if this were a normal conversation, "how are you going to spend today? What do you have planned?"

"Nothing."

I was at a loss.

"You talk to Nina yesterday?" Annette asked, coming to my rescue.

"That the one that called?" Betty asked.

"That's right," Annette said.

"I talked to her."

"Did you like her?"

Silence, except for the television.

Annette tried again. "How about you tell him about some of the things I did to help you get started?" she said.

There was another long pause, and then Betty spoke: "She helped me work on paperwork for a program where somebody'll do work for you in the home."

"That's good," I said. "You have trouble seeing, don't you, Betty?"

"Right now, I can't see nothing."

"And I understand that you're taking care of your grandchild?"

"Yeah," she muttered. "He stays here."

"How old is he?"

"Four."

"Four?" I said. "He must be quite a handful. Does he behave pretty well?"

"Sometimes."

More silence. The cartoons had ended, replaced by a medical soap opera of some kind, and despite her apparent inability to see, Betty's blank gaze was still fixed on the TV screen.

"Betty," Annette said, "did Rodney say he's going to get a meal delivered for you today?"

"Rodney didn't say nothing," Betty said.

"Well, I need to find out," Annette said. "So I can make sure we get you a meal. What do you have a taste for?"

"That's the problem. I don't *have* a taste right now."

"I'll tell you what," Annette said crisply. "I'll get some lunch here for you in a few minutes. Or I might send Rodney back with it, okay?"

"Okay."

Annette got on her cell phone, presumably for somebody to bring Betty lunch.

"That's a beautiful television you've got there, Betty," I said, trying to make conversation while Annette was on the phone.

"It cost enough," she said.

"I can believe it."

"I'm fixing to let it go back," she said dully. It didn't sound as if she cared much one way or the other.

Annette snapped her phone shut and slipped it back into her purse. "We've got to be going now, Betty," she said, moving toward the door and motioning for me to follow her. "Somebody'll be bringing you lunch in a few minutes."

"Okay."

"It was nice meeting you," I said as I backed out the door, its hinges screaming again. "And thank you so much for talking to me. You have a good day now, Miss Betty."

"I'll try," she said.

"I can't believe she's taking care of a four year old," I said to Annette once we were back in the car.

"Oh, she was *good* today," Annette said. "But somebody is in and out with that four year old. He's in school during the day, and like I said, Rodney has moved back in there now that his sister has moved out."

"And what's the story on that television?"

"That's not hers," Annette said. "It can't be. Her older daughter's probably the one that bought that. Because, you know, Betty had the two girls living there. The oldest girl left first—she's the one that left this child behind. And that happens a lot, you know what I'm saying?"

Annette went on to tell me that she'd put together a support group for grandparents who were taking care of their grandchildren, which sounded a lot like what Sylvia Forster was running back in Petal.

"It's a bad situation. I was in the support meeting, and this seventy-year-old grandmother was saying that she's afraid to go to sleep. I wondered why, and she said because she had these grandchildren that were out of control—and she was afraid for her life. Now what kind of stuff is that?"

The Family That Prays Together

Over lunch at Leon's Catfish and Shrimp Restaurant, a bustling local institution where she stopped at every other table to say hello, Annette talked about what it had been like growing up in Pine Bluff. Her father-in-law had been head of the local NAACP, and her own family's house had been fire-bombed—although fortunately, she said, nobody had been hurt.

"What happened was, when they got ready to start integrating the schools, my dad and his brothers would take the three blacks that attended. My cousin was one, and Mr. Dove—my father-in-law—had a child, and there was one other child that went. And so my dad would drive the kids up there. And a lot of times they would threaten them."

"This was at a white school?"

"That's right," Annette said. "A lot of times, things that were done were done at night. We were little kids, and we knew we had to run and get under the beds and hide when things were being thrown."

"You must've been terrified."

"Sure. Not knowing what's really happening and all that. But we weren't as bad off as my husband's family. Because, you know, they had crosses burned in their yards and things like that." Annette's voice trailed off.

"So when did all of that end?"

"I remember when we started having a lot of attacks on our house, we had the black college students who began to retaliate," she said. "They began to burn some of the buildings downtown. So the National Guards were called in, and then a lot of that stuff kind of died down—you know what I'm saying?"

I nodded.

"I was young, but I remember all this. We used to ride the bus, but we had to stop riding it, and my dad would take us. It was a safety issue. And then I remember when my brother and I started back on the bus, when we got off the bus, some boys in a car—about four of them—started following us. And I remember my brother telling me to run home. But they got him. And they took him to the cemetery and they beat him."

"Was he badly hurt?"

"He was badly beaten. But you know, that's life. Those are the things you live through. It just bothers me that our kids aren't taught any more about their history—for them to appreciate and to value the opportunity that they have."

I told Annette about the first day of my trip on Martin Luther King Day and how there had been so many families with their children at the Civil Rights Museum.

"That's good," she said, gazing past me. "That's good."

After lunch, we stopped by Lisa's place, Miss Bea's volunteer, but she wasn't home. "That's too bad," Annette said. "She must be out somewhere with the kids."

"How many kids does she have?" I asked.

"Seven. A couple of teenagers, and the other ones are younger."

"How old is Lisa?"

"I'd guess she's about twenty-seven or twenty-eight," Annette said. "And back before she got involved with Faith in Action, she was depressed all the time."

"I can imagine," I said. "I mean, wouldn't *you* be depressed if you were twenty-seven years old and you had to take care of seven kids?"

Annette laughed.

"You're right," she said. "But, you know, she would just cry all the time. And then one day she called me and started with all that when *I* was upset myself, and I said, 'Look, Lisa. Get up and do something for somebody else. Because I don't want to hear it anymore.'"

That, Annette said, was a turning point.

"I really wanted you to meet her because of how she's changing. Like I used to call her cell phone number and I'd get all this rap music and stuff you don't ever want to hear. Now you call it and the message is, 'The family that prays together stays together.'"

"That's wonderful," I said.

"It's small," Annette said. "But it's a change."

Rodney

The wind had picked up again and was rattling the loose ends of the insulation when we got back to the office. The sky was still solid gray, with no sign that the weather would relent any time soon.

According to the schedule that Annette had prepared, I still had a couple of people to talk to this afternoon: Dietrich Jones (home repairs) and Rodney (meal delivery). Neither Rodney nor Mr. Jones had arrived yet, so Annette started returning some of the phone calls that had come in while we'd been gone. After about ten minutes, there was a knock at the front door, and a loose-limbed young man with two gleaming silver front teeth, sleepy eyes, and a black wool cap pulled down over his ears stepped into the room.

"Mr. Rodney!" Annette cried. "How you doing, Mr. Rodney?"

"I'm doing all right," Rodney said, shedding his coat but leaving his cap on. He had a cell phone clipped to his belt and a chain around his neck with a silver pendant hanging from it that looked like a miniature grenade. He walked up to me and shook my hand; his hand was still cold.

"Hi," he mumbled, obviously ill at ease. He slumped into a chair across from me, draping one of his arms over the back and sprawling his legs out in front of him. It didn't look as if he particularly wanted to be here.

"It's nice to finally meet you, Rodney," I said. "Miss Dove has been taking me around the community, meeting with some of the people who are being helped by the program, and your name keeps coming up."

Rodney chuckled softly. "I don't know why."

"They say that you've been delivering a lot of meals to the elderly."

"That's true," he said.

When I asked him to tell me a little bit about himself, he said that he was born here in Pine Bluff in 1975, that he was twenty-eight years old now, and that he had three sisters and three brothers.

"And what was it like growing up here?"

"Well," he said in a sleepy drawl, "I've always been involved in the community doing something. Helping some elderly person mostly. You know, cut their yard, paint their house—anything like that."

"How come?"

"You know, I really don't even know. I guess because I'm the only one they would let come in their yard. I guess because of my personality. You know, I would talk to people, and they would say, 'Can you help me with this?' You know, with the elderly folks, their kids was already grown and moved out of town or whatever, so there was nobody there to give them any help."

Curious, I asked him, "How come you haven't moved out of town?"

Rodney looked down at the floor. "I ain't got nowhere to go."

"Did you ever want to leave? Or do you like it here?"

"Well, it ain't that I like it," he muttered. "You know, it's just home, you know what I'm saying?"

"Well, you could've joined the service, right?"

"Oh, no," he said, shaking his head.

"You didn't want to do that?"

"No," he said. "It's just . . . I guess on account of my mom being here, you know what I'm saying? I didn't want to move. I could have, you know, but I chose not to."

I told Rodney that Annette had taken me out that morning to visit his mother and that I understood that he was helping to take care of her.

"I do a little something," he replied. "You know, me and my sister. . . . Everybody just does what they can, you understand? My mom's on that program where my sister takes care of her—she'll cook for her and clean and take her where she's got to go. So basically, I just help on the outside. And like I took the CNA class to be a certified nursing assistant just in case she gets real sick and she needs a nursing assistant. I took that about five years ago so that I'd know what to do for her."

"Speaking of taking classes," I said, "did you finish high school?"

"No," he muttered. "I didn't finish high school."

"How far did you go?"

"To the eleventh."

"So you almost finished."

"Yeah," he said. "But we're going to start the GED program here in this office, and I am going to take that class myself, you know. And I'm going to get all my friends that didn't graduate. Because I've been talking to them, and they've been like, 'We're ready.' You know, basically the problem is we don't want to sit in class for four or five hours. But if you can do it in two hours, it'll be all right. They're willing to do that."

I remembered that Annette had mentioned that Rodney was a former gang member, and I was trying to figure out how to bring up the subject tactfully.

"Now I understand that you've made some big changes in your life," I said.

Rodney didn't respond. He just looked at me.

"Is that right?" I asked. "I mean, when you started getting involved with the volunteering and everything—was that a big change for you?"

He broke into a grin. "Keeps me out of trouble," he said.

Annette laughed.

"So why did you decide to make that change?" I asked him.

"Well," he said, "as you get older, you get wiser in making decisions, you know."

"Did something happen that made you decide to change your mind? I mean something in your life?"

"Yeah," he said. "I got real sick. Back then, I couldn't hardly walk. I had to have a cane. Today, God's forgiven me for what I did. I said, 'If you bring me out of this, I'll, you know . . . '"

"So you cut a deal with God?" I asked. "You said, 'You get me out of this, and I'll change my life'? Is that how it went?"

"Yeah," Rodney said. "That's how it went."

"Rodney," Annette said, "tell him about working with the youth department and the time that we have spent with the youth."

"Oh," he groaned. "Well, we developed basketball teams, you know, and then I got the boys out there, and the clergy. And we won the championship twice."

"That's terrific!"

"And the boys that we had, all of them had problems, you know," he added. "But we got them to where they was coming to church and making new friends, and most of them got it together, you know what I'm saying?"

"And you did that?"

"Me, Miss Dove, everybody. It was like a group thing, you know, where everybody'd come together. I had a part where I'd say, 'Okay, y'all come.' And they had a part where it was, 'And we'll keep you.' So we developed that and it was nice. The two years that we actually had it, it was real nice."

I asked Rodney why it had ended.

"Like they say, times have changed real hard," he said. "It's hard to get a list of team players. You can *get* them, but most of them get locked up in the juvenile jail, so it's hard to get *to* them, you know."

Annette broke in to tell me that Mr. Dietrich Jones had arrived and that he had only a few minutes because he had to get back to work. So I apologized to Rodney and asked him if we could continue our conversation after I had talked with Mr. Jones. He seemed relieved and said that would be fine.

Mr. Jones, it turned out, was a barber. In fact, he said, his customers at the shop were waiting for him to come back, so I kept the interview to a bare minimum. The gist of it was that in addition to cutting hair, Mr. Jones was an active member of the Southeast Arkansas Male Chorus, an interdenominational Gospel group that had branched out beyond singing to begin doing good works, including helping some of the elderly folks who were being served by Faith in Action.

"What do you do to help them?" I asked.

"Oh, you know," he said. "Painting their houses, keeping their yards cut—things like that. And we give 'em box fans. Maybe air-conditioners too."

I asked him whether, as a barber, he had a pretty good sense of what was going on in the community.

"Oh, yeah," he smiled. "You hear it all."

But when I asked him to be more specific, Mr. Jones looked at his watch and said he had to be going. "I told 'em I'd be back in fifteen minutes," he said as he headed out the door. "And I can't keep 'em waiting no longer."

After Mr. Jones left, Annette told me that her husband had been a member of the chorus, and that now they were represented on her board. "Anything I need done, they'll do it. Just last week, we had a family that got burnt out, and they needed some money to get into a place. So I called them on the phone, and they wrote a check."

"Just like that?"

"Just like that."

When Rodney came back to the office a few minutes later, I asked him how much time he put in as a volunteer.

"I'm in and out," he said.

"It seems like you put in a lot of hours," I said.

"I guess."

"So why do you keep doing it?"

"I don't really know," he said. "I guess maybe so that some day, I'll be able to start my own program. I always really wanted to be able to help people anyway. But, you know, I ain't never been in a predicament where I can."

"He doesn't realize, you know," Annette said to me. "During the summer months when we bring the kids in to the activities at church, he'll go out and collect hundreds of kids."

"Is that right?"

"I mean, people say, 'Just give it to Rodney, and tell him how many busloads you want.' And he'll come back with three busloads of kids. That's 130 or 140 kids. I've told him he'd make a good politician because he can convince anybody to do something."

Rodney grimaced.

"Tell me a little bit about the neighborhood," I said to Rodney. "Has it changed since you were growing up?"

"Yeah," he said. "It's changed a lot."

"In what way?"

"Most everybody I know moved," he said. "But I mean, you know, the kids. . . . It's a shame, because when we were growing up, we had people like Miss Dove who'd come and help out. You could call them up if you needed help or something like that. But you see, now these kids, they ain't got nobody really like we had."

"Well, aren't they calling you?" I asked.

"They call me, but . . . I can't take care of them like *that*," he said, trying to explain. "I can help them out, but I'm saying it ain't like, 'Miss Dove, can you come and get me out?' They don't have that."

Annette laughed.

"Because most of their parents is like on drugs and stuff," Rodney continued. "So it ain't like it was when I was growing up. You know, we'd probably have one parent on drugs. But these days they got both parents on drugs, and grandma on drugs too. And it's really hard, you know. Because like in my neighborhood, there's three or four boys, they'll be out every night. And the reason they'll be out is because they got nowhere to stay.

"They don't know where their folks are at. And like this one boy, I know he ain't got no place to stay, and he'll just be sleeping in cars and stuff. And I'll be wanting to let him stay with me, but you know, I'm at my mom's. So he really can't stay with me. But I'll be like, 'You can sleep in my car, man.'"

Rodney continued, the anguished words pouring out now. "But it's hard, you know, because they ain't got nowhere to stay. They got nowhere to go. They got no water to take a bath. It's stuff like that. When my mom ain't there, I'll tell them, 'Come on in, and take a bath.' But it really hurts to look at them because, you know, they're your friends. And they ain't got nothing."

I asked him what kinds of drugs were out there now.

"Oh," he said, "crystal meth, crystal, acid, crack, weed, ecstasy . . ."

"So it's all still out there?"

"Yeah, it's all still out there," he said despondently. "It ain't going nowhere. It won't never go nowhere. When we're gone, it'll be out there. They won't never get rid of that."

He shook his head. "But it's just rough, you know. It gets so bad when they have to steal. And then if they got kids, they're selling their games and their TVs. And then they can't feed the kids—and that is really rough. That's why they steal. You know, and that's why the kids steal: because they ain't got nothing to eat. So it's a big problem out there. And I can't do nothing about it. I mean, I can help somebody—but I can't fix the problem, you know what I'm saying?"

"Well, it seems like you're doing a lot to try to help," I said.

"I try," he said. "But like I said, I can't do it by myself. If I help you, who's going to help the other person? Because I can't help you *and* the other person, you know? You know, you might not have no lights, and she might not have no water. And the kids are suffering real bad."

I nodded.

"So that's the problem out there," Rodney said. "Like right now, I got one boy, I pick him up from his house and bring him over here. You know, he stays with his mom—he stays with her, but he ain't got nothing. He'll be hungry, but that's all: he's just hungry. You can see it in his eyes. Because I know where my next meal is coming from, but he don't know where his next meal is coming from. And so if you go out and buy you something to eat, and if he's with you, if you was fixing to get two hamburgers, you give him one and you get one. When I was that age, I always did something to keep a little change in my pocket. I'd rake leaves or something, you know."

"Sure."

"But, you know, people don't want them coming in their yards. Because they don't trust them. When I was growing up, there was a lot of kids in the neighborhood, but I was like the only one they would let in their yards. They'd have locks on the gates. And they'd say, 'Okay, Rodney, you can come in. But your friend can't come in.' And that really hurt me, because I'm like, 'My friend really want to come.'"

"But they didn't trust him?"

"That's right. And they really don't trust them now. Because they know they ain't got nothing. And if you ain't got nothing, what are you going to do? You're going to take it."

"Right."

"But if we could get them jobs. . . ." Rodney paused. "See, the basic thing is, a person, when they steal, it's because they ain't got no money. They ain't got no money. But if they had a job, you wouldn't have to worry about them being in the streets. You wouldn't have to worry about them stealing. And you wouldn't have to worry about no police being called—because they're doing something to occupy their minds."

PART FOUR

ALASKA

NORTH TO ALASKA

I HAD BEEN TO NEW ENGLAND; I had been to the Deep South. Where to next? Probably somewhere out west for geographical balance. I thought about Los Angeles or San Francisco, or maybe Seattle.

And then there was Alaska. The last frontier.

There weren't a lot of Faith in Action programs up there, but there were some: four, to be precise. I was tempted. I'd never been there. In fact, Alaska was one of only two states that I had never visited (the other was Hawaii).

Then, out of the blue, came a totally unexpected factor that clinched it for me. In order to find out whether there was enough going on at the four Alaska-based programs to make it worth the trip up there, I decided to call Paula McCarron, who was listed as the director of the Faith in Action program in Anchorage. I figured that because Anchorage was the biggest city in the state and more or less centrally located, she would be the person most likely to know what, if anything, was going on in the other three programs, as well as her own.

The good news, she said when I reached her, was that all four programs were going strong, including hers. The bad news was that in a few weeks, she was moving to Florida. But she assured me that an interim director would be in place when she left, and in the meantime, the hospital where her program was based was already actively recruiting a permanent replacement. "So by all means, come on up," she said. "By the way, do you mind if I ask you a question?"

"Go ahead."

"Do you happen to know a gentleman by name of George Mohr?"

"Sure do," I said. "He's my grandfather's cousin—sort of my great uncle."

"Well," Paula said, "he's being served by our Faith in Action program here in Anchorage."

"You're kidding!"

"He's a wonderful man. One of our favorite clients."

"But how on earth did you make the connection?" I asked.

The fact is, I barely knew George Mohr. I knew that, like my grandfather, he was originally from Vienna, that he had moved to Anchorage long ago, and that my brother and my father had both visited him up there. But I remembered meeting him only once myself, back in the late 1970s when Susie and I were living in Tampa and he'd had a stopover at the Tampa airport. I remembered liking him, but I hadn't talked to him since that brief encounter almost thirty years ago.

"Well," Paula replied, "his volunteer is a retired nurse by the name of Loralee Willis. And one day when she was visiting him, she was wearing her Faith in Action pin. Well, he saw the pin, and he told her that he thought somebody in his family—a man by the name of Paul Jellinek—was involved with Faith in Action. So she told me about it, and then when I got the message that you had called, I decided I just had to ask you."

How in heaven's name, I wondered, had George known about my connection to Faith in Action? The only thing I could figure was that my father must have mentioned it to him somewhere along the line, and that somehow he had remembered the name.

Coincidence or fate?

It didn't matter. Whatever the explanation, I decided there and then that my next trip for the book would be to Alaska—and that the first person I would interview when I got there would have to be George.

Although there were only four Faith in Action programs operating in Alaska, working out the logistics for this trip turned out to be more complicated than the planning for the first two trips combined. In fact, in the end, after a lot of hours on the phone and on the Web, I realized that on a two-week trip, I would have time to visit only three of the four programs. The main reason was Alaska's sheer size—about a fifth the size of the entire United States. Also, there aren't a lot of roads, and there are vast mountain ranges, giant glaciers, and lots of islands that make getting from one place to another much more complicated than it is in the Lower Forty-Eight.

I could have flown from one place to another, which is what most of the people I talked to recommended. But I decided to drive. Although I would certainly fly *to* Alaska, once I got there I wanted to have my own wheels, just as in New England and the South. I wanted to see Alaska from the ground, and I wanted to be able to visit people in their homes without having to impose on the local Faith in Action directors to chauffeur me around.

However, there was a price: time. Two of Alaska's four Faith in Action programs—the one in Haines and the one in Sitka—were located in the southeastern part of the state on the Inside Passage, a long island-studded waterway that runs between British Columbia and the Pacific Ocean. And while there were roads that I could take to get from Anchorage to Haines, the only way to get a car from Haines to Sitka was by ferry. The ferry, I discovered, stopped in Sitka only twice a week, and it took eighteen hours to get from Haines to Sitka.

Moreover, although there were roads that could take me from Anchorage to Haines, there were also several enormous mountain ranges between Anchorage and Haines, which meant that I would have to drive north of the mountains and cut through part of the Yukon to get around them—probably a two-day drive, I was told.

Then once I got to Sitka, the only way to get the car back to Anchorage would be to retrace my steps—in other words, another very long ferry ride back to Haines, followed by another two-day road trip from Haines to Anchorage. I did ask Avis what it would cost me if I wanted to leave the car in Sitka and just fly back to Anchorage, but the girl on the phone just laughed. "You might as well buy the car," she said.

I left for Alaska on July 13, almost six months after my trip to the South. Susie asked me that morning whether I was excited about the trip. And while I had expected that I would be, the truth is that I didn't feel much of anything. After all of the planning and preparation of the past few months, the trip itself seemed like just one more step in the process.

But at least I was ready. I had booked my flight, reserved my car, made my ferry reservations on the Alaska Marine Highway, and booked my rooms at all of the bed-and-breakfasts where I would be staying.

In fact, I was pretty sure that I had thought of everything this time—clothes, tickets, reservation and contact information, maps, the Western Canada and Alaska Triple-A book, camera, cell phone, cell phone chargers, tapes, film, batteries, books, CDs, even a spare pair of glasses—until I got to the security gate at the airport, and they were telling us to take off our shoes and our belts before going through the metal detector. Sure enough, I had forgotten my belt. So much for three months of planning.

Fortunately, there was a high-end men's clothing store conveniently located at the airport where I was able to buy myself a perfectly adequate new belt for only about twice what I would have paid for it in the real world.

The flight was uneventful until the end, when the pilot announced that we were starting into our descent. "Folks," he said, "those of you on the

left-hand side of the jet might want to take a look out your windows."
Luckily, I had a window seat on the left-hand side.

First came a sprawling archipelago of densely forested islands; then, on
what appeared to be the mainland, row after row of snow-covered mountains leading right up to the edge of the sea, each laced with fine silver
threads that, as we got closer, turned out to be furious whitewater rivers
and crashing waterfalls. Then more snow—an immense glittering expanse
of snow and ice studded with raw black mountain peaks that dwarfed any
other mountains I had ever seen.

So this was Alaska. At last, I really was excited.

ANCHORAGE, ALASKA

IT WAS 8:18 P.M. Alaska time when we touched down—eighteen minutes after midnight for me. But outside on the runway, it looked more like
two o'clock in the afternoon. Although Anchorage lay about 350 miles
south of the Arctic Circle, sunset on July 13 wasn't until 11:21. Not quite
the midnight sun, but almost.

My rental car this time turned out to be a brand-new silver Nissan
Sentra—so new that it didn't yet have a license plate, just a paper license
taped to the rear window. The woman at the Avis desk had told me to
check for dents before leaving the lot. "If there's any dents bigger than a
golf ball, let me know."

The Oscar Gill House, the bed-and-breakfast where I would be staying
in Anchorage, was teeming with flowers: flowers in wooden tubs out in
front by the sidewalk, flowered vines on the wrought-iron fence, big pots
of flowers on the porch steps, hanging baskets overflowing with flowers,
window boxes full of flowers hanging from every window ledge—reds,
whites, oranges, violets, yellows—each color taking on an iridescent glow
in the pale northern summer light. A woman in a green dress stepped out
the front door and waved. "Are you Paul?" she called.

"Sure am," I said. "You must be Susan Lutz."

"How'd you guess?"

Susan and I had talked a couple of times by phone and had exchanged
e-mails when I arranged my stay. I followed her inside through a small
foyer hung with walrus tusks, native prints, and a framed poster for the
movie *North to Alaska,* starring John Wayne and Fabian.

Susan turned out to be quite a talker. Within minutes I learned that she
and her husband, Mark, had originally come from Oregon; that Mark had
been a conscientious objector during the Vietnam War; and that they had
moved to Alaska at that time in order to do social work—"back when

social work was *real* social work." Then she told me which room I'd be staying in, gave me the key, and told me that if I still wanted dinner, there was a restaurant within easy walking distance that was open until eleven. You could eat at the bar, she added, and they had a great view of Knik Arm (which turned out to be a body of water).

I woke up at 3:30 A.M. local time, just four hours after I'd turned off the light. My body was still on Eastern Standard Time. After spending a futile half-hour desperately trying to fall back asleep, I gave up, switched on the light, and started reading Jonathan Raban's *Passage to Juneau,* about a sailing trip he had taken a few years earlier from Seattle up through the Inside Passage to Juneau. My ferry would be stopping in Juneau for a few hours on the way from Haines down to Sitka, so in a sense, our paths would cross. Eventually, as Raban drifted up the Puget Sound in his sailboat, I drifted back to sleep for another hour or two.

Breakfast at the Oscar Gill House—as at most other bed-and-breakfasts— was a communal affair, and I was joined by a friendly retired couple from Ontario and a single mother with two jet-lagged teenage sons from Buffalo. The mother, who played the saxophone and taught music in the Buffalo public schools, was taking her boys to Denali National Park. The retired couple—Don and Audrey—were in the middle of a long-awaited road trip across Canada's immense northern territories and Alaska.

"What's been the biggest surprise on your trip so far?" I asked them.

"Just the sheer beauty," Audrey said without hesitation. "Some of those mountains . . ." She shook her head.

"There was this one stretch of road," Don added, "with the red fireweed growing in the ditches on both sides. Just this incredible red border as far as you could see in both directions."

"Mauve," Audrey said. "It wasn't red; it was mauve."

Don shrugged. "Looked red to me."

"You do have to watch out for the moose though," Audrey warned me. "Tell him about the moose, Don."

On the road down from Eagle, Don said, they had spotted something black and shiny in a ditch up ahead. It turned out to be a brand-new SUV. "Then when we got closer, we saw a moose in the ditch on the other side of the road. The people in the SUV were okay, thank God. They had their seat belts on. But the SUV was totaled—and so was the moose."

Linda Shepard had just been hired two weeks ago to replace Paula McCarron as Anchorage's Faith in Action director. A slim woman wearing a small silver cross around her neck, Linda was an experienced home health and hospice nurse who had moved up to Alaska from her native Wisconsin in 1988 when her husband, who'd been in the military at that time, had been stationed in Fairbanks. He was a state trooper now, and they had been in Anchorage for several years. Linda said that she had been attracted to Providence Hospital by its mission and to the Faith in Action job by the name. "That's what I want to do," she said. "Put my faith into action." She was employed by the hospital and was working on Faith in Action full time.

I was impressed. "You mean the hospital fully funds your program?"

"That's right."

I told Linda how unusual that was, and how fortunate for her—not only in terms of her job security, but because it meant that she could devote all her time to the program instead of fundraising. What I didn't say was that it probably also made financial sense for the hospital itself, since patients who needed the kind of in-home support that the Faith in Action volunteers provided could be discharged that much sooner.

My schedule for this first day was simple. I would be meeting with George Mohr at 10:30, and then that afternoon, at about 2:30, I would meet with Loralee Willis, George's volunteer who had worn the Faith in Action pin that had triggered this whole trip. She lived in the same apartment complex as George, which made it easy for me. Then that evening at seven, Linda said, she had scheduled an open house back at the hospital for anyone who might be interested in becoming involved the program. Would I be willing to come and talk about Faith in Action—maybe share a few inspirational stories?

"Of course," I said. "I'd be happy to."

That was the right answer, because Linda had already placed an announcement in the local paper four days before saying that I would be there to "share inspirational stories of the people and lives that are touched by Faith in Action."

George

I was stunned when George opened the door. He looked like my grandfather's twin—except about a foot taller. The same laughing eyes, the same protuberant nose, the same set of his jaw. Even his baldness was the same as my grandfather's, with the identical white fringe that stuck out in small tufts behind his ears like the crest of a snowy egret. The effect was all the more striking because it had been twenty years since I had last seen my grandfather. It was almost as if my grandfather had suddenly come back to life.

"Come in, come in," George beamed.

After more than fifty years in this country, George's English was considerably better than my grandfather's had been, but his Viennese accent was still every bit as strong.

"You just missed Janet," he said. "She was here until yesterday, but she had to fly back to California."

Janet was George's daughter—his only child—and I had had a long telephone conversation with her a few weeks before about my upcoming visit with her father. She had warned me that her father's health had been declining steadily over the past year and that she wasn't sure what his condition would be by the time I got to Anchorage.

Janet had left behind a bundle of maps and other information about Alaska for me, which George dutifully handed over. George and I sat down on a tan sofa by the window. Bookcases lined the walls, and a low wooden table in front of the sofa was strewn with recent issues of *Newsweek* and the *New Yorker*. A big round magnifying glass lay on top of one of the magazines.

Dressed in a sporty blue-and-white checked shirt and sharply creased navy blue pants, he leaned back against the armrest and peered at me.

"So how is Susie?" he asked me.

He remembered that Susie had been with me that evening almost thirty years ago when we had met during his stopover in Tampa. I told him that she was doing fine.

"And your trip?"

My trip was fine too, I told him.

He went on to ask me some fairly detailed questions about our kids, which made it clear to me, first of all, that he was remarkably well informed about my family, and second, that at age ninety, his mind was still plenty sharp.

I knew from my earlier conversation with Janet that the past few years had not been easy for George. Apart from his own declining health, his wife, Nellie—Janet's mother—had Alzheimer's disease, which by now had advanced to the point where George was no longer able to take care of her. Nellie's illness came up when I asked George how he had been matched with Loralee Willis, his Faith in Action volunteer.

"I got picked up for service by Mrs. Willis when my wife got sick," he said. "My wife was very sick with Alzheimer's and is now in an assisted living facility. Mrs. Willis, who was involved with hospice and with Faith in Action, was visiting my wife and was also visiting me. She still does. They are very nice people—Loralee and her husband. And also she is quite mobile, as distinguished from me: I have sunk into almost complete immobility lately. Just last week they told me I have to use a walker."

"How come?"

"I had various operations. I broke my hip and had my hip replaced. I had ankle fractures. But the latest condition was finally identified as being related to my heart, which was starting to act up. I have a leaking valve, which in younger people would be operated on, but with me they say that it's too great a risk. Even if the operation were a success, I wouldn't heal. So I walk very slowly with a walker now. In other words, I'm in a condition in my life now where I have to take every day as it comes along." He sighed and suddenly sounded very fragile.

"And when did things start getting worse?" I asked him.

"Two months ago."

"Oh, so it's very recent."

"Very recent," he said.

I asked George if I could take his picture.

"Sure," he said, brightening a little.

"You know," I said as he pulled himself up and smiled gamely at the camera for me, "you look just like my grandfather."

"You mean Paul?"

"That's right."

"You know he was here in Anchorage once," he said. "He fell into a lake."

"Is that right?"

"You don't know the episode?"

"No."

"He broke through the ice," George said. "And it was important enough in his life that it appeared in his obituary when he died. That he had fallen into an ice lake in Alaska."

I laughed.

"Anyhow," George went on, "he was a delight to talk to. I liked him very much. He was my favorite cousin."

That got him back on the subject of my family, and along the way he asked about our oldest daughter, Lisa, who lived in New York City with her husband.

"What does she think of New York?"

"Oh," I said, "she loves it."

"I'm an exile from New York myself," George said. "I lived in New York for eight years, and then I couldn't stand it any longer. You see, I had a physical disability that made me go north. I had two heat strokes in my life, and they told me that if I had another one, it could be fatal. So they told me to go as far north as I could."

"Which you did."

"That's right," he nodded, smiling faintly.

George asked me to tell him about Faith in Action. "I know the name, but I don't really know what it is," he said. And so I told him some of the history of the program and how it worked.

"And so, Paul," he asked me when I'd finished, "what is the official relationship of Faith in Action toward the Jewish religion?"

"There's no official relationship," I said, a little surprised by his question.

"Can they participate with equal status?"

"Oh, yes," I said. "Absolutely. In fact, there's a synagogue involved in Faith in Action here in Anchorage. There are twelve congregations that participate in the Anchorage program, and one of them is a synagogue."

"We only have one synagogue," he said. "And you say it is already involved?"

I assured him that it was and asked him whether he himself was an active member.

"Yes," George said; then hesitated. "Well, 'active'. . . I actually have very little Jewish religious background. My family was conscious of their Jewishness, but as it was in central Europe before World War I—and before World War II actually, too—it was mostly Zionists and secular Jews. The emphasis was on the hope to return to Palestine, not on the Orthodox religious aspect."

"Let's go back," I said. "I want to go back and talk about *you*, okay?"

"Okay," he said. "Now you can ask your questions."

"Let's start at the beginning," I said. "What year were you born?"

"Nineteen-thirteen," George said.

"So you're actually a lot younger than my grandfather. He was born in 1897, I think."

"That's correct."

"And you were born in Vienna?"

"Yes," he said. "In Hitzing—the Thirteenth District."

"And did you have brothers and sisters?"

"One sister," he said. "Alice."

"And is she still living?"

"Oh, no," he said. "She was a victim of the Holocaust."

"And your parents . . . ?"

"Holocaust." George spit out the word like a poison.

Then he went on. "My father was Viennese. So was my grandfather. My grandfather was a typical easygoing Viennese character of the 1870s and 1880s, which was a very glorious period in the Imperial City."

"And do you have good memories of growing up in Vienna?"

"Mixed," he said, frowning.

"Talk a little about that."

"Well you know, anti-Semitism was growing while I was going to high school. It grew stronger and stronger. It was originally a religious phenomenon; then it went over into an ethnic phenomenon."

I nodded.

"Especially with the success of the Hitler party in Germany, I saw that there was no future for me to stay there. I finished school, and I had originally thought that I would become a lawyer. But when I saw what had happened in Germany, it was completely hopeless as a Jew to try to become a professional. Of course, I didn't realize the severity of what would happen with the Holocaust, but for my own development, I thought that I would probably leave Austria."

I asked George when the anti-Semitism had really started to intensify.

"At the end of the 1920s," he said. "And finally, of course, there was the Anschluss in 1938"—Nazi Germany's annexation of Austria. "But, anyhow, I had integrated very well into my class in the *gymnasium* in Meidling, which was a workers' district of Vienna adjoining Hitzing, where I lived. And it so happened that the relationship was very friendly between me and my classmates. When the graduation year occurred—that was 1931—I was on good terms with all of them."

"So then what happened?"

"I registered in a branch of the Vienna University which was for economics. I wanted to prepare myself for international trade, because I figured that if I left Austria, I would find something if I had an academic degree in economics. I finished the degree in 1934.

"So I got a job in Vienna. By then, already the times were pretty critical. The Nazis—who were an opposition party at that time—committed terror acts. There were bombs and assassinations. As a matter of fact, in the house in Meidling where your great-grandparents lived, there was a bomb explosion. There was a Jewish jeweler in the ground floor, and they were in the upper floor. The bomb killed the jeweler and his employees. It scared your great-grandmother a lot."

I shuddered.

"Anyhow, this company I worked for had knitting factories in rural Austria, and they exported a lot," George said. "They were looking for somebody who could take care of some of their correspondence in English, and I had studied English as a second language in school. So I was qualified for the job. The office was in central Vienna, and that's where I went to work until 1938."

"And what made you decide to leave?" I asked him. "Because a lot of people stayed—including your family." It was a question that I had wondered about for years—not about George specifically but about the Holocaust: Why had some people left, while others had stayed behind?

"They couldn't get a visa," George said.

"How were you able to get one?"

"You want the story? It's about five minutes long."

"Please."

"The Anschluss was in March of 1938," he began. "The racial laws already prevalent in Germany were now being applied to the newly acquired Austrian territory. And so the things that had happened in Germany happened from then on in Austria too—including the increasing violence against the Jews. There was one particular night called the Crystal Night—November 9, 1938."

"In Berlin, right?"

"Not just Berlin. It was all over Austria and Germany. And it hit me. I had just gotten married in September, and Nellie and I were renting two furnished rooms. I was on my way home that night when I noticed a commotion and Nazi SS troops running through the streets breaking windows. Anyway, I came home, and a friend of Nellie's came and said, 'Do you know they are tearing people out of streetcars and breaking windows and destroying the synagogues?' It was a concerted holocaust. Well, hardly had he finished telling us this when there was a pounding on the door, and an SS man came in and arrested me."

"And Nellie?"

"Only the men," George said, his voice barely audible. "They were looking for the men in this large apartment building. There were maybe eight or ten Jewish men. They lined us up on the wall in the entrance lobby of the building and threatened either to shoot us or to take us to Dachau. So I got the idea that I could save myself only with a bluff. I said, 'Who is the commander here?' They pointed him out, and I went up to him and said, 'You want to shoot me or send me to Dachau?'

"He said, 'Yes.'

"I said, 'Now?'

"He said, 'Yes.'

"I said to him, 'You know, I have an appointment for tomorrow morning at the Gestapo headquarters in the Hotel Metropole to discuss willing my total property to the Nazi party as a way to be allowed to leave the country. I have an interview with the SS commander concerning this, and if I don't turn up and they find out that you shot me against the program that was outlined for me . . . Anyway, I have to be there tomorrow, so please leave me off that transport that you are assembling here.'

"And he did," George said. "He was a very primitive person, and I used very vernacular Viennese dialect that sounded like someone who was really Germanized. So he said, 'Okay, you can get the hell out of here.' So I went upstairs to Nellie and said, 'I have to go underground before they find out tomorrow that I used a trick.' So I packed a few things, and the mother of a friend of mine, a Christian in Hitzing—she concealed me."

"Do you know if they ever looked for you?"

"I don't know," George said. "But at that time Nellie already had applied for a visa to England. The only way for people to get out—to get an exit visa and a temporary visa for Britain—was to prove that they had a job."

"Right."

"And in Britain, they were not allowing people to get a visa unless they had a permit from the Department of Labor. Anyway, it was well known in Jewish circles that domestic help was short in England, and that if you said you would like to do domestic labor in England, you could get a job. So Nellie had applied through the consulate, and somebody responded who was a vicar—a clergyman in Cornwall. He was looking for a nanny for his little girls. It seems that his wife had so much parish work to do that she couldn't attend to the children as much as she wanted to."

And so Nellie—who, like George, had studied English in school—got the job and wound up on the outskirts of the Cornish town of Penzance. "So she left," George said. "She got her visa."

"But what about you?"

"I was still stuck in Austria. I had left the shelter of that lady, who had put herself in a very dangerous position by concealing a Jew."

"Sure."

"And so I went back to the apartment from which I had been arrested. That was over, and I could be there. But I had no job, of course, and no income. And I saw no possibility. I didn't know anybody in the United States whom I could immigrate to. Besides, the U.S. immigration quota was blocked because so many people had applied.

"Then I got a letter from my wife after she'd been in that vicarage for a couple of weeks. She said the vicar—a Mr. Hoskins—had asked her if her husband would want to come and join her. And she had told him, 'Well, he can't get a visa.' And he said, 'Well, I know the MP [member of Parliament] for Cornwall very well.' So the MP intervened with the home secretary, and the home secretary ordered the necessary paperwork."

"So you got a personal intervention."

"I got a temporary visa. I remember the wording of it: 'While awaiting immigration into the United States.' I was very much envied by most people that I was able to get a visa."

"I'll bet."

"So when I got my visa, I said good-bye to my parents, and I boarded a train to the English Channel. I arrived in London, and I lived in London for a few weeks. Then the vicar told Nellie to contact me there in London to see whether I wouldn't want to come and live there with her in the vicarage in Cornwall. So I lived in the vicarage in Cornwall for several months, until September 1939."

"And you lived off Nellie's income?"

"I was a house guest. It was a huge vicarage dating from the eighteenth century, and there were rooms there. It was cold, but I was very lucky."

Just then the phone rang.

It was someone named Bonnie.

"She's from Beth Shalom," George explained after he'd hung up. "A group of these ladies from Beth Shalom, when they found out about my own status and Nellie's sickness, they got together and they're giving me rides to see Nellie. Bonnie takes me every Friday."

"So you go to see Nellie every Friday?"

"I try to go more often than that," he said.

Going back to George's story, I said, "I didn't realize you'd actually been arrested."

"Oh, yes."

"It must have been terrifying."

"You know," he said, "the people that did not use a trick like me to bluff the commander of the SS troop—they were never heard of again."

"They disappeared?"

He nodded. "And my own family. I know nothing about my father or my mother. I don't know where they perished." His sister, he said, died in Vienna, and he had found the names of one of his uncles and his uncle's wife in a book that listed all those who had died in Theresienstadt, an SS concentration camp in Czechoslovakia.

"And so was your last contact with your parents when you left for England?"

"Yes," he said. "My father took me to the train, and I knew that it was the last time. Because they were old and not in good health, and so they couldn't get a visa."

George stopped, his eyes closed.

"That must have been very, very difficult," I said.

"You know that your own great-grandmother—your grandfather Paul's mother—she perished in a concentration camp," he said. "But at least I know that your grandfather had some communication from her. I had one letter from my mother after she was deported that came many months after she wrote it, through the Red Cross in America. It was only to say, 'I'm all right,' or something like that."

"So you were in England for how long?" I asked.

"From February 1939 to September."

"Only six months. So you left in 1939."

"There was a steamer from Liverpool to New York. We got the tickets through a Jewish aid organization. We left on the twenty-eighth of August, and on the first of September the Germans invaded Poland."

"Right."

"And Britain declared war," George continued. "So we were on the high seas when the war broke out, and we were told over the loudspeaker that there were German U-boats in the North Atlantic so we would have to take a very northern route. It reminded me of the *Titanic,* which took a northern route.

"Fortunately, we didn't see any icebergs, but we had to sail in complete darkness—a complete blackout. Everybody was unsettled because it was the first day of war, you know. Nothing had been prepared. England was completely unprepared for war.

"Anyway, eventually we landed in Boston, and the newspaper boys came on board with newspapers that said, 'War Breaks Out in Europe: US to Stay Neutral.' So I bought a paper, and under the big headline, it said, 'FDR Declares US Will Sell Weapons But Not Go to War.' I knew, of course, about Roosevelt, but FDR was not an abbreviation that I was familiar with. So I asked the newspaper boy, 'Who is FDR?' And I remember so well the look on his face—that here is another one of those low-caliber immigrants who knows nothing about America. He said, 'He's the president of this country!'"

Although the boat had initially docked in Boston, it continued on to New York, where a cousin of Nellie's, whom she had never met before, lived. It was because of this lucky family connection that George and Nellie had been able to get into the United States at a time when, according to George, there was something like a thirty-year waiting list for those without such connections.

From New York, they had moved to Fall River, Massachusetts, where George worked for several years in the shipping department of a sweater firm that he had had dealings with when he'd worked for the knitting company in Vienna.

Next, they had moved up to Boston. But Boston was no longer the international commercial hub it had once been, and so in 1944 they went back to New York City, where he got a job in an export house on Wall Street—only, as George had told me earlier, he literally could not stand the heat.

"Then I saw in the newspaper that the army was recruiting people for Alaska, and so I applied. I didn't hear anything for six months. In fact, I'd forgotten that I'd applied. But then suddenly I got a notification from the U.S. Army, and it says: 'You will report to the Port of Seattle on such-and-such date for movement to Alaska.'"

"When was this?"

"In 1952," George said. "At that time, they were building up Alaska because they thought the Korean War would extend to Alaska. So they built up Anchorage, and Anchorage was really booming, with Fort Richardson and the Elmendorf Air Force Base."

"Before that, it had just been a small railroad town?"

"That's right."

So George, Nellie, and Janet landed right in the middle of the boom, and George became a transportation office employee—a civilian job—at the Fort Richardson Military Reservation just northeast of the city. Gradually he worked his way up inside the system, going back to the Lower Forty-Eight for special training, until eventually he was given the specially created position of traffic manager for the armed forces in Alaska. "It had to do with shipping—ocean shipping, railroad transportation, and aviation," he explained.

"You were in charge of all of that?"

"Yes."

I was duly impressed.

"By this time," he said, "the Cold War had intensified, and they built the so-called DEW Line"—the Distant Early Warning radar system. How could any child of the Cold War forget those grainy black-and-white classroom films and their chilling reassurance that every hour of every day, America's mighty DEW Line was standing guard and protecting us all from certain nuclear obliteration?

"It was along the Bering coast and the North Slope," George said. "It had to be built, and supply ships had to go in. And then once the line was active, it had to be resupplied every year, and I set up the system. It was called Operation Mona Lisa, and I was the traffic manager for it. So I traveled extensively. I investigated the landing possibilities."

"And this was all kinds of travel? Air? Rail? Ocean?"

"Everything," George said proudly. "And so I flew around a lot—on the North Slope, Kotzebue, Point Barrow on the coast—all the DEW Line sites. And I had a nice opportunity to advance myself."

George retired from the army in 1975 and immediately took a job with the state's Department of Transportation, helping Alaska to make the transition as a newly admitted state to the regulatory requirements of the federal Interstate Commerce Commission. He did that for three years before retiring permanently.

"So you must have traveled all over the state," I said.

"Oh, yes," he said. "And it was a small state then. When I would go to Valdez or to Point Barrow and I'd walk into a restaurant, they'd all say, 'Hello, George. How are you?' I knew the governor and everybody."

"So did you enjoy that work?"

"Certainly," he said. "You see, aviation is very important here, and especially small-scale aviation. We have two hundred landing strips in the state. And back then a bush pilot license was very easy to obtain. Some people couldn't even read and write, and they became pilots." He chuckled. "They had to be regulated and taught how to file a tariff and all that—and that was my job."

"So you retired in 1978," I said. "Then what?"

"We bought a house—we'd been living in an apartment until then—and we decided to stay here," he said. "Our roots were here now. We'd lived in Alaska longer than anywhere else—even Vienna. I was twenty-six when I left there, and now we've been here in Alaska for fifty-two years.

"So everything was good until a few years ago when Nellie got sick. It was evident to me that her memory was fading, but I didn't know how severe it would be. People can have so-called dementia without having Alzheimer's. But Alzheimer's is devastating."

After his retirement in 1978, George said, he became active in Anchorage's civic life, especially the Anchorage Concert Association, a venerable local institution devoted to bringing artistic productions to town. "It was our geopolitical situation on the route between Europe and Japan which brought a lot of concert groups here who were on their way to give concerts in Tokyo," George said. "So we were able to get the London Symphony Orchestra, the Paris Chamber Orchestra, the Vienna Philharmonic—a lot of big names."

We finally broke for lunch. By now it was too late to go down to the dining room, so I made us a couple of cheese sandwiches. As we ate, I said, "You've lived through a lot. You've been through some of the most horrible times of the past century—some of the most terrible things. And also some very good things. So what do you think now, at this point in your life, are the most important things about life—that make for a good life and that are important in life?"

George thought carefully before answering me.

"I would say security," he said at last. "That was always absent in my life until I came to Alaska."

"Even when you were in New York and Boston and England?"

"You didn't know how long you'd have a job," he said. "Whether you could advance; whether the political situation would hold up; whether your child would be accepted where you wanted her to go. It was insecurity. I think that under American ideology, security is not a very welcome concept. The concept here is to be adventurous—that taking risks is what makes a man. Well, I'm not a risk taker."

"It's funny you say that," I said. "Here you came, to a brand new country—to America—with very few contacts, no prospects, nothing."

"Yes, but I was forced into it."

"But you weren't forced to come *here*. You could have stayed in England, right?"

"Some people did, yes."

"But you decided that, no, you were going to keep going to the United States," I said. "And then you took another chance by going up to Alaska in 1952, when it wasn't even a state. It was still pretty rough and tumble."

"That was the one exception," George acknowledged. "And that worked out very well. I'll never forget the discussion when I came home from that recruiting office and I called my wife and my daughter together. And I said, 'How would you like to go to Alaska?' Because I couldn't go without the willingness of my family to endure it. I mean: Alaska! We discussed it for hours. And finally the consensus was yes."

He took a bite of his sandwich.

I nodded. "That was a big chance you took. You knew nobody here. It was thousands and thousands of miles from anybody that you knew. And in those days, it was a lot harder to get up here, I'm sure. No frequent flyer miles, no e-mail."

George chuckled. "The people who later came to visit me from the East Coast would say, 'I can't understand it.' The Jewish saying is, 'He doesn't belong in the market; he belongs in the café house.' And they'd say, '*You* belong in the café house—and now you're shooting *bears*?' I shot a bear," he added nonchalantly.

I was curious about the bear, but I wanted to get back to his belief in the importance of security.

"Why is it so important?" I asked.

"Well, as I say," George replied, "I'm not quite sure whether the concept is correct that if you are secure—that if you are taken care of, like in a welfare state—you're less of a human being, striving for improvement, than you would be if you were confronted with constant risks and fail-ures. But looking back, I think I would have led a more acceptable life if I'd had the assurances that previous generations had. But, of course, the uncertainty of existence goes along with being Jewish. The eternal wan-derer. There is something to it."

He sighed deeply.

"The emancipation of the Jews is fairly recent," he said. "It comes from 1848 or something, at least in Europe. So it hasn't gotten very far."

"But you feel that here in Alaska . . ."

"Here in Alaska, it's the minimum," he said. "I mean, some people don't really know. They hear my accent, and they know a little bit about my history. But they don't visualize that I'm different—that I'm Jewish. It's so American to have an accent—to be a foreigner. And especially in Alaska, everything is new; everybody is a *cheechako*."

"*Cheechako?*"

"You don't know the expression?"

I shook my head.

"It's the greenhorn," he said. "It's an Athabascan word."

"Interesting."

"So I was accepted here on an equal basis," George said. "A very equal basis. For instance, I think Loralee at one point said, 'What? You're Jew-ish? I didn't know that.'"

"And it doesn't matter?"

"It doesn't matter. She's a member of the United Methodist church, and she took me to services there on a Sunday. And she introduced me to a man who is very active in interfaith and interdenominational rela-tions, and that's when I found out that there are church organizations that make a big deal out of observing the Holocaust memory. So he asked me to speak in the church, and I did. I mean, that wouldn't have hap-pened anywhere else. I was really overwhelmed by the kindness of these people."

"That's terrific," I said. "So finally you found a place where you could be yourself."

"That's right."

"And that's the most important thing?"

He nodded, chewing on another bite of his sandwich. "But I never learned to make such a good sandwich as you," he said.

"What?" I wasn't sure I had heard right.

"With all my background, I never learned to make such a good cheese sandwich as you," he said earnestly. "I enjoyed this tremendously."

"I'm glad," I laughed.

Where There's Tok

"Lot of forest fires up that way," Susan Lutz said when I told her that I was going to be heading up to Tok. She handed me a cup of coffee. "It's been so hot this year. And almost no rain."

It was the morning of my third day in Alaska. After my interview with George on the first day, I had interviewed Loralee Willis, his volunteer; had dinner with George; and then gone to the hospital for Linda's Faith in Action event, which had drawn a crowd of about a dozen very nice people. The next day, I had interviewed four more volunteers, including a woman from Philadelphia who had recently become a Buddhist priest. But now it was time to hit the road: Tok tonight, and on to Haines tomorrow.

After breakfast, I told Susan that I would see her again next week, piled all my gear back into the Sentra, and headed up Sixth Avenue through downtown Anchorage and out to Alaska Highway One.

At first, Alaska Highway One was like any interstate in the Lower Forty-Eight: four lanes of high-grade blacktop with a median strip down the middle and monster eighteen-wheelers barreling past at eighty miles an hour. But forty minutes later, in Palmer, it dropped to two lanes, and it stayed that way the rest of the trip.

The road ran through a valley, and the mountains surrounding it were magnificent, with wisps of cloud trailing from their peaks. But I also drove past Wes Bob's Tire Service, a Job Corps center, a VFW post, a McDonald's, and a Taco Bell. A roadside sign warned DON'T TRASH ALASKA, threatening a thousand dollar fine if I did; another sign announced RHUBARB FOR SALE; and a third sign informed me that it was still 273 miles to Tok Junction. Fortunately, the tanker truck in front of me was moving at a good clip.

After Palmer, the scenery continued to improve. A brash young river the color of tarnished silver roared alongside the road, and bright fireweed and delicate queen ann's lace lined the shoulders on both sides. The Chugach Mountains formed a wall to the south, punctuated with what looked like genuine glaciers.

I had lunch at the Eureka Café, where a skinny guy with tattoos and a baseball cap was talking to the pretty girl behind the counter about some demonstration that he said was going on in Valdez protesting the dumping of oil in the environment.

"They're all out there in their fancy powerboats waving their signs," he said. "Seems to me there's something wrong with that picture."

"I don't like it when they get so extreme," the girl said as she refilled his coffee. "But on the other hand, you've got to have balance, you know.

Because there's people that'll just go out and dump oil any old place and ruin everything. So like there has to be a balance—you know, harmony."

The skinny guy shrugged and sipped his coffee.

"I guess," he said.

After lunch, I drove on to Glennallen, which, according to my map, was where the Alaska Pipeline crossed the road. For some reason, I didn't actually spot the pipeline, but I did pass the Trans-Alaska Pipeline Camp, as well as the Moosehorn RV Park (With Full Hook-Ups) and the Hitchin' Post Restaurant (Breakfast Special $3.99). And a colossal mountain. The mountain was right there in front of me, but I almost didn't see it. In fact, at first I thought I had imagined it. But then I saw it again: a giant snow-covered white hump looming in front of me. It was shrouded in haze—or maybe it was smoke—so that one moment I could just barely make it out and the next moment it was gone.

The road, which had been going mostly east so far, turned north at this point, running along the western edge of Wrangell-Saint Elias National Park, the biggest of all of America's national parks. Although the park was said to contain "the largest collection of peaks over 16,000 feet," all I could see as I drove up the road was more fireweed, more trees, and signs that warned: NO SHOOTING FROM ROADWAY.

Determined to get a better look, I turned off onto the Nabesna Road, one of only two roads that penetrated this vast national park. I stopped at a ranger station near the junction, where a friendly ranger by the name of Thelma assured me that the Nabesna Road was in pretty good shape at the moment, although I might have to cross some water here and there. "The only problem is the smoke," she said cheerfully. "It's been pretty thick, so it kind of obscures the view—which is a shame."

Sadly, Thelma was right. Even though, according to my map, I was flanked by the Mentasta Mountains on my left and the lofty Wrangell Mountains on my right, I couldn't see a thing. The only change from the main road was that the Nabesna Road was mostly unpaved, so I was leaving a magnificent plume of dust in my wake. Still, I persevered, hoping that sooner or later I would get close enough to one of these invisible behemoths to actually see it. Twice the road was overrun by wide streams of rushing water, and although I hesitated, I decided to trust Thelma's assurances and plunged ahead, just like in the truck commercials on television—except that, of course, my Sentra was no truck.

About thirty miles out, I passed a cluster of weather-beaten wooden buildings with a big hand-painted sign nailed to a tree out front that read: SPORTSMEN PARADISE LODGE: BAR, LIQUORE, COLD BEER TO GO, BURGERS,

POP, FURS. The only sign of life was a mangy yellow dog that slowly rose to its feet and trotted toward the road as I drove by, its tail wagging list-lessly. Beyond the lodge, the condition of the road began to deteriorate. Thelma had told me that it was only forty-two miles long, so I was get-ting fairly close to the end anyhow. And then, to top things off, there was a sudden burst of thunder, and it started to rain.

I turned around and drove back to the lodge, hoping that someone besides the dog would be there and that maybe I could have a beer while I waited for the rain to pass. Happily, there was someone behind the bar— her name, she said, was Judy—who handed me an ice cold can of Bud-weiser and a bag of Cheetos. She was reading a magazine, and the television, which was tuned to a satellite juke box station, was playing "Mama Said" by the Shirelles.

Judy was the first person I had met so far who was actually from Alaska—born and raised in Fairbanks. Her husband, who was working on something in the back room, had grown up right here, she said. His father used to run the place until he died three years ago, and his mother had turned it over to him and Judy to run. "I like it out here," she said. "It's peaceful."

I asked Judy about the smoke.

"Yeah," she said, "it's pretty bad this year. They were saying there's something like seventy fires burning now. Something like 2 million acres. They say the worst one's about twenty miles out of Fairbanks. I just talked to my brother in Fairbanks and he said it's getting bad. And I heard it was pretty bad around Tok too."

I told her that that's where I was going.

She nodded. "You want another beer?"

"That's okay. I'd better get going. Nice to meet you."

"You, too," Judy said, turning back to her magazine.

The rain had passed—it turned out just to be a brief shower—and by the time I got back to the main road, it was 6:15. Another sixty-five miles to Tok. At last I began seeing some serious mountains—the first since that mystery mountain back at Glennallen. I was winding through the eastern edge of the Alaska Range now. Towering peaks of raw granite, one after the other, pierced the gray clouds overhead as if they were holding up the sky itself. With the windows wide open and the new Jeff Beck CD roar-ing from the speakers, I was thrilled to the core: this was Alaska.

Tok, which according to my atlas has a population of 1,393, is just the junction where Alaska Highway One connects to Alaska Highway Two— better known as the Alcan Highway, which runs 1,488 miles from Daw-

son Creek, British Columbia, to Fairbanks. In other words, if you're coming up the Alcan Highway from Canada or the Lower Forty-Eight, Tok is
where you turn left if you want to get to Anchorage without having to go
all the way up to Fairbanks. I was stopping there because it was about
halfway between Anchorage and Haines, and because there didn't seem
to be many other places in this part of the state where you could stop for
the night—not if you wanted a bed.

Getting a bed that night turned out to be a little more complicated than
I had expected. I had made my reservation more than a month in advance
at the only bed-and-breakfast that was listed in my Triple-A book for Tok.
But when I arrived at about eight o'clock, nobody was there. Not only
that: the bed-and-breakfast, it turned out, was out in the woods, off a side
road several miles up the Alcan Highway from the junction—and the
woods out there were thick with smoke.

The smoke had been building gradually all day as I'd gotten closer to
Tok, but now that I was actually here, there was no getting away from
it. A pall of acrid gray wood smoke hung over everything. And as I'd
driven up the road from the junction to the bed-and-breakfast, it had
only intensified.

How close *was* this fire anyhow? Did I really want to spend the night out
here in the woods? I left a message on a board beside the door of the bed-
and-breakfast and drove back to the junction to get something to eat. I
would come back later to check in—maybe. Visibility out here was down to
a couple of hundred yards at best, and I could feel the smoke in my lungs.

Fortunately, I did find a good place to eat back at the junction, where
I had what may have been the best slice of pie I had ever had at a restaurant. "What kind of pie is this?" I asked my teenage waitress when she
came over to refill my coffee.

"You like it?" she said. "It's a combination of peach and cherry and
huckleberry. The ice cream is huckleberry too."

"Well, please tell whoever made it congratulations. It's terrific."

She said that it was a fourteen-year-old ninth grader.

"You're kidding!" I said.

She blushed. "I'll tell her you liked it," she said, quickly heading back
to the kitchen.

Meanwhile, the couple at the next table was asking their waitress about
the fire. They asked her how close it was, and she told them that she had
heard it was about four miles away. As she was talking, I spotted a fire
truck silently heading up the Alcan Highway in the direction of my bed
and breakfast.

I asked my waitress about the fire when she came back with the check,
and she told me that she was scared. She said a fire here about twenty

years ago had done a lot of damage: a lot of people had lost their homes. "If this one jumps the river, it could do a lot of damage, too," she said.

"Well," I said as I got up to leave, "I sure wish you guys luck."

"I'm praying," she said softly. Her lip was quivering.

After dinner, I drove back out to the bed and breakfast—into the thickening smoke—only to find that the couple who ran the bed-and-breakfast had inadvertently given my room to someone else. They were mortified.

"We've never had this happen before," the wife stammered when I showed her the e-mail confirmation that she herself had sent me. The husband, meanwhile, got on the phone and called a friend of theirs named Helga who, he said, also ran a bed-and-breakfast and might still have a room for the night.

She did.

At first, I was relieved, thinking that wherever they were sending me had to be safer than they were out here. But I should have known from its name: the Off the Road House. If anything, the name was an understatement. The place wasn't just off the road; it was off the map. Surely this is more than four miles from Tok, I thought as I followed dirt road after dirt road into the dense spruce forest, leaving the relative safety of the blacktop farther and farther behind.

At last I came to a clearing, in the middle of which stood a ramshackle two-story wooden house with a huge rack of antlers hanging above the front door. This was the place. As I parked the Sentra and climbed out, a trim round-faced woman with close-cropped brown hair walked up from the house, smiling broadly. "You are Paul?" she asked with a strong German accent. "I'm Helga. It's very nice to meet you."

We shook hands.

"Let me show you," she said. "I have two rooms: one in the house and one in the back. You can choose which one you like. Oh, and please forgive the mess," she added. "As you can see, we're putting an addition on the house."

An addition? In the middle of a major forest fire?

But sure enough, there were two workmen banging away with their hammers, busily putting up a wooden frame along the side of the house, as if it were the most natural thing in the world to be doing.

The room inside the house was full of angry mosquitoes, so I opted for the cabin behind the house, which seemed a little better. Fortunately, the hammering stopped a few minutes later, and the workmen drove off, leaving behind the kind of profound stillness that you can find only in the complete absence of traffic noise and humming appliances. As I drifted off, my last thoughts were about how in heaven's name I would ever find my way out of here if and when the flames arrived.

The flames, fortunately, did not arrive—at least not that night. Much relieved, I gazed around me when I woke up the next morning and, in the morning light, discovered that I was surrounded by art: small stained-glass creatures on the walls, the dresser, and the window sills.

A little later, Helga, wearing an apron with OFF THE ROAD HOUSE stenciled across the front, fixed me a mushroom and herb omelet for breakfast, cutting the herbs fresh from her garden. As she cooked, I mentioned how I liked the artwork in the cabin.

She smiled. "I'm glad you like it." It was all her work, she said. She was a professional artist, with a gallery in Fairbanks and another one nearby. She had been here in Alaska for twenty years now. "I came from Stuttgart to Minnesota, where I was teaching art," she said. "Then one summer I came here to Alaska for vacation and fell in love with the place—and with a man from here."

So she had moved up here and married the man, and now they had a nineteen-year-old daughter who was at the University of Fairbanks majoring in music.

"You don't mind the cold?"

She laughed. "You get used to it."

"What about the fire?" I asked. "Do you worry about that?"

She said that two weeks ago, she had been worried. But now they were saying that the fire was pretty much under control. "Of course," she added, "they said that in 1990, and it wasn't. First they said it couldn't jump the river—and it did. Then they said it couldn't jump the highway—and it did. But then finally, just before it reached Tok, it turned. People still say it was the hand of God."

Although it was a sunny day and the sky was clear, the smoke that morning remained strong and thick the entire ninety-three miles from Tok east to the Canadian border. I could smell it, see it, taste it, and feel it in my lungs. Then shortly after I crossed into the Yukon, the smoke mysteriously disappeared.

I stopped in the town of Beaver Creek ("The Most Westerly Community in Canada") at a place called Buckshot Betty's, where I had a cup of weak coffee and a slice of unremarkable cherry pie.

After that, it was pretty much one breathtaking panorama after another. In the Yukon, I had the Nisling Range on my left and the massive Saint Elias Mountains on my right—including Mount Logan, the second-highest mountain in North America. In British Columbia, coming down the Haines Highway, I was flanked by the heavily glaciated Alsek Range. And finally, as I pulled into Haines late that afternoon, there was the monumental Chilkat Range, utterly dwarfing the town and everything in it.

HAINES, ALASKA

THE POPULATION OF HAINES is only 1,811, not much bigger than our kids' high school. The metal sign indicating the town's city limits was so shot full of holes that I could barely read it, but soon after it came a large unscathed wooden sign, suspended between twin totem poles, that made it official: WELCOME TO HAINES, ALASKA. Continuing on into town, I passed the Mountain Market ("Natural Foods, Deli, Espresso Bar"), the Haines Volunteer Fire Department, the Haines chapter of the American Bald Eagle Foundation—and then suddenly, to my left, I saw the water.

Haines sits at the head of one of the northern forks of Alaska's Inside Passage, a long fjord known as the Lynn Canal. On this particular afternoon, with the naked sun slanting down from the west, the Lynn Canal was an immense expanse of pure aquamarine bounded by towering ice-packed mountains that rose straight up from the water's edge. Minutes later, as I pulled up in front of Norm and Suzanne Smith's Fort Seward Bed and Breakfast, I noticed a bumper sticker on the old Lincoln parked out front that summed it up nicely: "I DIED & WENT TO HAINES."

Beth

Beth MacCready, the Faith in Action director in Haines, showed up at 8:30 the next morning, Sunday, to take me to church. Beth was about my age, with shoulder-length brown hair, a sprinkling of freckles, and a smile so broad that it made her squint.

"You really don't need to come with me," I said. "Just tell me how to get there, and I'll be fine."

"Oh, no," she said. "I *want* to go. Besides, there's someone else who I want to bring with me. Just follow me."

I jumped into the Sentra and followed her Toyota pickup truck down the hill into town. At one point, as we were driving through town, she slowed down and pointed out her window at what looked like a nursing home, shouting something back to me that I couldn't understand; then she drove a few more blocks onto a residential street and parked along the curb. I pulled up behind her.

"That was Senior Village we drove past," Beth explained as she climbed out of the truck. "I wanted to show you where it was so you'd be able to find it, because that's where I've scheduled most of your interviews. I thought it'd be easier for you than driving all over the place."

We walked up to the house across the street, and Beth banged on the door. "Hello, there! It's me. Who wants to come to church with me?"

"Come on in," a woman's voice called back. "We're almost ready."

Inside were a woman combing her hair in front of a hallway mirror and a young girl in a wheelchair.

"Hi, Janice," Beth said to the woman, and then she turned to the girl. "Nicki, I've brought along a visitor. His name is Paul, and he's writing a book. He's going to interview me after church."

"Interview you?" Nicki said.

Beth laughed. "Can you imagine that?"

I walked up to shake Nicki's hand and realized that she was blind. She smiled when I took her hand. "Nice to meet you," she said.

"I'm ready," Janice said, and the four of us started up the street to the church, Beth pushing Nicki's wheelchair.

"It's just a couple of blocks," Beth told me.

"Do you know Isabel?" Nicki asked me.

"Isabel is Suzanne and Norman's daughter," Beth explained.

"No," I said to Nicki. "I'm afraid I don't."

"I think she's away at camp," Beth said to Nicki.

The sky was a deep blue, with just a few clouds hugging the tops of the mountains, and the morning sun warmed my face against a cool breeze blowing up from the water below. The church was a small, simple building on the corner with a white cross on top and a sign out front with the name of the church superimposed on a picture of an eagle flying over the mountains. A newly assigned priest said the mass.

What struck me most was the genuine warmth with which the people offered one another the sign of peace—the handshake or embrace—following the Lord's Prayer. These people smiled and made eye contact with each other. And after the mass was over, they didn't just make a dash for the parking lot. Several came over to say hello to Nicki, and Beth took me around the room, introducing me to some of the other parishioners.

"Jellinek," one of the women said loudly. "Isn't that a Polack name?"

"Czech," I said, a little taken aback.

"This is Mary Price," Beth smiled. "You'll be interviewing her tomorrow."

As Beth and I walked back home with Janice and Nicki a few minutes later, Beth started telling me about her daughter's wedding, which they were going to be holding out at their place next month. They were expecting over two hundred people. She then talked about an upcoming retreat.

"Is the retreat connected to hospice?" I asked. Beth ran Hospice of Haines, the organization that had received the Faith in Action grant.

"No," she said. "We have a building on our property that we let the public use. We've had board meetings there and prayer gatherings, meditations, all kinds of things."

"Any rock concerts?"

"No," she laughed. "Although my husband would like that."

Her husband, Greg, she said, played the banjo and the bass, although he made his living as a commercial fisherman. In fact, he was out fishing now. "He was out for ten days, and he came in for one day. He looked pretty bad—no sleep this time of year."

"What's he fishing?"

"Salmon. They put a few halibut strings out too, but mostly salmon. They had sixty-two thousand pounds in ten days."

"Sounds like a lot," I said, having no idea whether it was.

"It's about ten pounds per fish," she said. "So that gives you some idea of how much you're pulling out of a net. July is our biggest income month for fishing."

"And is Greg from around here originally?"

"He's actually from Detroit, but he grew up near Seattle. His dad worked for Boeing."

"How about you? Where are you from originally?"

"Michigan originally," Beth said. "I came up here in '73 to visit."

When we got back to the house, Beth and I said good-bye to Nicki and Janice.

"Why do you have to go?" Nicki moaned to Beth.

"I'm going to take Paul on over to my house now," Beth explained, squatting in front of Nicki's wheelchair. "And he's going to interview me for his book."

Beth's house turned out to be several miles from downtown Haines. As I followed her speeding truck up and down the twists and turns of Mud Bay Road, I caught occasional glimpses of glaciers and cliffs and the shimmering water of Lynn Canal, but it wasn't until we got to her house that

I realized what a spectacular spot it was. From the small driveway where we parked our vehicles, I followed her down a steep wooded slope to the house below, which was like no house I'd ever seen before: sort of Frank Lloyd Wright meets Daniel Boone.

"What a place!" I exclaimed.

"Yeah," Beth said. "I started out here in a little cabin, twelve by sixteen, and I've been working on it ever since. In fact, we started the roofing on the porch four years ago—and it's only going to get finished next week."

"Because of the wedding?"

"That's right," she laughed as she opened the door. "We're getting ten years' worth of projects done just because family's coming."

I stepped inside.

The entire back wall was floor-to-ceiling windows that faced out onto the water, the mountains, and the huge Alaskan sky. Inside, everything was polished wood and plants, with big plush couches, a wood-burning stove, a spotless modern kitchen, and a state-of-the-art office space. A cello, perched on its stand, stood in front of the center window as if it too were mesmerized by the view. I asked Beth who played it.

"I'm trying to teach myself," she said. "Would you like a cup of tea?"

"Just a glass of water would be great," I said.

I started by asking about Nicki.

"She has optic gliomas," Beth said. "Children normally don't survive that past age four or five—and Nicki's eleven. So she's been the subject of a lot of intense treatments. In fact, they just took out the first tumor that they've actually been able to remove; it was growing, and it was going to kill her.

"And of course, she's getting to the age now where she's asking a lot of questions. So when they were going to do the operation, she asked the doctor, 'Why do I have to do this?' And he told her, 'Because you're going to die, Nicki, if you don't.' She's awful little . . ."

"You mean, to have to deal with something like that," I said.

"She has all her life. You know, with the shunts in her head and everything. She used to tell me that she was having fits over her speech difficulties, because language is everything to her. Our relationship is based on jabbering. You know, we talk, talk, talk."

"Is she mentally with it?"

"Oh, yes, she's totally there. You bet."

"So she's actually watching herself fall apart."

"Right," Beth said sadly. "And, of course, Janice and Jim . . . Well, they're happy today, you know, because she survived this operation a couple of weeks ago, so they know they have her a little longer."

She told me that Janice and Jim had adopted Nicki, and that they'd never had a child since because taking care of Nicki had turned out to be a full-time job. Beth herself had started out as one of Nicki's care providers when Nicki was two or three years old. Later she had become Nicki's teacher, teaching her at home because her immune system was too depressed for her to be in school with other children. She was also Nicki's godmother.

"She's a wonder," Beth said. "A miracle child."

"Let's go back," I said. "When you first moved up here, were you on your own?"

"I had a boyfriend for a couple of years, but he didn't work out," she said.

"And did he come up with you?"

"Yes," Beth laughed. "He was my Volkswagen mechanic."

"So you guys drove up here in a Volkswagen?"

"Right. We drove in a Volkswagen and landed in Haines, and within two weeks I had a job working for a woman bush pilot. An awesome woman. I was her dispatcher, her bus driver, her babysitter—everything."

"And then what?"

"Well, I worked for Head Start, I had a pizza parlor . . . "

"Wait a minute," I said. "You worked with the bush pilot for how long?"

"A couple of years. I've probably had forty different jobs, plus I also went back to school since I've been here. You know, you do whatever you need to in order to live here."

"Including running a pizza parlor?"

"Yeah," she said. "I started it with a couple of teachers whose husbands were lawyers. So we had a combination law office–pizza parlor."

"What else?"

"Let's see, I worked for Head Start. . . I did artwork—I was the first person here who did desktop publishing on my Macintosh. I worked for the Indian Arts carving place. I had a popcorn wagon for a couple of years on Main Street and sold burritos. I worked for the movie *White Fang*— I cast the extras for *White Fang* when Disney came to town, and I have a credit in the movie. I guess I'm kind of a Jill-of-all-trades. Let's see, what else did I do? I worked for number of years with developmentally disabled kids."

"Was that before or after you went back to school?"

"After," Beth said. "I went back to school in my mid-thirties. I wanted to get a Ph.D. in psychology. I was in the master's program at the University of Oregon. But instead, what happened is that I had a new boyfriend who got killed by a sniper."

"*What?*"

"Yeah," she said. "One day I had a lunch date with him, and . . ."

"This was in Oregon?"

"In Eugene."

"He was killed by a sniper in Eugene?" I said, incredulous.

"I liked him a lot." Beth paused. "I was totally blindsided by that."

"Was this a random thing?"

"Totally random. A nineteen-year-old kid. My friend was a two-time Olympic runner. He was a senior counselor at a youth detention center. So in another world, my friend would have been this nineteen year old's counselor. But instead this kid was dressed in camouflage, broke into a sporting goods store early one morning, climbed into the stadium where my friend was jogging, and shot him."

"My God."

"In the meantime, my mother had been diagnosed with a terminal illness, and so just the week before I had signed up with a hospice group there in Eugene. And so, with their support, I finished the semester—but barely. My brain was fried. I said, 'You know, I think I need to go back home.'"

"And your mother was in Michigan?"

"Right. My mother was in Michigan, and I ended up in Michigan actually caregiving for her for a couple of years."

"A couple of *years*?"

"On and off. I traveled between here and Michigan. That's when I did a lot of temporary jobs. The artwork, the popcorn wagon—seasonal things like that. And then when my mom died, in 1987, that's when I started building this house."

I asked Beth how she had gotten started with the hospice here in Haines.

She laughed. "We had this home health nurse here, and one day we both just sort of said"—in a singsong falsetto—"'Let's start a hospice!' Kind of like Spanky and Our Gang, you know: 'Oh yes, let's start a hospice!'"

"Did you know anything about hospice?" I asked.

"No, I didn't, really. Only that they'd rescued me back in Eugene from my trauma."

"Tell me about that."

"Getting rescued in Eugene?"

"Right."

"Well, I called them immediately when I realized that my friend Chris, who was plastered all over the paper, was the same person who was killed. I found that out the next morning."

"You didn't know?"

"He didn't show up for my lunch date. So I didn't know until my girl-friend showed me the paper the next morning."

"You're kidding," I said. "I mean, that must have fundamentally changed . . ."

"Everything," Beth broke in. She stared out at the mountains behind me. "For me, it was my big turning point," she said slowly.

"In what way?"

"Spiritually, I was raised in a family without much. My dad was an atheist who said that if you're agnostic, you're too chicken to admit that you're an atheist. And so it wasn't until this happened that I started to realize that I *did* have faith—and it was partly because Chris . . ." She paused. "There were just too many things that happened. Too many things. Meeting him, having this happen, the hospice thing. Even crazy stuff that I don't tell people about." Her voice broke. "I don't want to get emotional," she said thickly.

"It's okay. . . ."

"I mean, I'd say, 'Chris, what is this *about?*' And the light above my head would start flickering on and off. Silly stuff that I put meaning to. And I remember the big question that I had in my mind was: Did he suffer? They'd found him about an hour or so later, lying out on the field. And so, after that, I thought, What am I doing away from Haines? Because this place is such a recharge for me. There's just something pretty intense about this valley."

I nodded.

"You know," Beth said, looking up at me, "in the Tlingit culture, this place was called Deshu, which means 'the end of the trail.' Or," she added, "sometimes it's interpreted as 'the beginning of the trail.'"

I asked Beth about her program.

She said that Hospice of Haines had been up and running for about eight years now—"a lot longer than the popcorn wagon"—and that it had received its Faith in Action grant last year. The grant was being used to bring local congregations into the coalition—ten so far—and also to expand the organization's services beyond hospice care to help people with chronic health problems, through what was called the Bridge Program. At this point, there were about twenty active volunteers, and she was just about to train two groups of new volunteers who had signed up from the congregations.

"I've lined up some of the volunteers to talk to you," Beth said, handing me a neatly typed schedule. "And also some of the care receivers and family members."

I looked over the schedule and glanced at my watch. "It looks like I'm supposed to meet Beverly Jones in fifteen minutes over at the Bamboo Room."

"That's right," she said. "She wanted to meet you there for lunch."

"Guess I'd better head over there."

You Can't Miss It

It was right after my interview with Beverly that I managed, against all odds, to get lost in Haines. I needed to get from the Bamboo Room to the Haines Senior Village, where the rest of my interviews were scheduled—and which Beth had pointed out to me earlier that morning on the way to church.

Looking back now, armed with an actual map of downtown Haines, I can clearly see that the Bamboo Room was just a block and a half from Haines Senior Village. Had I simply turned left from Second Avenue onto Main Street and then taken the first right onto First Avenue, I would have been fine. But instead, I crossed Main Street and continued driving straight down Second Avenue until I found myself all the way back at the turnoff for Norm and Suzanne's bed-and-breakfast.

At that point I realized, first of all, that I was lost, and second, that I was running late. My first interview at Haines Senior Village, which I had thought was at 1:30, turned out (on a more careful reading of my schedule) to be at 1:15—and it was now 1:20.

But I didn't panic. I simply pulled into a handy parking lot, turned the car around, and headed back toward the downtown area, confident that there was no way that I could possibly get lost in a town the size of Haines.

Unfortunately, almost immediately I got stuck behind an enormous black SUV that had stopped dead in the middle of the lane to make a left turn. So I waited—and waited. But he couldn't make his turn because of the steady stream of cars coming the other way. Now, exactly the same thing happens all the time on Quakerbridge Road, a busy two-lane road around the corner from our house in New Jersey. And in New Jersey, when that happens, all you do is pull onto the shoulder and drive around the guy.

But not in Haines. Because when I did, suddenly a police car came up behind me from out of nowhere with his blue lights flashing, signaling me to pull over.

I must say that the officer was very polite, and when I explained to him how we did things in New Jersey, he pointed out very patiently that I was in Alaska now and that wasn't how they did things in Alaska. He asked for my license and slowly ambled back to his car with it so that he could run a check on me—a process that took about ten minutes. By now, of course, I was hopelessly late. But at least the officer was kind enough to let me off with just a warning, reminding me again that this was Alaska and not New Jersey. He then showed me exactly where to turn off to get to Haines Senior Village.

"You can't miss it," he grinned.

Mary Price

My ten o'clock interview the next morning was with Mary Price, the woman Beth had introduced me to in church yesterday. This should be interesting, I thought as I waited for her to arrive.

Suddenly Mary burst into the room.

Wearing tinted glasses and dressed in vivid red pants and a brightly flowered blouse, Mary seemed even bigger and louder in the stillness of the Haines Senior Village lounge than she had in church.

"Good morning," she boomed in a deep raspy voice. "I hope I'm not late."

"Not at all. You're right on time."

"Well, I try to be."

Getting up to greet her, I asked her—as I always did—whether it would be all right if I taped our conversation.

"All right," she said as she took her seat on the couch. "Just be sure you tell them that this is a lady and not a man. I've got a big voice, and a lot of people mistake me for a man. Like when I worked here at the clinic. I worked here for eighteen years."

"Doing what?"

"I was a nurse," she said. "For eighteen years. By the way, didn't you tell me yesterday that your name was Czech?"

"That's right," I said, surprised that she remembered.

"Well, I'm Slovak. Price isn't Slovak, but my maiden name is: Petrokubi. So where are you from?" she asked.

"New Jersey."

"Oh, my God," she said, "You see, I'm from Pennsylvania, but I trained in New Jersey—Orange, New Jersey. You know where that is?"

"Sure."

Born in 1931, Mary was from Hazleton, a small city in the eastern Pennsylvania coalfields, where her father had worked as a miner. After finishing her training in New Jersey, she had worked there for a few years but then had gone back to Hazleton.

"So when did you come to Alaska?" I asked.

"April 1961. My girlfriend and I came up to Sitka."

"Sitka's a long way from Hazleton. How did that happen?"

"She saw an ad. She worked for the VA up the road in Wilkes-Barre, and there was an ad up on the bulletin board that said, 'We need nurses in Mount Edgecumbe, Alaska.' And she said, 'Should we go?' I said, 'Sure, let's go!'"

"That's a big jump," I said.

"Well, I'd never really been anywhere outside of Hazleton—except New Jersey—and I wanted a new experience," Mary said. "So we both went and I worked for two years at a TB hospital for the Native population that was run by the Bureau of Indian Affairs."

"Were you married?"

"No. I met my husband in Sitka."

"So you were thirty years old, single, and free to do what you wanted."

"Footloose and fancy free," Mary chuckled. "Both of us."

"So what was it like when you first came to Sitka?"

"Well, first we came into Annette Island"—at the southern end of the Inner Passage, just south of Ketchikan. "And then from Annette Island we had to go to Sitka on a PBY."

"What's a PBY?"

"It's a water plane," she said. "It holds more than four passengers— it's kind of a big one that was used in World War II. Anyway, we landed on the water. And if that ain't scary—I mean, there was water coming up over the *plane*."

"And where did you stay?"

"Why, at the BOQ, of course."

"The BOQ?"

"Bachelor Officers Quarters," Mary explained. "Mount Edgecumbe used to be a base for the Army during World War II. You know, the Japanese were coming up the Aleutians, and they were getting closer. So there were all kinds of military buildings there on the island left over from the war, and the Bureau of Indian Affairs had converted them into a school. The kids came in from as far away as Barrow—anywhere up north where there wasn't a high school. And my husband worked there. He was the dorm attendant. So that's how I met him."

"This was in Sitka?"

"At Mount Edgecumbe. See, Mount Edgecumbe's on an island, and so is Sitka. And so the only way we could get from Mount Edgecumbe to Sitka was on a boat—what they called the shore boat. It cost you ten cents. I met my husband on the shore boat."

Mary's husband, Warren, had three children by a previous marriage when she married him. Over time, Mary and Warren had eight more children, so that Mary wound up raising eleven children in all. In 1963, shortly after their first child was born, Mary and Warren moved to Haines, Warren's hometown.

"Before we moved up, he told me to go up and take a look. Well, that was in the middle of winter, and the snow was this high," she said, pointing at the ceiling. "But I liked it. It was kind of like living in Hazleton, you know."

"Only no coal," I said.

"Right," she said. "No coal. But I liked this place—I still do. I don't think I'd go back to Hazleton now."

"Do any of your children still live in Haines?"

"Just one," she said. "Wayne. He's carving a boat and a totem pole. You should go up and see it if you're interested in carving. He's up on Major Road."

I asked Mary what life was like when she first arrived in Haines.

"Slow paced," she said. "A lot more easy-going."

"Did you feel like you fit in?"

"I did."

"And did you get along well with your husband's family?"

"I did. Maybe *he* didn't," she chuckled, "but I did."

"Is your husband still living?"

"No," she said, shifting uneasily on the couch. "He died in April. April of this year."

"Oh, I'm sorry."

"That's how come I got to know hospice."

I asked Mary how she'd first learned about hospice. She couldn't remember for sure. She thought it might have been Vince Hanson who had first told her about it; he belonged to her church. "I didn't understand what the whole program was," she said. "Because, you know, when I was still working, hospice was only for those who were dying—period. And my husband was . . . Well, he was in no way ready to die at that point." There was a tremor in her voice. "Anyway," she continued, "Beth came and talked to me about it, and I thought, Gee, this is a good program. Better than me trying to find someone and paying them twenty-five dollars an hour."

"What kind of help did you need, Mary?"

"Well, my husband was in a wheelchair, so he didn't do any cooking. He could get himself in and out of bed, but at some point it got to be hard for him. He was diabetic; he had some heart problems. And he was an above-the-knee amputee."

"Because of the diabetes?"

"Yes. And he was pretty independent at first. But I could see where he was going downhill. Down one day and up the next. You know, it came to the point that if I wanted to go somewhere for a day—or if I had to go to Juneau overnight . . . "

"You couldn't leave him alone?"

"No," she said. "I had to have somebody who could check on him at least. Somebody that could go to the house and see that he was all right."

"Was your son able to help you out at all? The one who lives here?"

Mary shook her head sadly.

"No?" I asked.

"He just didn't," she sighed. "He just didn't."

"That must've been hard."

"Him and his dad didn't get along," she said, looking up at me. "What can I say?"

We lapsed into silence. A truck rumbled by outside.

"So you needed some help so that you could get out," I said.

"That's right. I could go out for an hour, you know—to the store or the post office, that kind of thing. But then last December, he wound up in the hospital for a week. And then he was in the nursing home for six weeks."

"This was down in Juneau?"

"Yes. And then about three days before he was supposed to come home, I fell and broke my wrist. Beth had helped me get a hospital bed for him— maybe that's when she told me about this Faith in Action thing—but then when I fell and broke my wrist, I could hardly do anything. I couldn't even help him get up in bed."

"And so hospice was able to help you?"

"Some of them. And some of the ladies from the church were really good about helping. And Father Blaney, he would help. But then I would have to go down to Juneau to get my arm checked—and that time of year, with the weather being what it is, you don't know how long it's going to take. You don't know if the ferry's going to be able to go or if the planes'll be able to fly, you know."

"Sure."

"So that's when Beth really helped me out. She would have people come stay with him in two- or three-hour increments—whatever the person could do. And they'd be there until I came back. Like one day I went down there, and I didn't get back until the next afternoon."

"They stayed with Warren the whole time?"

"That's right. He had his mind, but he just wasn't able to take care of himself. He was wearing Depends; he had accidents. And he could not get out of bed by himself."

"Did he have any kind of nursing care?"

"Me."

"By yourself?"

"I was the nursing care," Mary said firmly. "And so from January to April, I just didn't go anywhere. And then two of our kids came up for two weeks while I had my arm in this stupid sling—one came for a week, and then another one came for a week."

"So they were able to help you out."

"That's right. Because at that point, I just couldn't do it."

I asked Mary whether Warren had died at home.

"Yes," she said.

"Were you with him?"

"Well . . . yes," she said, more tentatively. "I was home, and I was taking care of him. I went in early in the morning. Around five-thirty or six o'clock, I'd go in because he'd be awake, and I changed him, washed his face a little bit. And, you know, he was a grumpy old man, telling me: 'Don't *do* that. Leave me *alone.*' He was always like that: 'Don't *tell* me what to do. I'll do it *myself.*'"

A look of tenderness crossed her face.

"Finally I told him, 'You can't stay wet like this.' So he let me do that. I changed the bed, and then I left him. He says, 'Leave me alone. I'm gonna watch TV.' And I said, 'Okay. Then we'll see if you want something to eat.' He was eating poorly.

"And . . . of course, I knew eventually this was going to happen," Mary said, her voice still quavering. "Because I was talking to Father Blaney a couple of weeks before, and I said, 'He doesn't want to live like this. He's ready to die.' But you know," she said, blinking back tears, "you're never prepared for it."

"Was he in pain?"

"All the time, I think. But he would never say."

Mary pulled herself up straight.

"So, anyway, I left the room," she said. "I would usually check e-mail, and I'd make coffee. But that day he didn't want coffee when I had it made, so I said, 'Okay,' and went back out again.

"At about seven o'clock, I looked in on him again, and he was sleeping. I was sure he was sleeping. A little while later, I went in again— around seven-thirty—and . . . I looked at him . . . and he was gone."

She paused.

"And you know," she said, her eyes glistening, "who's prepared for that kind of thing? I mean, you spend forty-two *years* with the guy. . . ."

"And you still loved him," I said.

"Of course!" she exclaimed. "Of course!"

Vince

Vince Hanson, my final interview in Haines, showed up just before five, wearing sandals, white shorts, and a white T-shirt with the words "California Authentic" across the chest in gold letters.

It turned out that Vince really was an authentic Californian—born in Ukiah, about a hundred miles north of San Francisco and raised in nearby Upper Lake, which he told me was even smaller than Haines. His father had been a civil engineer with an insurance business on the side, and his mother had spent much of her time raising their ten children.

"Ten kids? Where were you in birth order?"

"Number seven. You kind of fended for yourself in a way. They opened the doors in the morning and let us back inside in the evening."

Vince had first come up to Alaska after college, landing a summer job at Denali National Park, and it was at Denali that he met his wife, who was from Juneau. After a nine-month detour working for an electronics firm in Illinois, Vince realized that his heart was in Alaska, so he returned to Juneau, where he and his wife got married, had three daughters, and lived quite happily for the next fifteen years. Then about six years ago, they decided to move to Haines.

"Why Haines?"

"It's a small town, which we like," he said. "It's close to my wife's family in Juneau. And it's connected: you can get pretty much anywhere in Alaska from here, really—although it might take you a while."

His wife had been a teacher in Juneau and got a teaching job in Haines. Vince wasn't sure exactly what he would do when he got there. But it turned out that the city manager's job had just opened up, so he threw his hat into the ring and wound up getting it.

"What did you know about city administration?"

"The state agency that I'd worked for in Juneau worked a lot with small communities," he said. "But really, I didn't know anything. When I started, I said that if I lasted a month, it'd be a miracle. After a month, I said two months would be a miracle; then six months. Finally, after two years, I quit. They got a real good replacement, but unfortunately he died on his way to work one day—so I went back for another six months until they found another replacement."

"And what are you doing now?"

"I've got a consulting business. Community development and government."

"Are you finding enough work to keep going?"

"No," he said. "But my wife is still working as a teacher, and the kids are at that age where I want to do more with them. So I've done some consulting, and I've also worked as a school bus driver—a typical Haines thing."

Besides changing jobs, Vince said, he had made some other changes in his life. Having grown up in the Catholic church, he had agreed to become a deacon. And he had signed up to become a hospice volunteer.

"How did that happen?"

"There was something about it on the radio. They were going to have a training session for people who wanted to volunteer. And it was something that I'd been interested in ever since my father was ill and then died. He had Alzheimer's for twelve years."

"Twelve years?"

Vince nodded. "My mother's the one who took care of him. I'd go down and visit—to try to give her a break. But it was very difficult."

I asked Vince whether he remembered his first match as a volunteer.

"Oh, yes," he said. "I've really only had two. It's only been a little over two years since I got involved."

"So who was the first one?"

"The chief," Vince said fondly. "He was a great guy. An old Native man, probably in his late sixties. He had throat cancer. He'd obviously been living with it for a long time, and he couldn't eat, so he was totally tube-fed."

"Was he with it mentally?"

"He was, but he had difficulty speaking. I'd sit down with him, and he'd look out the window and start talking to me about his hunting and fishing days. See, here's a guy that has cancer in his throat—so it's probably very uncomfortable for him to talk—and he would talk to me for hours. I had to listen really close because he was so hard to understand."

"But you were able to follow him?"

"Oh, sure. After a while you tune in."

"And how long did he survive?"

"Well, they gave him to me as a hospice client, which meant that he wasn't expected to live very long. But the guy was tough as nails." Vince smiled. "I'd go see him, and he'd be the same every time. I was mainly going so that his wife could go to an exercise class, and I did that for several months. Then the guy who'd been tube-feeding him had to leave for a while, and Cornerstone"—a home health care agency—"asked me if I'd be willing to train to do it while he was gone."

"And did you?"

"I'd go out there every other morning at six o'clock. But then the city manager died, and they called me to come back. So I told them that I'd do it, but that I had this commitment. So I kept on going out there to Klukwan doing the tube feeding for the chief."

"How far is Klukwan?"

"About twenty-eight miles up the highway. But the thing about it is that he never seemed to get any worse. He'd go down to Sitka once in a while to get his things straightened out; then he'd come back, the same as always. So I was just shocked when he died."

"What happened?"

"I don't know. He went down to Sitka, got the flu, got pneumonia, and suddenly . . . that was it." Vince looked down at the floor, blinking.

"So you guys were friends?" I asked after a pause.

"Yes, I'd say we were. I'd see him in town. It was really sad, you know, because he seemed like such a . . . a bubbly kind of person. But he was so hindered by his condition. Still, I always felt good after being with him."

"In what way?"

"Well, I guess I feel like I got to experience a lot of growth by getting to know a person of his caliber."

"Was he actually a chief?"

"No, I think that's just what they called him. But he was well respected in the community, and he was the person in charge of the building they have out there in Klukwan with a lot of their historical artifacts."

"How did you find out that he'd died?"

"Beth called me. I was pretty shocked. And I was sad for his wife. You could tell that she was really attached to him."

I asked Vince whether he had had any contact with the chief's wife since his death.

"I went over for the funeral," he replied. "There was a big crowd of people there, but she saw me out of the corner of her eye. And she came over to me in the middle of that crowd and thanked me for spending time with the chief. She said that it had meant a lot to her. But the truth is that I was honored to have had the opportunity to spend time with the chief. And I just hope that he's in a better place now where he doesn't have to suffer anymore."

About two months after the chief's death, Vince was assigned to his second match: Warren Price, Mary's husband. I told Vince that I had just talked with Mary that morning.

"She's another incredible person," he said, smiling. "The priests call her Mother Superior."

"I can imagine."

"But she needed help," he said. "She was just bogging down there at the end—and he was just the opposite of the chief. They told me that he was a Bridge client and that Mary just needed some respite—she'd broken her arm. But Warren wasn't eating and he wouldn't get out of bed."

"Did you get the feeling that he'd given up?"

"Oh, he was dying. We'd talk a little bit, but he was ornery."

"Is that right?"

"Oh, man, yes." Vince shook his head. "He didn't want people around. You know, 'I don't need no help.'"

"Did you ever feel like you made a connection with him?"

"Not really."

Vince had stayed overnight with Warren one time when Mary had had to go to Juneau for her arm, and he did once get into a conversation with him about Korea. But for the most part, he said, Warren just wanted to be left alone.

"I was actually kind of proud of myself," Vince chuckled. "He could cut me up, you know, and I wouldn't let it bother me. I'd just say, 'Whatever, Warren.' A lot of that wasn't him, though. Mary said that a lot of it was after he'd had this stroke—and that was right before I came in."

"So you didn't take it personally?"

"Oh, no," he said with a grin. "I'd been the city manager. I could take anything."

I asked Vince how his experience with hospice had affected him.

"Well," he said, the words coming slowly, "I think it helped me to realize, you know, that this is where I'll be some day. And it won't matter how many other things I've done, I'll still be in the same spot. And I'll be there sooner if I don't change my ways."

"So it's changed your priorities?"

"I think so."

"And how does your wife feel about that?"

"Oh," he said, "I think she likes having me around a little more—although I'm still a little bit ornery."

I laughed.

"The other thing," he went on, turning serious again, "is that I've always taken death pretty well, but I think I'm better equipped to deal with it now."

"Including your own?"

"Yes."

"That must be mostly because of the chief," I said. "It doesn't sound as if Warren was much of an inspiration in that respect."

"Well, you know . . . "

"Or *was* he?"

"He still was," Vince reflected. "Because, you know, he'd lost his leg, he had diabetes—he had every kind of problem you could imagine. But he was always very independent right to the end. And he had a lot of grit. So even though I didn't really get to know him until it was near the end, I count myself lucky that I did."

The Alaska Marine Highway

It was a few minutes after six when Vince and I finished our conversation, so I still had time for dinner at the Bamboo Room before heading to the ferry terminal. According to the woman at the Alaska Marine Highway office with whom I had booked my passage to Sitka back in April, I was supposed to be at the terminal at 7:30 for a 9:30 departure.

"Two whole hours?"

"Yes, sir," she told me. "That's what we advise."

I ordered the fish and chips dinner and sipped my beer as CNN brought me up to date on its version of world events: another rash of forest fires in southern California (no mention of the fires in Alaska), Yasir Arafat once again under intense pressure from the international community, a security breach at London's Heathrow Airport—apparently a document had turned up showing all the different spots around the airport from which a rocket attack could be launched against incoming and outgoing flights. No wonder most bars kept their TVs tuned to the sports channels.

I got to the terminal at 7:30 and went inside to check in. The woman behind the counter told me to pull my car into lane 8, handing me a sticker to put on my windshield. Quite a few cars and trucks and recreational vehicles were already there, parked in their designated lanes. People were hanging out, leaning against their vehicles in conversation with one another or walking their dogs. A little red-headed kid in a black T-shirt ran past my car gleefully kicking a plastic bottle.

I got out and walked around and spotted a bald eagle perched near the top of the cliff across the road from the terminal. I watched as the magnificent bird lifted into the air and soared far out across the water, eventually disappearing into the evening sky.

At about quarter to nine, the ferry workers began waving us onto the ferry, the *Columbia,* one lane at a time, starting with those going to Bellingham, Washington, and ending with the Juneau lane. Somehow they got us all onboard in less than fifteen minutes. After dutifully setting my emergency brake and locking my doors as instructed, I followed my fellow passengers up a metal stairwell to the bridge deck. As the *Columbia*'s diesel engines rumbled to life far below and we got under way, I made my way back to the stern and watched as the scattered lights of Haines receded in our wake.

By now the sky had dimmed to a gray half-light, and broad sheets of charcoal-gray clouds had moved in from behind the mountains, streaked with deep red where the sun caught them from below. The breeze was strong and cold and seemed to blow right through my dungaree jacket. I felt sorry for the people stretched out in sleeping bags in the designated "tent and camping area" on the deck behind me. I was glad that I had booked a cabin for the night.

I had a drink in the *Columbia*'s smoky bar sitting beside a young guy from somewhere in rural Pennsylvania who told me that he had been up here in Alaska for a month with a bunch of his friends. He said that when they had first come up from Bellingham on one of the other ferries, he and his friends had gone to the bar every afternoon when it opened at four and stayed there until it closed at eleven. "Then we'd go out on deck and howl at the moon until two."

I went back out on deck. By eleven o'clock, the last vestiges of color had drained out of the night, transforming the surrounding mountains into looming black giants, their jagged peaks sharply etched against the gray midsummer sky. Every so often, I would spot a massive wall of ice and snow crammed between two adjoining peaks or a sheer rock cliff plunging thousands of feet into the black water below. But more than anything, it was the profound stillness of this vast and ghostly world that moved me.

The next morning, after a hot shower, I went to the dining room for breakfast. The sky outside the dining room windows was thick with low-hanging gray clouds, and the water was the color of dull pewter. If the mountains were still there, you couldn't see them—just banks of low hills seamlessly carpeted with tall black spruce that came right up to the water's edge. There were no towns, no houses, no docks—no sign of human life whatsoever.

My french toast was dry and the bacon was limp, but the coffee was strong and hot, so I had a second cup, and then a third, which I took out on deck. When a light drizzle set in, I moved to a covered area on the rear deck where a middle-aged woman in a turquoise windbreaker and a burly man wearing a blue cap were sitting together quietly smoking cigarettes and gazing across the water. I said hello, and they introduced themselves as Jeannie and Spike.

They had just boarded in Juneau where they had been visiting some of Spike's grandchildren, and were on their way down to Bellingham. From

Bellingham, they would drive to Portland to visit some more of Spike's grandchildren, and after that, they would probably head down to the Ozarks, where they were thinking of retiring. "Lived here in Alaska all my life," Spike said in a raspy voice, "but it's getting to be too much."

Born in Anchorage, Spike had been an oil rigger since he was fourteen, and he had worked in some tough places, including the North Slope and Siberia. But he was getting older, he said, and his body wasn't what it used to be.

"We live down on Kenai," he told me. "This last winter, I went out to get something out of Jeannie's car. Well, it was forty below and the snow was six feet deep, and for a little while there, I honestly didn't know if I was going to make it back to the house. So I figured maybe Jeannie was right, and we should go some place warmer."

But it wasn't an easy decision. Spike said that when his grandparents had first come to Alaska back in 1936, they had walked from Dawson Creek, British Columbia, to Anchorage—about fifteen hundred miles. And although Jeannie was originally from Corning, New York, she had been up here since the seventies and loved Alaska almost as much as Spike did.

"It's changing, though," Jeannie said, stubbing out her cigarette and lighting a fresh one. "Like in Juneau, there's only two bars left that aren't owned by the cruise ship companies. So when the cruise season's over, that's it: all the other bars in town shut down."

Spike said it was the same on Kenai: "Lot of the best fishing's reserved for the tourists now. So where are the rest of us supposed to go?"

"So what was it like working in Siberia?" I asked him.

"Cold," he said. "But that wasn't so bad, because we were used to it, and we had the right gear. But those poor Russians, they got paid almost nothing. So they'd be out there in fifty below with nothing but old blue jeans and jackets like what you're wearing."

He had become friends with one of the Russians on the site, he said, and so when the job ended, he had left him his duffel bag full of arctic gear. "That was seven years ago, and the guy still sends me a Christmas card every year."

Spike added that the oil rigging business was hard on families. He and Jeannie had been married fourteen years now, but he'd been married twice before. And being gone four or five months at a time, he hadn't gotten as close to his kids as he would have liked. "I'm trying to make up for it now with my grandkids," he said. He sighed heavily, releasing a cloud of blue cigarette smoke.

For a while, none of us spoke. We watched the heavily wooded hills and the small islands slip by through the light rain and fog, and every so often a silver salmon would slap the water with a splash.

Then Jeannie pointed at the shore. "Spike, look over there," she said, her voice suddenly animated. "Isn't that the place we stayed that time we came over here salmon fishing?"

He squinted in the direction that she was pointing. "Yeah," he said. "I think maybe it is. It does kind of look like it."

"That was a great place," Jeannie said.

"Sure was."

SITKA, ALASKA

AS I WAS GETTING MY THINGS together just before we docked in Sitka, it suddenly dawned on me that I had no idea where I was supposed to go once I got off the boat. I knew that I would be staying at the bed-and-breakfast that Auriella Hughes, Sitka's Faith in Action director, and her husband, Fred, operated, but as I thumbed through the numerous e-mails from Auriella that I had printed out and brought with me, I realized that none of them gave her actual street address—only a post office box. Fortunately I did have a phone number. But I was out of my cell phone's service area, so I would just have to find a pay phone.

As I drove down the *Columbia*'s ramp, I spotted Spike and Jeannie sitting by the side of the driveway, smoking and holding a pair of long-haired dachshunds on a leash, but I didn't see any pay phones at the terminal. So I turned south onto Halibut Point Road and headed toward Sitka, which, according a sign, was seven miles away.

On my left was forest; on my right, open water, studded with small wooded islands like the ones I had been seeing all afternoon. Gradually the forest gave way to houses and businesses of various kinds. A roadside sign in front of the First Baptist Church proclaimed that FEAR OF THE LORD IS THE BEGINNING OF KNOWLEDGE, and immediately after it, as if to underscore the point, came several signs indicating tsunami evacuation routes. But no pay phones.

Then came Petrol Express, Sea Mart Quality Foods, Sitka Bottling Company, True Value Hardware, Dewey's Party Trix and Things, House of Liquor, even a McDonald's—but still no pay phones. Finally, on the wall of a Cascade Convenience Center, just south of Sitka, I spotted one and swerved in—only to find that it was out of order. Frustrated, I turned around and drove into downtown Sitka, where I found a whole bank of pay phones down by the harbor—also out of order. Then, at last, in the empty atrium of what appeared to be a civic auditorium, I found a pay phone that worked. Elated, I took my calling card out of my wallet, dialed Auriella's number and got—what else?—her answering machine.

Not having any other options, I left a message with the pay phone number, and sat on the bare terrazzo floor and read *Passage to Juneau,* hoping that she would get my message and call back. Ten minutes later, a breathless woman with long brown hair and sparkling blue eyes, wearing blue jeans, sandals, and silver earrings, bounded into the atrium, and looked down at me.

"Paul?"

Embarrassed, I scrambled to my feet.

"Auriella?"

"You must have a car," Auriella laughed. "I don't know why, but I didn't think you'd have a car, so I was waiting for you to come off the pedestrian ramp. Of course, I had no idea what you looked like. I waited for a while, but I didn't see any men coming off the boat alone, so I decided to check my answering machine, just in case you'd called to say that you'd missed the ferry or something.

"Actually," she said apologetically, "I hate to do this to you, but I scheduled your first interview for five o'clock. It was the only time Mary could do it, and I really thought you'd be interested in talking to her."

"Mary?"

"Mary Chambers," she explained. "We helped her with her husband, Kerry, before he died. He had Huntington's disease."

"Like Woody Guthrie?"

"Right. It's quite a story. But we have time to drop your things off at the house first. Then we'll come back here and meet Mary over at the dock at five. She teaches marine safety."

Mary Chambers

Mary Chambers was already out on the dock when Auriella and I got there, loading some boxes into an aluminum motorboat. Although her husband had died on June 15—only a little over a month before—she didn't strike me as the least bit fragile. With short jet-black hair and a strong, almost masculine jaw, she shook my hand firmly and looked me in the eye as Auriella made the introductions.

"You've never seen this boat, have you?" Mary said, turning to Auriella.

"Actually, I haven't," Auriella said.

"So what's the story about this boat?" I asked.

"Well, you know, Kerry—that's my husband, who just passed away—he was a commercial fisherman. He had a wooden boat—the *Majestic*—that was parked right over there. I'd say he had the *Majestic* for about twenty years. But then, once he got his disease, he eventually could no longer fish it, so he had this one built, with the thought that he could still operate a smaller boat that was all aluminum. So this is the boat that Kerry used. And he hit rocks with it a couple of times. I mean, he always used to be a really safe character, but once he got the Huntington's . . ."

"He couldn't control it?" I asked.

"He could control it. I think it was more about not really caring anymore and living on . . . a different edge. I mean, you know, his judgment was impaired, but . . ."

"You think he knew what he was doing?"

"That was always the controversy: Should he be driving the boat, or should he not be driving the boat? There was no license you could remove, though, so he was operating the boat anyhow. And he was hitting rocks and things. But at least he made it through without hitting or hurting anyone else."

"And meanwhile, you're teaching marine safety," I said.

"That's right. In fact, one time I was down here teaching some high school kids, and suddenly Kerry shows up in the boat."

"Did he have clothes on?" Auriella asked.

"Probably he did that time," Mary said. "But anyhow, he comes in and just drives right in the middle of these kids. I mean, it was nonstop stories like that. To him it was all just a big joke."

Auriella and I followed Mary to a smaller open motorboat bobbing peacefully in the late afternoon swell near the end of the dock.

"This is the commuter boat," Mary said as she climbed in. Auriella and I carefully stepped in behind her, clutching the gunwales to keep our balance. Mary pulled a bright orange life vest over her jacket. "You can either put them on or not," she told us, pointing to the other vests piled in back. We did. Mary cast off, started the engine, and steered the boat out of the harbor into Sitka Sound.

"So I understand you just got here," Mary said, making conversation above the drone of the motor and the screaming of the gulls. "Where'd you come in from?"

I told her, and she said that she hadn't been to Haines in a long time but that she still had friends there. "I used to dance with a Russian folk dance group, and we used to go up there."

"No kidding."

Sitka, I knew, had once been one of Russia's major Pacific ports and still had plenty of Russian street names—not to mention the Russian Cemetery, the Russian Bishop's House, and the onion-domed Saint Michael's Cathedral. It made sense that there would be a Russian dance group too.

"Do you have any kids?" I asked Mary.

"Two," she said. "Lucas is sixteen, and Maya's thirteen."

"How about you?" I asked Auriella.

"One," she said. "In fact, my son and Lucas play on the same baseball team."

We passed a couple of heavily loaded old fishing boats slowly making their way toward the docks, and then, without any warning, Mary threw the throttle wide open. There was no more conversation as we practically flew the rest of the way out to one of the small islands on the far side of the sound, slamming the waves hard, the wind and the cold salt spray whipping our faces. Minutes later, as we eased up to a low wooden dock sheltered from the open Sound, I asked Mary whether this island had a name.

"Bamdoroshni," she said. "It's a Russian name that means 'on the way.'"

"On the way where?" I asked.

She laughed. "Depends which way you're going, I guess."

After mooring the boat, Mary led us down a boardwalk that wound through large stands of blueberry and huckleberry bushes, and along the way she pointed out some of the houses set back among the Sitka spruces.

"There are plenty of people who wouldn't want to live out on an island like this," Auriella said. "They wouldn't want the hassle of commuting. But for others it's a dream come true to be out here, away from town and everything."

"If you look out over there, that's the Eastern Channel," Mary said, pointing out across the water. "That's where the big cruise ships come in. And when the wind blows in the winter, it gets really rough out there. So for the people who live out there on those farther-out islands and have to cross the Eastern Channel, it's a much bigger deal than for us. I mean, we took the kids to school every day, and we never missed a day because of weather—although it is a little tougher to commute in the winter because it's so dark."

She reached down and picked up something slimy looking from the boardwalk and flung it into the bushes.

"What was it?" I asked. "A slug?"

"Innards from a fish," she said, making a face. "An eagle must've dropped it."

Walking on, we turned left at a fork in the boardwalk and moments later stopped at the base of a giant spruce tree that had a flight of wooden steps winding up its trunk. At the top of the steps, perched high above the ground, was a house. At the base of the steps was a gangly aluminum contraption that looked like a crude open cable car, with a metal track that ran straight up the trunk to the house. "This is the lift," Mary explained. "The same guy who built Kerry's boat built this."

Auriella chuckled. "When I'd come out here with Mike to see how Kerry was doing, he'd say, 'You've got to take the lift.' Because he'd built it, you know. So we'd ride up the lift together."

"Kerry used it for about ten years," Mary said. "In fact, he never once used the stairs."

But we did. "This is amazing!" I said as we reached the top of the stairs and stepped onto the porch.

"Kerry built this house," Auriella said. "And you can't see it today, but we have a volcano over there—Mount Edgecumbe. It's pretty well covered with clouds today, but I'm sure you've seen pictures of it."

"And where's the Pacific from here?"

"Right past that island," Mary said. "Kerry never liked the sound. He always wanted to be on the outside. In fact, we're pretty much on the outside here. You can really tell in the wintertime—it's blown a hundred knots up here. But we haven't lost a window yet."

We stepped inside. The living room was a wide open space, with windows on all sides, and a beautiful wooden floor. The floor, however, was covered with small black spots, like a leopard hide.

"Are those burns?" I asked.

Mary nodded.

"That's the one thing that reminds me of Kerry," Auriella said. "He'd light a cigarette and just flip it onto the floor."

"You're kidding."

"Kerry got to where he was pretty much just living on the floor," Mary said. "He'd lost his balance, and so he'd just squat. He'd eat on the floor . . . It all just happened on the floor, you know."

At this point, Auriella left to go visit some friends on the island, and I told Mary that I would like to back up and start her story from the beginning. "Where and when were you born?" I asked.

"Berkeley, California, in 1954."

"Tell me about your family."

"There were five of us kids," she said. "I was number four—although the youngest didn't come until eight years after me. So I guess for a long time, I was the baby. My dad was a dentist in Danville, California—a town of about eight thousand, the same size as Sitka. That's really where I grew up."

"And your mom?"

"Mom raised the kids. We had a loving, healthy family—a great upbringing."

At eighteen, after sailing from Hawaii to San Francisco, Mary went to college for a year, spent the following summer sailing again, and then decided that instead of going back to college, she would head north to Seattle, where she got a job building boats. Meanwhile, her older sister had taken a nursing job in Sitka and was encouraging her to join her. She decided to give it a shot.

In the beginning, Mary lived in Sitka part time, either fishing or working at the cannery during the warmer months and heading south—usually to Mexico—for the winter.

"And how long were you able to keep up that lifestyle?" I asked.

"Until I got married and started having kids."

She and Kerry got married in 1983, five years after they had met on the docks. They were the same age, but Kerry had been here longer: he had come to Sitka straight out of high school in Los Angeles, following his older sister, who had also settled here.

After meeting on the docks, Mary and Kerry had fished together, dated, and eventually moved out to a small cove here on the island. But their decision to get married was not taken lightly: Kerry's mother, she said, had Huntington's disease. "When I met him, he'd go down to see her maybe once or twice a year. She was still living in LA."

"So what are the odds?" I asked.

"Fifty-fifty chance if your parents have it."

"Fifty-fifty? And you went in knowing that?"

Mary nodded. "I went in knowing that."

In the beginning, married life wasn't all that different from life before marriage, except that now, when Mary went south for the winter, Kerry came with her. Fishing was still good in those years, and with the money they made during the season, they were able not only to travel but also to buy this piece of property and begin building the tree house. Then after about four years, they decided to start a family.

"So how did that change things?" I asked.

"Well, it was a wonderful deal. We were thrilled about it. It took some time to decide whether we were going to have kids because of the whole situation."

"I can imagine."

"Kerry was very, very directed. He knew what he wanted from the start. He had in mind that he might get this disease, and he was adamant about building a house, preparing, making sure that he had an income—all that."

"And you?"

"I . . . I guess I was a little more hesitant about having kids," Mary said, her voice suddenly dropping low. "It took me about five years to get to the point that I decided maybe we should take that chance. I guess I looked for someone to tell me that it was okay to do this."

"You found someone?"

"No."

"So you had to take that on yourself," I murmured.

"Right."

For the first five or six years after Lucas was born—followed three years later by Maya—Mary and Kerry's life of fishing and traveling continued pretty much as before, although now Mary mostly stayed home with the kids while Kerry fished. Then, ten years ago, when he was forty, Kerry decided to get tested for Huntington's.

"At this stage of the game, they'd come up with a way of testing that was 99 percent accurate for whether you had the gene," Mary said. "It was still a pretty recent discovery that hadn't been available to us when we were trying to decide whether to have kids."

"So you knew ten years ago that he had it?"

"Well, first we looked at whether we wanted to have it done. I mean, why would you want to get tested? There was no cure. But for Kerry, he always approached life like, 'If I get it, I'm going to be set up. I'm going to assume that I'm going to get it. But I'm going to build my house, get everything all set up—I'm going to give it my all. And if I get it, I get it.'"

Mary shook her head. "You see, he was brought up with having this disease," she said. "His dad died when he was seven—from a brain tumor. And his mom had the disease. He was the youngest of four, and there wasn't much money—a whole different setup from mine. I was in an upper-middle-class family; we all had our health . . . a model family. Everybody happy, healthy, loved, the country club. We had that sort of setup."

"And he didn't."

"He didn't. So he had a very different approach. He looked at it like, 'Well, if I get it, that's life.' Well, it wasn't life to *me*. To me, it was a whole different thing."

"So did he get tested?"

"He did."

They had to go down to Seattle for the testing and then come back three months later for the results. "They made sure you wanted to know," Mary recalled. "And then we went in and they told us: 'Yes.' And, you know, even though you think you've set yourself up for it, it still hits you like a brick. Even for him, that's what he said it felt like. Like a brick."

Mary sat still for a moment, gazing past me at the dull gray afternoon sky. I could hear the wash of the surf below and the cry of a couple of gulls off in the distance. When she turned back to me, her eyes glistened.

"What happened to us after that was pretty dramatic. I mean, that really was an important time when we should have had counseling because there'd been a big change between yesterday and today—even though physically we couldn't see that change yet. Up until that time, Kerry was always busy with all kinds of projects—fishing, working on the house. But after that, his momentum absolutely changed. Up until then, it was always about providing for everybody else. But now he said, 'It's about me.'"

"And you weren't prepared for that?"

Mary shook her head.

"He made some big changes," she said, "and I did too."

"What kind of changes?"

She took a deep breath and let it out slowly. "I think I acted in fear, looking at the future and thinking: What could I do as a mother with two young children? I didn't really have a profession, and I knew that Kerry wasn't going to be around to help me out.

"As for Kerry, I think he retreated in the exact same way. He had quit smoking; he started smoking again. He said, 'I don't care if I smoke. I'm going to smoke in the house'—things that we'd decided together that he wouldn't do. He basically wasn't about compromising anymore."

"So did he pull out of the relationship?"

"I would say we both did," Mary said, her voice flat.

She said that for the first few years after Kerry's diagnosis—with the support of friends and neighbors—she had stayed on the island. But after four years, it all became too much, and she moved into town with the kids.

"I think he had an expectation that I was going to react the same way that he'd reacted to his mother. He was a beautiful caregiver for his mom—except that he only saw her twice a year. He loved her very much, and I'd watched how he'd cared for her. He didn't care how she looked; he'd change her if she needed changing. Whatever needed doing, he'd do it. Only he didn't live with her."

"Right."

"But I think he had high hopes that I would just . . ." Mary looked down at the black scorch marks on the floor as her voice trailed off.

"And so that's where some of the anger came from?"

"I think so. Sure. I mean, I'd be scared too. He knew what was coming. So he became more independent, and we drifted further and further apart."

Auriella and the Faith in Action program didn't enter the picture until about the last year of Kerry's life, Mary said.

"He was still living out here on the island well past the point that I thought he should have—as much as I wanted him to be able to die out here. It was totally his dream, and I really wanted him to be able to. But the hard part was that I didn't believe in a lot of the phases that he went through."

"Phases?"

"Well, he just sort of let go. You know, 'This is how it's going to be, and this is what I'm going to do.' And the more I tried to control things, the worse it got. Because he was losing control—so he needed to be able to control whatever he could. And so he got more and more aggressive about maintaining that control, and I had less and less say. Yet I was responsible for it all."

"How do you mean?"

"The finances, the kids—everything."

Most of all, Mary said, she tried to make sure that the kids had as normal a life as possible under the circumstances. "And once we were in town it worked out pretty well. They loved their dad; he loved the kids. He was there as much as he could be; we'd come up and see him on weekends.

"He didn't eat much," she added. "But whatever he wanted, you had to get it. If it was five hundred dollars' worth of cheese candy, you had to get it—and we did that for years. We got him all kinds of junk food. He went completely into whatever he wanted."

"And this was all part of the disease?"

"It *is* part of the disease, but not everybody plays it out that way."

"So you think he had some control over that?"

"Oh, yes," Mary said firmly. "He definitely had control."

"So it was manipulative?"

"Very."

I nodded.

"In the meantime, his brother and sister, who both also lived here in Sitka, they also had Huntington's," Mary went on, her voice calm again. "So it's had a pretty big impact on the community." She paused. "Everybody would try to help. But the hardest part with Kerry was that he absolutely didn't want any help. And if he was not going to accept help, there was no way you could work with him. On any level. So you just had to keep at it and keep at it."

"Why? Why didn't you just give up?"

She looked at me, surprised.

"I think because I loved the man," she said softly.

We sat quietly for a while, and I watched out of one of the big windows as a large flock of gulls and other seabirds began circling above the water, their screams barely audible from where I sat.

"How did he die?" I asked.

"His last two months, he bottomed out in his depression," Mary said. "He'd been self-medicating until then. He had these pretty strong pills that he did himself. He knew what he needed, and he would take a Zoloft whenever he needed to. But then finally he just stopped taking them.

"There's a psychotic part to this disease, and I think that's what affected him. He would call up constantly, almost driving the kids crazy. He would come into town—just show up at our doorstep. He'd get a cab to just drive him around, and he could still drive the boat. So he'd show up at a ball game or whatever—and he was scary. He *looked* scary. He wouldn't be in very good clothes—sometimes not in very many at all." She paused. "It got kind of frightening, really."

"Sounds like it."

"He got very depressed, and he wanted to kill himself. The people who were helping him at that point were not in town, so we got him to the hospital, and we pretty much kept him there until he died. And I would say that he probably died of starvation. He stopped eating. And he kept saying that he wanted to die, but he couldn't quite let go."

Mary paused again. "Anyhow," she said, taking a breath, "what Auriella had done during that last year—well, we didn't even ask Kerry if he needed help: *I* needed help. And Auriella was able to facilitate that. There was one man who was already a Faith in Action volunteer who had fished with Kerry years ago—he was already going out to visit Kerry. But then Auriella put a whole team of people together."

"What did they do?"

"A person would come out every day, and they would basically bring Kerry whatever he needed. I had charge accounts at various places, so they'd bring him food and visit with him. I'm not sure what all of them did because everybody did their own thing. And the kids and I still had a day that we would come out. But it was a great relief to us to have help."

I asked Mary whether Lucas and Maya had been tested yet. She shook her head and said that you couldn't be tested before age eighteen.

"Right now, I feel like we've gotten through one crisis," she said. "But that doesn't mean that we're free of it. Huntington's will always be in our lives. And so we still have to find the blessings. And you know, we've been fortunate. Like with this home: we gathered the logs, we milled the wood—we have the memories.

"And we have pictures. I wish I had them out here for you to see. We just had so many memories. We'd go hunting together in the winter. We'd take the boat up north and get a bunch of deer . . ." She broke off. "I'm going to miss Kerry," she said faintly. "In spite of . . ."

"In spite of everything?"

She nodded.

Auriella

Auriella had just finished making a fresh pot of coffee when I walked into the kitchen the next morning for breakfast. "You may want some sugar in this to cut the bitterness," she said as she poured me a cup. "We like our coffee really strong." After pouring herself a cup too, Auriella set a basket of steaming muffins on the dining room table between us. The kitchen window was open wide, letting in a cool draft of damp salt air, straight off the Pacific. "Let me know if that gets too cold for you," she said as she wrapped a blue knit shawl around her shoulders.

"It feels good," I said.

As we went through my schedule for the day, Auriella told me that unfortunately my first interview of the day—with one of the volunteers who'd worked with Kerry—was going to have to be rescheduled for that evening. "Jamie's a nurse, and they called her to come in to work this morning."

"No problem," I said. "Why don't we use the extra time to get started on my interview with you?"

"Do you really *have* to interview me?" she said, blushing.

"Absolutely."

Born in 1958, in Park Forest, Illinois, a suburb of Chicago, Auriella was the youngest of four children, with a ten-year gap between her and her next oldest sibling. Her parents, she said, were both "controlled alcoholics," and while she'd never quite felt unwanted, she told me that her childhood was pretty much a case of "benign neglect."

"Are your parents still alive?"

"My dad just died this past March," she said. "My mother is still living, but she has senile dementia."

After high school, Auriella went to a small college in western New York State, intending to major in ceramics, but—like Mary Chambers—she had dropped out after her first year. With a girlfriend, she headed south to Mexico and Central America, living in Guatemala for eight or nine months.

"That's when I was kidnapped," she said, so softly that at first I wasn't sure that I'd heard her right.

"Kidnapped?"

Auriella nodded. She and her friend, she said, were abducted from a bar by some very scary-looking men and taken off to a locked compound. Fortunately, she said, at the last minute she had managed to persuade the guy who had driven the truck into the compound to drive them back out. "But it was a terrifying experience," she said, still sounding shaken all these years later. "I guess it really opened my eyes."

Despite the kidnapping, Auriella stayed on in Guatemala until she came down with a bad case of hepatitis. "That's when I came back to this country and went to nursing school," she said. "Actually I wanted to do massage and alternative medicine, but my dad told me he wouldn't pay for it unless I went to nursing school." And so, not having any resources of her own, Auriella went to a nursing school in Santa Fe, New Mexico, and got a nursing degree.

In the meantime, she had been reading about Georges Gurdjieff, a Russian mystic whose teachings had influenced the lives of several of my own friends. "That was really the beginning of my spiritual journey," Auriella said. "I became involved in Sufism, and I actually got to see the Whirling Dervishes dance—an absolutely *incredible* experience." Her eyes flashed.

"You were doing this while you were going to nursing school?"

Auriella nodded. "I was actively involved in a meditation community in Santa Fe, and it was a very important part of my life. In fact, after I graduated, I went to India for six months, where I was the guardian for a small boy who was being taught by the Dalai Lama."

"Wow!"

After living among the Buddhist monks for six months, Auriella returned to Santa Fe with a stopover in Hawaii, where she first met her husband, Fred. But she didn't marry him—not yet. "I still had a boyfriend back in New Mexico," she said. "But then he went back up to Idaho, where he was from, and I didn't want to go with him. So I went to California and became an AIDS nurse at the Kaiser hospital in Oakland."

"When was this?"

"Oh, around the mid-1980s, I guess. Early in the epidemic. We weren't even wearing gloves back then."

Not long afterward, however, Auriella went back to Hawaii, and this time she and Fred did get married. They stayed on in Hawaii, where she ran a rural diabetes prevention program funded by the Robert Wood Johnson Foundation, and it was at one of the foundation's meetings that she first heard about Faith in Action. She loved the concept, but it wasn't until Fred's job took them to Sitka several years later that Auriella applied for a Faith in Action grant to help the homebound elderly in her new home community. "And I guess the rest is history," she concluded. "We feel pretty good about how it's turned out."

Jamie

Jamie Panzero, the nurse I had originally been scheduled to interview that morning, was out in her front yard playing with two dogs when Auriella and I arrived that evening—a big fluffy white one on a long rope, and a much smaller one, also white, that was running in circles around the larger one, yipping fiercely. "They won't bite," she assured us as we got out of the car.

Auriella left to go to the baseball game that she had told me about yesterday, and I followed Jamie inside and into the living room. The little white dog trotted in after me, climbed onto my lap, and stayed there for the duration of my visit.

"I was born in 1961," Jamie began. "In Cleveland, Ohio."

"What was it like growing up in Cleveland?" I asked.

"Actually I had a nice childhood," she said. "Pretty spoiled. But then my dad died when I was thirteen, so that kind of colored the rest of my childhood."

"Was it sudden or was it . . .?"

"Yeah, it was a sudden death. He had a heart attack at home and I saw him and . . ."

"You *saw* him? You were there?"

"Oh, I saw him die, yeah. I even tried hitting his chest," Jamie said with a bitter laugh. "And then, afterward, my mother couldn't cope. Or, really, the way she coped with her grief was by not talking about it. And so we weren't really allowed to talk about his death or him dying. That was real hard for both myself and my sister."

"And you couldn't talk about your dad?"

"No. And that was the hard thing. It changed my whole life." The direct, almost aggressive tone in Jamie's voice was very different from that of most of the people I had talked to so far in Alaska.

"So then what happened?"

"Eventually I went to college and became a nurse. My mother got sick when I was twenty-five. I was waitressing and going to Kent State at the time, and she told me that I'd be a good nurse, so I went into nursing. We were lucky and were able to get hospice for her, but I was her primary caregiver. So actually in my life I've just seen a lot of death. Which is kind of how I ended up as a volunteer."

"Well, let's go back a little bit before we talk about that. What kind of a teenager were you?"

"A wild child," Jamie laughed.

"Is that right?"

"A bad grief reaction," she said. "Depression. It was the 1970s. I was self-medicating, if you know what I mean."

I asked Jamie what had turned her around.

"Good question. Well, I quit doing any kind of drugs."

"Why?"

"Actually, I was in a psych ward for my depression, and I met a bipolar patient who sat down and prayed with me. So it was like a born-again deal. And then once I prayed, I knew that I didn't need the drugs anymore. But I ended up leaving the born-again church maybe a year afterward."

"This was when you were how old?"

"Seventeen."

After high school, Jamie spent the next seven years waitressing, finally enrolling at Kent State at age twenty-four. "I was going to major in philosophy or anthropology or psychology," she said. "But then, like I said, when my mother got sick, she told me that I'd make a good nurse."

"And why did she think that?"

"Oh, even though I'd been a wild child and the black sheep, I was always the one that did the work," Jamie said. "And after I was such a wild, bad teenager, I always tried really hard to be good to my mother. And so I guess that being able to take care of her when she died was like the least I could do."

"So how was nursing school?"

"It was kind of interesting. My mother had told me that she wasn't sure that I could do very well in nursing school because of being such a wild teenager and hurting all those brain cells. And then she died. And I think subconsciously I showed her and graduated summa cum laude—the top of my class."

"Wow," I said. "Congratulations!"

"Yeah," Jamie said, blushing.

"But that was after your mom died?"

"Oh, yeah. She got diagnosed in March and was dead in July."

"Were you actually present when she died?"

"Oh, yeah."

"So you were there when both your parents died."

"Right."

Because Jamie kept working while she was going to school, it took her eight years to get her bachelor's degree in nursing. But before she finished, she wound up taking care of two other terminally ill relatives: a favorite uncle, who was on peritoneal dialysis, and an aunt with cancer.

"How did all of that experience with death and dying affect the way that you look at life and think about life?" I asked her.

"Quite a bit," she said with a laugh. "Much different, I think, than most people."

"In what way?"

"Just . . . that it's fragile. You don't know how long you're going to be here. In a way, it's made me a little bit of a hedonist. But then, in other ways . . . I don't know, I've kind of lost my ambition. Like I don't want to work and bust my butt to have everything, because I realize . . ."

"That you can't take it with you?"

"That things don't matter. You know, I'd rather have fun along the way. So it's just a different kind of philosophy. Plus I don't have any children. So I can live like that, you know. If I had kids, of course, it'd be different."

In her early thirties when she had finished nursing school, Jamie went to work in a hospital for a while before switching over to home nursing and hospice nursing, which she loved.

"This was still in Ohio?"

"Right. I stayed in Ohio until 1998, when I moved to Washington State."

"Why did you leave Ohio?"

"I think I kind of had a midlife crisis, and I actually lost my best girlfriend," Jamie said, sighing heavily. "Like I hadn't had enough of the dying thing? She came down with breast cancer, and she was only forty-six—a little bit older than I was. But she had kids; she didn't want to die. She resisted it to the moment she left her body."

"Did you take care of her?"

"No, her family took care of her. But I was there as a friend. And it was real hard. Hard for them; hard for her."

"And hard for you," I added.

"Hard for me too," Jamie agreed. "And then, after that, I thought, 'Well, shit, there's nothing left. What am I doing here?' So that's when I left Ohio and went to Washington."

"Why Washington?"

"I happened to have a friend in Washington who actually became like a boyfriend. He lived in Seattle, and I lived in Bellingham, where I was doing hospice nursing. So we had like a weekend relationship. But then *he* got ill and died of Creutzfeld-Jakob disease. Mad cow genetic form—very rare.

"And so he moved in with me in Bellingham. Actually we'd gone on a trip down to Belize before he was diagnosed, and I knew then that something wasn't right. He knew he had this gene, and he'd gotten genetic testing, but he never wanted to know the results. So when he got a little bit strange, I thought, 'Oh, oh.' That was in March, I think it was, and he was dead by the end of August—a very rapid progression. It was funny—it *wasn't* funny, really—but he would yell and he would swear, and I would swear right back at him. But it was hard."

It was shortly after his death—about three and a half years ago—that Jamie had made the move to Sitka. A friend of hers from Ohio, she said, was living in Sitka and "charmed" her into coming up to Alaska.

"And what do you think so far?"

"I miss hospice," she laughed. "There's no hospice here in Sitka."

Instead she had worked as a psychiatric nurse in the community for a while, and now she was working at a clinic in town.

I asked Jamie how she had become involved in Faith in Action.

She thought for a few moments. "I guess I saw something in the paper about it, and I definitely wanted to get involved. I wanted to be a volunteer. And in fact, the first person I went to visit—a little lady in the Pioneers Home—I guess she was the first one of our clients who died. She was from Fairbanks. A real independent spirit. She had no family or anybody."

"So you would visit her?"

"I'd just go and sit with her for maybe an hour, an hour and a half. Go back the next day, just to keep her company. She was having a little bit of dementia, and I think it was a little hard for her to understand what was going on. She always seemed happy to see me, but I don't really think she knew who I was. So I would just sit with her."

"And then she passed away," I said.

"She passed away," Jamie nodded. "So now I see this cute little lady . . ." She got up and rummaged through a desk drawer, retrieving a newspaper clipping that she handed over to me. "See, they had her picture in the paper. Isn't she cute?"

"Sure is," I said, handing it back to her. "Is she still coherent, or does she have dementia too?"

"No, she's pretty with it."

"So you can have more of a relationship?"

"Oh, sure," Jamie said. "We have a nice relationship. We laugh, you know. I mean, I have to feel like I'm doing something kind of worthwhile. Like I'm giving. Really for my own well-being."

"And where does that come from? Is that something your parents did?"

Jamie frowned as she thought about the question. "I actually think part of it I was born with," she said sheepishly. "I mean, I know that's . . . Maybe from a past life? And maybe from my dad. He was kind of religious."

"Are you religious yourself?"

"Not *religious,*" she said emphatically. "I don't deal with any organized religion. But I do have faith—my own faith."

"And now what about Kerry?" I asked.

"That was hard," Jamie said.

"That's what I hear."

"Because it didn't go the way you wished it would go," she said. "It's always nice to see people go gently, but Kerry didn't."

I asked Jamie whether she had ever worked with anyone with Huntington's before.

"Not end stage," she said. "But it was similar, actually, to my boyfriend in Washington. You know, the agitation, the anger."

"So what was Kerry like?"

"He was so cute," she laughed. "He was a wild, independent spirit. When I first went to visit him on the island, I went to his house and I would help him with his bath and try to straighten up his immediate living area. He would stock the fridge with this very good beer and root beer, so that when his guy friends would come over, they could get beer. He'd be watching porn on the TV, and he'd be smoking pot. To me it was comical. I mean, I didn't laugh—I try to keep an open mind about what people do—but it was kind of cute, you know, the way he wanted to have everything good for when the guys came over."

Jamie paused. "He was a character," she said. "He was headstrong, and he had real mixed feelings about dying—to the point where he'd want you to actually help kill him. But then on the other hand, he had these two beautiful children that he was so proud of. So I think he was just torn—really torn."

I nodded. "So did you feel like you were able to relate to him?"

"Sometimes. Not all the time." Jamie sighed. "He had a hard time. He had a hard dying. It wasn't . . . Finally at the end, I guess he did sleep. And Mary and the kids came. And that was good—to see him peaceful."

As the disease progressed to its final stages and Kerry began requiring almost constant care, Jamie started to get paid for her time. "I would sit with him for like five, six hours at a time. And sometimes it could be heavy duty. Because, unfortunately, during those times when he was awake, he was pretty tormented."

"Were you ever afraid for your own physical safety?"

"No, not really. I mean, he'd swing at me sometimes—but," she laughed, "I have good reflexes."

I asked Jamie whether, given how much time she'd spent with him, it had been hard for her when Kerry died.

"No," she said. "I was very glad. I was so . . . I was *very* glad."

"Why?"

"Because I knew that finally he was freed, you know. He was free from the way his life had been in the months and weeks before. In his case, there weren't as many good moments as there were hard moments. Usually you still see a lot of good moments. But he was just *so* agitated. So, no, I was really happy when he died. And then all the skies were bright for days afterward—like he opened the heavens. It was weird. Because it'd been raining and miserable. But the day he died, all of a sudden it was bright and sunny—and it stayed that way for days."

Doris

"There are a lot of cats and litter boxes, and it's kind of closed in," Auriella warned me as I drove us up Halibut Point Road to Doris Baker Wilson's house the next morning.

"Does she live alone?" I asked.

"No, she lives with her husband and her son. Dick, the husband, is the primary caregiver for both Doris and Fred, who's the adult son, who had a brain tumor."

"A brain tumor?"

"Fred is functioning," Auriella said. "But the brain tumor created a bizarre disorder where he has no control over his eating. So he'll just eat until he's sick. They have to actually lock the refrigerator and dole out food to him."

It was a cool, overcast day, with a bank of white clouds piled against the horizon, again obscuring Mount Edgecumbe from view.

"But Fred helps with Doris's care," Auriella continued. "He helps Dick to transfer her and all that. But I don't think he's too keen on the cleaning thing," she added. "And I don't think Dick is either. And Doris is bedbound. So the environment is pretty . . ."

"Funky?"

"Yeah."

I mentioned to Auriella that last night I had read the collection of Doris's poems that she had given me to look through.

"They're good, aren't they?" she said.

"They really are," I said.

"And by the way, Dick used to be really active with NAMI here in Sitka—the National Alliance for the Mentally Ill—because their two daughters are both mentally ill," Auriella went on. "But I don't think he's as active anymore because of the increasing needs at home."

"And where does Faith in Action fit in?" I asked.

"Alita and Betty—they're Doris's volunteers—they come to visit Doris while Dick and Fred go out for a few hours and play pool. That's their outing. I really wish you had time to meet Alita and Betty. They're just amazing.

"I'll hang out with Fred while you're doing the interview," Auriella said as she motioned for me to pull up into a dirt driveway on our left. "He plays a type of Scrabble game that's three-dimensional—and he's got a surprisingly good vocabulary. I think it's a way for him to keep mentally engaged, you know."

Dick was waiting for us at the door as we got out of the Sentra. A bull-dog of a man, he wore a plain white T-shirt and a vest and blue jeans that were probably one or two sizes too small in the waist.

I introduced myself and shook hands, and Auriella and I followed him inside. Auriella was right about the litter boxes.

"This is my son, Fred," Dick said, and I shook hands with Fred, a pale, expressionless man of about my age whose full black beard was going to gray. He wore a stained checked shirt that was unbuttoned halfway down his chest, and his work pants were held up by a pair of blue suspenders. There was no feeling in his handshake.

"Doris is in the bedroom," Dick said.

"I'm going to chat for a little bit," Auriella said to Fred, "and then I was hoping that you and I could have a game of Scrabble."

"Sure," Fred said, his voice flat.

Auriella and I followed Dick into the bedroom, and there was Doris, propped up in a raised hospital bed with a pillow behind her head. She seemed tiny compared to Dick, with her right arm in a modified sling and a green towel clipped around her neck like a bib. She had short dark hair and glasses, and her skin was, if anything, even more pallid than Fred's. But her eyes sparkled, and her face was full of life.

"Hi, Doris," I said. "I'm Paul."

Auriella excused herself to play Scrabble with Fred, and Dick asked whether I would mind if he listened in.

"If you'd like," I said.

"That's up to Doris, isn't it?" Auriella said tactfully.

"It depends on what you want me to say," Doris said mischievously. "He'd probably be embarrassed. By the way, this is his birthday, you know. And we have been married—how many years now?"

"Fifty-four," Dick said as he climbed up onto the far side of the bed and propped himself up beside her.

"Fifty-four!" I said. "Not bad!"

"Especially in this day and age," Doris said.

I told Doris and Dick about the book and how I had been traveling to various places around the country interviewing people who were involved with Faith in Action, finally winding up here in Sitka.

"It is a beautiful place," Doris proclaimed. "Just heaven on earth."

"It sure is," I said.

"This man worked for the Forest Service," she went on, nodding toward Dick. "And he was up high, so they offered him a couple of transfers to Washington, D.C. No way," she said emphatically. "No way."

"Smart move," I murmured.

"And then he has done a lot of good as an advocate for the mentally ill," she said. "I am bipolar—he'd never even heard about it before he met me. But, of course, now he's so busy taking care of me since I had a stroke—on top of the polio, which happened years ago."

Bipolar? A stroke? On top of her polio, their son's brain tumor and their two daughters' mental illness?

Doris was born in Denver, along with three brothers. Like Dick, her father had worked for the Forest Service—which, she said, meant that the family was constantly relocating from place to place. "For instance, one of my interesting experiences was that I lived in Tombstone, Arizona," she said. "You've heard of the gunfight at the O.K. Corral?"

"Sure."

"Well, I lived there when I was four years old."

"But that was after the gunfights," Dick noted dryly.

It wasn't easy being always on the move, Doris said. She'd been a timid child, and so she didn't make new friends easily. Instead she threw herself into her schoolwork, which—apart from math—she was very good at.

"And were you close to your brothers?"

"Well, yes and no. Because, you see, I was one girl with three boys. I remember one time when I was about seven years old and we were at Payette Lake in Idaho. And I just threw a tizzy fit because my dad was going to take my older brother fishing."

"And he wouldn't take you?"

"He wouldn't take me. And you know, when you're little, you've got to stick up for your rights."

"So what happened?"

"Oh," Doris said, "I got to be his best fishing buddy. In fact, I've got a picture from way back in the past of me standing with my dad up in the willow thickets of the ranger district in Leadville, Colorado. And I think it's probably because of my experiences with my dad that I married *this* guy."

"You mean because of the forestry?"

"Well, no. You see, my dad was a very short man, and he was kind of cocky—a know-it-all. He was definitely a know-it-all. And I think that this big man was attractive to me because he was a very humble and sweet guy."

Dick grunted.

I tried to steer the conversation to Doris's poetry, but for some reason she didn't seem to want to talk about it. I told her how much I had enjoyed reading the poems that Auriella had given me, but she didn't respond. Then, when she started talking about school and how she wasn't very good at math, I told her, "Well, but you're a very good writer."

"I was a pretty good speaker," she said. "I remember in college one time I was in some kind of speaking contest. I was up there speaking, and the people who were adjudicating it said, 'Well, now, Miss Baker was really going strong—she was really going great—and then all of a sudden, she kind of lost it.'" Doris paused for effect. "*He* had come in," she said, turning her head and looking fondly at Dick.

"So you were distracted," I said.

"And so was I," Dick said.

Doris and Dick went to the same college—Colorado A&M in Fort Collins—and they met during Doris's freshman year. Dick was a junior by that time and had already served four years in the Marine Corps before going to college on the GI Bill. Before meeting Dick, Doris had intended to major in occupational therapy. "But instead," she said, "I graduated in two years—with an M.R.S. degree."

It took me a moment. "An M.R.S. degree?"

"I got married," she laughed.

"She paid for the marriage license," Dick recalled. "My brother paid the ten bucks for the minister and took us to a greasy spoon afterward for chicken-fried steaks."

Doris's father had given them his old Nash Rambler, and so after the wedding and the chicken-fried steaks, the two of them drove up to Missoula, Montana, where Dick had gotten a job as a smoke jumper parachuting into remote backcountry areas to fight the forest fires that the fire trucks couldn't get to. "He was there to pick up the bodies after the Mann Gulch Fire," Doris said. "Have you heard of the Mann Gulch Fire?"

"I have," I said. The Mann Gulch fire, a fierce forest fire that had swept through Helena National Forest in Montana during the summer of 1949, was notorious for having claimed the lives of thirteen firemen.

"He picked up the bodies and took pictures."

A month later, a job opened in the National Forest Service, so Dick grabbed it, and he and Doris made the first of many moves that they would make during the course of Dick's career in the Forest Service—this one to Zigzag, Oregon.

"Zigzag?"

"It was near Mount Hood," Dick said. "There was a ranger station there. But I was only there a month before they moved me out to Enterprise, over in the western end of Oregon."

"Sounds like you were moving as much after you got married as you had before you got married," I said to Doris.

"I guess that's true," she said. "But we lived in some interesting places, didn't we? Places with no running water and no electricity either—like Chico."

"Chico, Oregon," Dick said. "It was on the map because there used to be a post office there. And it had a population of two: Doris and me."

Fred, their first child, was born in June 1951. "You know about him," Doris said. "That he had a brain tumor."

"I do," I said. "Auriella told me."

"He is a dear, sweet, helpful person," Doris said, her voice breaking. "But I think that is much more the tragedy of my life than my own . . . whatever."

"But that's more recent, isn't it?" I said.

"He's been living with it for the last eighteen years," Dick said heavily.

We could hear Auriella patiently talking to Fred out at the kitchen table, where they were still playing three-dimensional Scrabble. I didn't hear Fred's voice at all.

"So what happened after Fred was born?" I asked.

"I put in a transfer request to the Forest Service, and in July of 1952 we came up to Ketchikan," Dick said. "You see, one of the problems down there was that the jobs ended with the first snow. So you'd be off with no pay during the entire wintertime—and yet somehow the expenses kept coming in, you know."

They liked Ketchikan—their first stint in Alaska—and eventually wound up living on a barge with a little wooden crew house on top of it.

"This was with Fred?" I asked.

"Oh, yes," Doris said. "And he was a mechanically minded boy from the time he was little. He didn't climb out of his crib: he took his crib apart."

The phone rang. It was one of Doris's volunteers checking to make sure that Doris was still up for a visit this afternoon. Dick told her that she was.

Then Auriella came back into the bedroom and announced that she and I had to get back to town for a lunch meeting with Father Dave, the chairman of her board, after which the three of us had a meeting scheduled with the mayor so that I could explain Faith in Action to him from a national perspective. "We still haven't gotten one penny from the city," Auriella said indignantly. "Can you believe it?"

Over lunch at a busy place called Ludwig's, Auriella and Father Dave did their best to fill me in on the intricacies of Sitka's political scene while I quickly bolted down my first-ever elkburger.

The three of us then walked over to the mayor's place of business, a bustling office that appeared to have something to do with the cruise-ship industry, where I did my best—in the ten minutes that he had to spare—to explain to the mayor that Faith in Action was a nationwide program that helped the elderly and the disabled and that, in addition to the Robert Wood Johnson Foundation, it was supported by a wide range of local funding sources, including local governments.

The mayor, who looked as if he had other things on his mind, nodded politely from time to time and, when I was done, thanked me for my comments and thanked us all for coming to see him. Raising money, I reflected as we walked back onto the street, really was harder than giving it away.

Freda

Freda Aron—my three o'clock interview—sounded as if she had just stepped off the D train straight out of Coney Island, with the strongest New York City accent of anyone I had interviewed since Lou Viscovitch, the Hell's Kitchen native back in Calais. And in fact Freda *had* lived in Coney Island—but she wasn't born there.

"I was born in the Bronx, New York," she told me proudly. "In 1915."

"You mean to tell me you're eighty-nine years old?"

"Eighty-eight. Don't rush me."

We were meeting in a room on the first floor of the Manager's House at the Pioneers Home, where Freda had just been visiting one of the residents. It was a little noisy out in the hall because people were beginning to set up the food and the chairs for a Faith in Action reception that was scheduled to start at 4:30. Auriella had offered us the use of her office upstairs, where it was quieter, but Freda had complained that her legs were bothering her, so we took the room in the back and opened the windows to let in some air.

"So did you have any brothers or sisters?" I asked her.

"Two sisters," Freda said. "I'm the oldest. I had one that was three years younger than me, and the one I go to visit in Florida, who is nine years younger."

"And tell me about your parents."

"I think this is what started me on volunteering," she said. "See, they came from Russia. And I think that the immigrants who came to this country were always very generous. We had a two-bedroom apartment, and there was never a morning that I got up that there weren't people sleeping all over the floor. Whoever came off the boat had a place to sleep. There was no hotel, and they had no money anyway. So when I went to bed, I never knew who was going to be there the next morning when I woke up—and it was perfectly acceptable. And I think that was a wonderful way to be."

"Sounds like it," I said.

"My father was very generous," Freda said. "And my husband was very generous. That's why we had no money. He was a doctor, but he wouldn't charge people. He'd say, 'It's bad enough that they have to be sick. Why should they have to pay for it?' So it was ingrained in me, and I tried to teach my kids that too. My one son went to Liberia with the Peace Corps. My other son has nursing homes in Chicago where nobody's refused, whether they can pay or not."

"And when did you leave the Bronx?"

"We moved to Coney Island when I was eight years old," Freda replied. "And I'll tell you a funny story about that. We kids were on the beach all the time. We'd swim, and our parents would come and bring us lunch. And so one day we decided that we'd have our initials put on our bathing suits.

"Well, my father had a bakery, and my mother worked there at night. So after work, she sat up all night putting my initials on the suit. And the next morning, all the kids were there and I walked out like this," she said, thrusting out her chest. "Because I was maybe twelve or thirteen and my body was just developing, you know. Well, the kids started screaming and laughing hysterically, and I was just mortified. My initials were F.U."

We both burst out laughing.

"I was so innocent. The girls didn't know, but the boys—the boys just started howling! I was so mortified that I ran straight home and my poor mother sat up all night again pulling my initials out of the suit."

"So what *was* your maiden name?" I asked.

"Umansky. My family came from a town called Uman, I think."

When Freda was sixteen, her family moved from Coney Island up to the Crown Heights section of Brooklyn, where she lived until, at age twenty-two, she left New York City to go to nursing school in Chicago. "My mother said, 'Nice Jewish girls do not go into training. It's okay if you marry a Jewish doctor, but God forbid you should be a nurse.'"

"Well, why did you want to be a nurse?"

"Why? Because when I was a kid, I saw the picture *War Nurse,* and all the doctors and nurses were having wonderful romances," Freda said. "And then, of course, the war came along, so I thought I'd join the war. But as I graduated, I met my husband, and we got married right after we met."

"Just like in the movie," I laughed.

"Right."

I asked Freda about her husband.

"He was a Holocaust victim," she said. "He came from Germany, and he was an intern in the hospital. One day a friend said to me, 'I've got a guy for you—a German.' And I said, "A *German*? I don't want Germans.' And she said, 'Yeah, but he's a young intern, and he's so cute.' So we got married. We didn't have a wedding, though. We couldn't afford it. So we just went to a justice of the peace. My mother said, 'You were never married, because you weren't married by a rabbi. You're living in sin.' And I told her, 'But it's wonderful sin, Ma, wonderful sin.'"

Freda stayed in the Chicago area for the next fifty years and was married to her husband for forty-seven of them, until he died in 1989. She had four children—two girls and two boys—and eventually gave up nursing to work for a newspaper.

"Which one?"

"The *Bugle,*" she said. "In Niles, Illinois. And then the Lerner papers, which covered about forty-eight different suburbs in the Chicago area. And then I had my own newspaper for a while—a feminist newspaper called *She.*"

"This was all in Chicago?"

Freda nodded. "Everything was in Chicago while my husband was living. Because he'd come from Germany, he only felt safe in Chicago. I couldn't get him to go anyplace else."

After her husband died, Freda hit the road. "My kids were all spread out, so the first thing I did is I went to visit them. Then I started volunteering for the government."

"The government?"

"Well, first I signed up with the Peace Corps. And they accepted me, but they wanted me to go to Morocco. And my son, who'd been to Liberia with the Peace Corps, told me, 'Ma, do not go to Morocco. They don't treat the women right—not even if you're with the Peace Corps.' So I volunteered for VISTA instead. I told them I wanted to work on an Indian reservation because I always loved the idea of working with Indians. And I said that I wanted to work in Alaska. But they had nothing open in Alaska at that time, so instead they got me a place in Utah."

Freda wound up spending the next ten years of her life in Utah, doing community nursing on the Ute and Navajo reservations. She went from house to house and got to know many of the families that she worked with.

"I remember one time I went back to Chicago for some vacation," she recalled. "And when I came back, some of my people from the reservation were sitting on a hilltop waiting for me. The woman said, 'I have to go to the hospital, and I knew you were going to be here today.' And I thought that was really interesting: I didn't even know myself when I'd be coming back. But there they were, waiting for me.

"They were very nice," Freda mused. "And they always wanted me to live out there on the reservation. But there was so much drunkenness— so much brutality. It just broke my heart. We'd have seminars and meetings for drunkenness, you know, and the guys would say, 'My father died of alcoholism; my uncle died; my brother died . . . and I'm going to die, too, so what do I care?' In one of my families, three people died of alcoholism: the mother, the father, and one of the sons. All three of them died together. It was awful to see that. And in another one of my families, with this guy who was very loving to his grandmother, I woke up one morning and they said, 'We have something to tell you.' I went to the reservation, and he had chopped up his grandmother the night before in a drunken frenzy."

"Oh, my God . . ."

"Oh," Freda cried, "when I heard that . . . It was so terrible. He had loved his grandma, and she was so good to him. And I had seen them together and taken care of both of them. I mean, the horrors I saw were just unbelievable. It was so sad."

She sighed deeply.

"Are you still glad that you did it?" I asked her softly.

"Oh, yes," she said, looking up at me. "I made wonderful friends. And after living my whole life in New York and Chicago, I was living in a town of three hundred people. It was a beautiful experience."

Finally, after ten years in Utah, a VISTA position opened at a women's shelter in Sitka, and Freda got her chance to go to Alaska.

I asked her what had drawn her to Alaska.

"I don't know," she said. "But there's something about Alaska. Everybody's fascinated with it. You know, when I was in Florida visiting my sister, everybody was asking me, 'Do you live in an igloo? Are you covered up with snow?'"

I laughed.

"The only question I had when they called me was if there was a place to buy chocolate in Sitka. Because I live on chocolate. And they said, 'A chocolate shop just opened up.' So I said okay, I'll come. And let me tell you, I love it so much, I'm staying here forever. I've finished with my VISTA assignment now, but I'm just volunteering all over the place—at Centennial Hall, at the Russian Bishop's House, at the Sheldon Jackson Museum. And of course with Faith in Action, where I go to the Pioneers Home and talk to people."

Curious, I asked Freda whether there was a synagogue in Sitka.

"No," she said. "There are only about thirty Jewish men and women here. So we just come together at one another's houses for holidays."

"Were you attending when you were in Chicago?"

"Well, I did because of the kids. I did like to go to the synagogue, but I wasn't that faithful. My husband never went, because he said there was no God in this world."

"Because of what he'd been through?"

"Because of the Holocaust. He said, 'If you saw how parents and children were torn from each other and saw what happened, you would have no faith, either.' And I don't really have too much faith in God either, to tell you the truth. But I did want my children to have a Jewish education. Then it's up to them. Some of them observe; some of them don't."

I nodded.

"Also, we've always taken our kids to different kinds of churches," she added. "I want to tell you something: when I was pregnant with my first baby, I went to a Catholic church—one of those special Christmas Eve services. So I figured I had to kneel with this big stomach of mine—and I couldn't breathe. And then the priest—a stupid young priest—says, 'And we have to pray for the Jews because they killed Christ.' I said to my husband, 'Is *this* what we came for?'" She laughed.

"But, yes, I've been to all the different churches—Catholic, Lutheran, everything," she continued. "Because, to me, there's only one God. It doesn't make any difference, no matter what anybody says. I don't like super-religious people, to tell you the truth. They think that their God is the only God and that their way is the only way—and that includes the Orthodox Jews. They're just as bad as everyone else. And I don't believe in that."

"Auriella mentioned that you have your own radio show," I said. "Is that true?"

"Oh yes," she laughed. "Frankie and Freda's New York Jazz Show."

"A jazz show? What do you do?"

"I play music, and I tell stories about my family."

"You like jazz?"

"Oh," she smiled, "I love it."

"Who's your favorite jazz musician?"

"Frankie Sinatra. That's why it's Frankie and Freda's Jazz Show. And Tony Bennett. I play mostly all the old stuff—the big band stuff, you know. Tommy Dorsey and all that. There's a lot of young people that never heard of any of them, but when they hear it on my show, they just love it. And then, like I said, I tell stories about my family. I'm going to tell a very funny one this week. Want to hear it?"

"Sure."

"I was married almost two years," she began, "and I started getting very nauseated. My husband, the doctor, took me to his GI man. He pumped my stomach, he X-rayed me, and he gave me medication. But I wasn't getting any better. And all our doctor friends said, 'Oh, she must have eaten something—something that's affected her.'

"Well, then my aunt Dora comes from Brooklyn to visit me, takes one look at me, and she says, 'You're pregnant.' And I said, 'No, it can't be.' She said, 'Why? Don't you sleep with your husband?' I said, 'Every chance we get.' She said, 'You're pregnant. Why do you say you're not pregnant?' I said, 'Because all our friends are doctors. They would know if I was pregnant.' She said, 'Did anyone give you a test?' I said, 'No.' She said, 'Did anyone examine you?' I said, 'No.' Well, sure enough," Freda laughed, "they gave me the test, and I was almost three months pregnant!"

She couldn't stop laughing. "There I had practically the whole medical society of Chicago, and not one of them had figured it out. And really I was very lucky that the baby came out okay, what with all those X-rays they gave me. I probably should have called her Aunt Dora."

I brought the conversation back to Faith in Action. One of the elderly women she had visited at the Pioneers Home had died, Freda said, but there were three others that she continued to visit.

"They're not talkative," she said. "And, actually, I don't even know if they comprehend. So my way of dealing with this is that I come in there and I kiss them on the head, and I touch them a lot, and I talk. Whether they comprehend or not, I don't know. But I do touch them. Because I didn't mention this, but I was a nurse in a nursing home for years and years—I told you that my son owned nursing homes in Chicago—and I would tell all the aides, 'When you go in to a patient that's blind or not capable of understanding you, touch them. Always touch people. Kiss them if you can—it doesn't hurt to kiss someone or to touch them—just to let them know that they have some *meaning* in this world.' So that's what I do too. And like I say, I talk."

"Even if they don't understand you?"

"It doesn't matter."

"And I guess you don't know much about them," I said.

"No. But that doesn't matter either. If this one dies, they tell me, 'Go see that one.' So I do. And I always touch them. Because I think the human touch is very important."

Sometimes You Have to Cry

There was a good turnout for the reception. A small band of musicians was playing vigorously in the entrance hall as people streamed in. Most headed straight for the tables in the back of the room that were loaded with smoked salmon, cheeses, and cakes and cookies of all kinds. I recognized several of the volunteers and some of the board members whom I had met the day before.

But there were also people whom I hadn't met yet, including an older Tlingit man by the name of Paul, with whom I got into a long conversation about Native politics, and a young fisherman named Dennis who told me that he and his wife had both signed up to become Faith in Action volunteers after reading about the program in the newspaper—only neither of them had realized that the other had signed up until they had both showed up at the same training session.

Eventually Auriella asked us all to take a seat on one of the chairs that ringed the perimeter of the room. She introduced me, and after I had talked for a few minutes about Faith in Action from the national perspective, some of the others spoke.

Father Dave, for instance, took the faith-based issue head-on: "A major concern for me is when people ask us about our organization that we can answer with a brave heart that we are a faith organization. And that faith is that we're called to act compassionately to one another. Whatever our religion might be, we're called to reach out and help each other. And I think that's the faith that motivates this community. So I think we need to bravely say: *that's* the faith that this is based on."

There was a murmur of assent.

Somewhat to my surprise, Auriella also focused on the "faith" part of Faith in Action. "You know, when we first started talking about doing Faith in Action, there was so much support right from the beginning that it probably wouldn't have had to have been an interfaith program," she said. "If we'd just made it a volunteer program without the interfaith part, I think we would have also gotten a lot of support for that."

Several people around the room nodded.

"But when I saw the interfaith requirement in Faith in Action, to me it was just so exciting," she continued. "Because for me personally, when I look at the world, one of the most painful things is to see so much of a breakdown that is based on misunderstandings between religious groups— a breakdown that results in everything from bad feelings to taking others' lives. So I'm very inspired by that aspect of the program. In my mind, it has this visionary piece to it. In other words, if you're going to create this program that's going to spread around the nation, why not have something that's interfaith where you're breaking down some of these artificial barriers? Because even though it's about caregiving, this interfaith piece has even further-reaching implications."

Again, heads nodded.

And then there was an old Tlingit story about a brave named Raven that my new friend Paul stood up and shared with the group. "Raven is walking along in the woods," he began in the resonant voice of a veteran storyteller. "He comes upon a clearing. There are no trees—just one big tree standing there alone in the middle. Well, he walks up to that tree and he looks at it, and there's sap running out of that tree. To Raven, it looks like the tree is crying."

Paul paused and gazed around the room at all of us. Everyone was listening. He went on gravely, "And so Raven, he looks up at that tree, and he says, 'Something has happened to you that has happened to me.'" Paul first cried out those words in Tlingit—which was incredibly dramatic— and then translated them for us.

"So Raven sits down—and he cries with that tree." Paul paused again, his gaze sweeping the room. "And that's what *you're* doing," he said softly. "Sometimes you have to cry with people to comfort them."

Doris Revisited

The next morning, after saying good-bye to Auriella, I headed back out to the Wilsons' place to finish the interview with Doris that I had started yesterday.

"Come on in!" Dick called when I knocked.

Fred was sitting at the kitchen table and nodded blankly when I said hello. Dick's voice called again from inside the bedroom.

"In here!"

It was the same scene as yesterday, with Doris propped up against her pillows and Dick in his T-shirt and his vest sitting on the far side of the bed beside her. Doris was wearing a blouse with an autumnal pattern with brown leaves and flowers. She seemed a little more upbeat than she had yesterday.

"So, Doris," I said, "let's go back to where we left off yesterday."

"Where was that?"

"I think we were in Ketchikan," I said. "And Fred was taking his crib apart."

"Oh, that's right," she chuckled. "And my mother said, 'Be careful or he'll take your whole barge apart, and you'll sink.'"

I laughed. "So how long did you stay in Ketchikan?"

"We were in Ketchikan from July of '52 to the fall of '54," Dick said. "Then we moved to Craig." Craig, he explained, was on the west coast of Prince of Wales Island, about forty miles west of Ketchikan. "It was a small community at that time—about 250 people."

"In the wintertime, the water would freeze up," Doris said. "So we always stored water in the bathtub."

"That was because our house was on pilings and had exposed pipes," Dick explained. "So when I had to go out on field trips for work, I'd shut off the water to the house. So we had some problems."

"But the people were very fine," Doris said. "Super fine."

"If the water main burst, which it did more than once, everybody'd be out with their picks and shovels to dig up the road so that we could fix it," Dick said. "And we never had any accidents, because there were only three cars in the whole town—and most of the time only one of them was running."

In August 1955, they had to leave Craig and go back to Ketchikan, and a month later Doris was stricken with polio. "They used to think you couldn't get polio in Alaska because of the cold," Doris said. "And it didn't really start up here until about the time that I got it."

I asked her how she had learned that she had polio.

"I had headaches," she said. "Horrible headaches. So I went to see Dr. Clark, and he knew what it was."

"And there was nothing he could do?"

"Oh, no," Dick said, shaking his head. "There was no cure. It was just a matter of putting her in the hospital."

"And also, I had the interesting experience of being transported to California on what they called the MATS plane—which stands for Military Air Transport Service," Doris added. "They were equipped with portable iron lungs, and they went all over the world and picked up polio victims."

"She was in the iron lung for about three or four months," Dick said. "And then they put her on the rocking bed and they taught her glossal-pharyngeal breathing . . ."

"Which is where you swallow air and then breathe it," Doris said.

"And how long did that go on?" I asked.

"Several months," Doris said. "I remember one time when I was in that iron lung, they were testing to see how I was breathing. And they weren't watching what they were doing. So they kept me inhaling without quitting."

"You're kidding."

"And they wouldn't turn it off!" she gasped—and for a moment there was real panic in her voice, almost as if she were reliving it. Dick reached over and gently clasped her hand with his much larger hand.

I asked Doris when she had started writing. "It's beautiful poetry," I said.

"That partly comes from the fact that I am bipolar."

"And when did that start?"

"Well, you know, you're born bipolar," she said.

"It shows up as part of a developmental sequence in childhood," Dick explained. "The more they look at it, the more they find it in early child-hood. But it's very seldom recognized in schools. The theory is that you'd be able to prevent any adverse effects if you could treat it early enough. But even today, most mental health people don't recognize it because it has different symptoms in children than in adults."

"They still like to blame the problems on bad parenting," Doris added sardonically. "They say it's just bad parenting. In fact—especially among some highly religious people—*they* sometimes claim that it's just evil."

I asked Doris when she had first discovered that she was bipolar.

"I don't really know," she said.

"Well, you had your first depressive episode when you were sixteen," Dick reminded her.

"Oh," I said. "So before you'd even met."

"That's right," Dick said. "But in those days they didn't have any way of treating it. In Europe, they had lithium in 1950—Winston Churchill was on it in 1950. But in the United States they didn't approve the use of lithium until 1970. So Doris never had any medications to help stabilize her."

"So you had that to deal with on top of the polio," I said to Doris.

"And I had my little stroke," she added. "Before that, I was up and walking and doing things and working. In fact, I walked five miles in the morning before breakfast right here in Sitka," she said proudly.

"When was this?"

"Six or seven years ago," Dick said. "When she first came home from San Leandro back in 1956, she was in a wheelchair. We were living in Bishop, California, then so that we could be close to rehab. She had braces on her legs, and she had to have help standing up. Walking was a difficult challenge, and her right arm was severely affected. They had a spring-loaded thing on her wheelchair that helped hold her right arm up so that she could do a little bit with her fingers. And it took quite a while before she got out of that stage."

They wound up staying in California for fifteen years, finally returning to Ketchikan in 1970. In 1975, they moved to Sitka, where they had been ever since—except for a short stint in Juneau before Dick retired from the Forest Service in the early 1980s.

It was in the 1980s that Doris had written many of her poems, and I mentioned to her that her religious faith seemed to come through very strongly in some of those poems.

"I do have a strong faith," she said. "But I don't have a conservative, narrow faith. And I really believe that Muslims, or whoever they are, are as okay as we are. But you find people who say not only that you have to be a Christian, but you have to be *this* kind of Christian."

"And you don't believe in that?"

"No," she said. "It's the way you live. Like Dick has always lived *his* life. He was raised to be helpful, and not prejudiced." She turned and gazed fondly at her husband, but he remained impassive.

GOING HOME

LIKE THE COLUMBIA, the ferry that had brought me to Sitka four days earlier, the ferry for my return trip—the *Malaspina*—was also named after one of Alaska's famous glaciers. In fact, the Malaspina glacier was reported to be bigger than the entire state of Rhode Island. But the ferry that bore its name turned out to be eleven years older than the *Columbia*, ten feet shorter, eleven feet narrower, and more than a thousand tons lighter. Not to mention that my cabin, when I first checked in, felt as if it was at least twenty degrees hotter and considerably dingier than my cabin on the *Columbia*.

But as soon I got back out on the deck and the *Malaspina*'s four thousand horsepower engines rumbled to life, all was well again. The sky was still gray, with banks of white clouds hovering just a couple of hundred feet above the water—and, after four days, there was still no sign of Mount Edgecumbe. But the breeze coming off the Pacific was brisk and cool, furiously whipping the nylon American flag on the *Malaspina*'s stern, and all of a sudden I was filled with that rare feeling of being totally and wonderfully alive.

A big red and white Coast Guard helicopter buzzed us for several minutes as we made our way across the sound, which puzzled me until I saw a family on the upper deck frantically waving at it.

"That's our boy up there!" the woman shouted.

"Hey, Randy!" one of the kids yelled.

After the helicopter returned to Sitka, I saw two more eagles drifting overhead, and a little later I spotted what may have been a whale. It was just a big black tail smacking the water before it went under, so it was hard to know for sure.

As we turned back into the sheltered Inner Passage, time once again seemed to stand still. The small wooded islands and low black hills drifted by silently, and the still gray water was broken only by the occasional slap of leaping salmon.

Paul

After a while, I got up and walked around to the other side of the ferry, where, to my surprise, I spotted Paul, the Tlingit man who had told the story about Raven at the reception last night. Wearing jeans and a blue T-shirt with an eagle emblem, he spotted me at the same time and asked if I wanted to join him in the dining room for a cup of coffee.

The dining room was almost empty, and we talked until the staff asked us to leave so that they could set up for dinner. So we moved back outside and continued our conversation on the rear deck. Paul, who was seventy-two years old, seemed to know every nook and cranny of the Inner Passage. He pointed out a dismal stretch of land off to the right that he told me was called Deadman Reach. "And that's Poison Cove on the other side. You know why they call it that?" When the Russians first came to this area, he said, they wanted the Aleuts they had brought with them from southwestern Alaska to fight the Tlingits for them. When the Aleuts refused, the Russians left them on Deadman Reach, which he said used to be an island. After a while, the Aleuts began to starve. So they ate the plants that grew on the island, but the plants were poison. After all the Aleuts had died from the poison, the Russians simply dumped their bodies in the water. "So that's why they call it Poison Cove," Paul concluded.

"That's awful," I said.

Then Paul talked about his own life. He had been in the army, he said—he was in Korea during the war. At one point, his platoon wound up in a minefield. Their officers were being picked off one by one, but Paul wasn't worried. Since he was a young boy, he had known that he would one day be killed by a bear. "Well," he said, "I looked around, and I didn't see any bears. So I just walked out of that minefield, and the other men followed me. One of them lost a leg, but none of us was killed."

Later Paul became a paratrooper. "My buddy and me—the one who'd talked me into becoming a paratrooper—we'd always jump together. And we said that the first one to open his chute had to buy the other one a drink. It was kind of like chicken. Well, I never looked at the ground. I just watched him. Because he was good—and I knew that *he* was watching the ground. So I'd always wait until he opened his chute, and then I'd open mine. He said I was crazy, but he had to buy the drinks."

After Korea, his buddy tried to talk him into staying in the army, but Paul loved the sea, and so he became a sea captain and spent the next forty years sailing all over the world. He had been all over the Alaskan coast too, up and down the Inner Passage and taking barges through the Bering Strait up to Barrow. For the last twelve years, he had lived on a tugboat—most recently in Sitka. In fact, just today, he said, he had finally sold it. And so now he was going up to Juneau to stay with his son.

"Did you get good money for it?" I asked him.

"Well, yes," he said, squinting at me over his coffee. "But it all goes to my ex-wife."

George Revisited

After we docked in Haines, I retraced my journey back to the Oscar Gill House in Anchorage, where Susan and Mark Lutz welcomed me back as if I were a long-lost friend. The next morning, my last in Alaska, I drove back out to see George Mohr again. Before I had left for Haines ten days ago, I'd promised George that I would try to stop by again before flying home. The instant I pressed the button beside his room number at the front door, he buzzed me into the building. He had obviously been expecting me.

As before, he was wearing a blue-and-white checked shirt with his glasses dangling from his neck by a black nylon strap.

"How are you this morning?" I asked as he ushered me back into his apartment.

"Reasonably well," he replied in his warm Viennese accent. "And you?"

"I'm fine too."

"And how was your trip?"

"Great," I said.

But it was clear that George didn't want a one-word answer. He wanted a detailed account. So I spent the next forty-five minutes retracing all of my steps over the past ten days. When I'd finally finished my account, I told George that I would like to hear more of the details about his experiences here in Alaska.

And so for the next hour, George talked about his life here in Alaska over the past half-century, especially about his years with the army. "And then, of course, there was the earthquake," he remarked.

"The one in 1964?"

"That's right. It shook Anchorage and the whole middle section of Alaska—including the Prince William Sound, which swept over Valdez. Here in Anchorage, things broke down—on Fourth Avenue especially. Businesses broke down and fell into the ground. Anyway, immediately after the earthquake, the military formed a cleanup operation using their trucks for the removal of debris, and so I had to set up the dispatch office to coordinate all the rescue and recovery."

"And where were you when the earthquake hit? At home?"

"No. That was on a Friday afternoon. It was Good Friday, actually. It was called the Good Friday Earthquake."

"Interesting," I said. "Because of course you know the story of Good Friday—how the earth opened up . . ."

"Oh, yes," George said. "The crucifixion. But, anyway, we had a custom in those days that the officers and the highest-ranking civilian employees went to the Officers' Club on Friday afternoons. So we were all downstairs in the bar at the Officers' Club when everything started shaking. And I still remember that somebody gave the signal, and we all started to run outside. I was standing away from the building, and I looked at the Chugach Mountains—and they were really trembling. I never thought I would see a thing like that."

"Did you think that you'd had too much to drink?"

"No," George chuckled. "But I looked around at the other people, and they all run upstairs with their drinks in their hands—although some of them didn't even want to get up from the bar on account of a lousy earthquake. But most of them were standing there looking at the mountains shaking with a drink in their hands."

I laughed.

"By that time," George went on, "I realized it was a major earthquake—although I didn't know it was the biggest earthquake ever to hit the United States. And it went on for four minutes, which is a long time for an earthquake."

Immediately after the shaking stopped, George tried to call home to make sure that Nellie was all right, but the power lines and the phone lines were down. So he tried driving home, but the road had collapsed. He then took another back road, and this time he was able to get home, but Nellie wasn't there. "So I looked in the back where there was a huge parking lot, and there she was, sitting in her car listening to the radio. All the power lines were down, but the car radio, of course, was still working."

"And where was Janet?"

"Janet was in California. It was Easter vacation, so she had joined a small group of friends to go skiing in the mountains. So she was on a mountain in California, on the upper terminal of a ski slope, when somebody came up in a cable car and said, 'Well, how do you like the situation in Alaska?' And Janet said, 'What's going on in Alaska?' And the person said, 'You mean you didn't hear about the big earthquake? It swallowed up the whole city of Anchorage.'

"So Janet yelled, 'My *parents* are in Anchorage! What can I do?' And so they told her that she could get information through the Red Cross. I don't know the details anymore, but I do know that people were asked to write down the names of the relatives they were searching for so that the Red Cross could send them a notification if they were found. So Janet did that, and after that, she was trying to get in touch with us pretty desperately.

"Meanwhile, we were trying to find some back-channel way to reach her. And eventually I found somebody who had a ham radio, and he contacted someone in the San Francisco area who started making telephone calls. And so after two days, Janet got the notification that we were alive and we were all right."

"Thank God."

"But six months later," George added dryly, "Janet got a letter from the Red Cross that said, 'We regret to inform you that we are unable to locate your parents. . . .'"

Just then, the intercom phone sounded.

"Oh," George said. "That is my ride to take me to Nellie." He stood up painfully, walked over to the intercom phone, and picked it up. "I'll be down in just a few minutes," he said to the person on the other end. "I have a visitor."

"How often do you go?" I asked.

"Usually three times a week," George replied. "Monday, Wednesday, and Friday."

"Does Nellie know at all who you are anymore?"

"No."

"And how long ago did she start to lose her . . .?"

"She's been in the severe stage for about a year," George said, and then he dropped the subject.

He pulled on a blue jacket, and picked up an aluminum walking cane. I followed him out the door and down the hall to the elevator. "Do you think you'll come back to Alaska?" he asked me as we stepped out onto the ground floor.

"I would love to," I said. "And I would love to bring Susie. I know that she would very much like to see you again."

"That would be very nice," he said.

Two smiling women—one blonde, the other brunette—were waiting for George as we slowly walked out of the building. "Ah," the blonde said, "you *do* have a visitor."

George made the introductions. "He's come all the way from New Jersey to see his Uncle George," he told them.

I took a picture of George smiling gamely between his two escorts. Then the blonde helped him into the back seat of a blue SUV that was parked at the curb, and a moment later they pulled out of the parking lot onto the highway. And although I had meant what I'd said when I had told George that I would very much like to bring Susie back for a visit, there was a part of me that knew even then that I wouldn't ever see George again. The final link to my grandfather's generation was gone.

Home

As I climbed into my mud-spattered Sentra in the parking lot of George's building that wet, gray Monday morning, my mission, for all intents and purposes, was accomplished. The rest was just a matter of getting home. I puttered around downtown Anchorage for a while, had a cheeseburger at Peggy's Airport Restaurant, returned the Sentra to Avis with 1,972 miles on the trip odometer, and boarded Continental flight 1280, which left Anchorage a few minutes after five o'clock that afternoon and landed in Newark just after six the next morning.

From the airport, I caught a New Jersey Transit express back to the Hamilton station, where our son, Rob, was waiting for me. Susie had already gone to work, he said, and he had to get to his summer job himself by nine.

But he still had time for a quick breakfast, so we headed to Fred and Pete's Deli over on Route 33, where Annie, the waitress, and my eighty-nine-year-old friend Jake welcomed me back. After we'd finished our cheese omelets and coffee, Rob dropped me off at home and went on to work.

As I walked up the driveway with my suitcase, I glanced at the house next door where Mary used to live, now home to a young family. It would have been nice, I thought, to have been able to tell her about my travels around the country and about all the remarkable individuals I'd met along the way: the directors, the volunteers—and especially the many wonderful people they were helping. She would have enjoyed it.